PRAISE FOR *BETTING THE HOUSE:*
THE INSIDE STORY OF THE 2017 ELECTION

"It's the political book of the year: a gripping inside account of what really went on behind closed doors as the Tories bungled to election disaster and just how close the fiasco came to toppling Theresa."
Mail on Sunday

"Read it in one sitting. Absolutely gripping stuff, a terrific story well told. This is likely to be the definitive account of a most unusual election, one of the great surprises of British political history."
John Rentoul, chief political commentator for *The Independent*

"The thrilling account of the most dramatic election in recent history."
Robert Peston, ITV political editor

"Excellent."
The Economist

"Compelling ... A well-constructed narrative which gives a lively account of the campaign while also reflecting astutely on the underlying forces that shaped the result."
Andrew Rawnsley, *The Observer*

PRAISE FOR *WHY THE TORIES WON:*
THE INSIDE STORY OF THE 2015 ELECTION

"This book is brilliantly clear about how it was done and who did it."
JOHN RENTOUL, *THE INDEPENDENT*

"Probably the most revealing of all the election books so far."
THE GUARDIAN

"Any activist wanting to better understand, or, dare I say, win elections, should read this book."
PROGRESS

LANDSLIDE

THE INSIDE STORY OF THE
2024 ELECTION

LANDSLIDE

TIM ROSS AND RACHEL WEARMOUTH

\Bb\
Biteback Publishing

First published in Great Britain in 2024 by
Biteback Publishing Ltd, London
Copyright © Tim Ross and Rachel Wearmouth 2024

Tim Ross and Rachel Wearmouth have asserted their rights under the Copyright, Designs and Patents Act 1988 to be identified as the authors of this work.

All rights reserved. No part of this publication may be reproduced, stored in a retrieval system or transmitted, in any form or by any means, without the publisher's prior permission in writing.

This book is sold subject to the condition that it shall not, by way of trade or otherwise, be lent, resold, hired out or otherwise circulated without the publisher's prior consent in any form of binding or cover other than that in which it is published and without a similar condition, including this condition, being imposed on the subsequent purchaser.

Every reasonable effort has been made to trace copyright holders of material reproduced in this book, but if any have been inadvertently overlooked the publisher would be glad to hear from them.

ISBN 978-1-78590-947-4

10 9 8 7 6 5 4 3 2 1

A CIP catalogue record for this book is available from the British Library.

Printed and bound in Great Britain by
CPI Group (UK) Ltd, Croydon CR0 4YY

CONTENTS

Introduction   ix

PART I   THE LEGACIES
Chapter 1   King Boris   3
Chapter 2   Trussonomics   23
Chapter 3   The Lawyer   45
Chapter 4   The Banker   67

PART II   THE STRATEGIES
Chapter 5   Tears and Rain   97
Chapter 6   On the Ground   113
Chapter 7   Digital   147
Chapter 8   Change   163
Chapter 9   Trust   183

PART III   THE CAMPAIGN
Chapter 10   D-Day   203
Chapter 11   Bad Bets   217
Chapter 12   Enter Farage   223

Chapter 13	Fall Guy	241
Chapter 14	Scotland	257
Chapter 15	Poll Axed	265

PART IV	THE ELECTION	
Chapter 16	Election Night	289
Chapter 17	New Dawn	317
Chapter 18	Landslide	323

Epilogue	Government	337
Appendix 1	The Results	345
Appendix 2	Key Dates for the 2024 Election	347
Notes		353
Acknowledgements		363

INTRODUCTION

At 10 p.m. on Thursday 4 July 2024, the transformation of British politics began.

The broadcasters' general election exit poll put Keir Starmer's Labour Party on course to take power, with an enormous landslide of 410 seats. That was more than double the total the party won five years earlier. Starmer's power would be unassailable, at the head of a huge House of Commons majority.

The seat forecast was a complete humiliation for Rishi Sunak's Conservatives. They were very nearly destroyed as a political force. After fourteen years in power and five Prime Ministers, the Tories were set for just 131 seats – the lowest ever tally in the party's 190-year history, the exit poll said. When the results came in, it was even worse.

On sofas at home with loved ones, and in campaign offices surrounded by aides, the protagonists in the drama of the 2024 general election were transfixed. The thing about a seismic upheaval is that it can take those involved a while to process. As Starmer hugged his family tight, watching the pundits discussing his imminent appointment as Prime Minister, his most loyal aides just stared at the screen in silence. One remembers thinking, 'I don't know how I'm meant to feel now.'[1]

Sunak's team, scattered hundreds of miles apart, also had mixed emotions. The Conservatives had been ruined but not quite eradicated. It was awful, and there was grief, but it could have been worse, they thought. At least the Tories would still get to be the official opposition.

Ed Davey's Liberal Democrats, finally out of the electoral doghouse, could not quite believe they were projected to grow from a band of eleven to sixty-one MPs. They hugged and screamed at each other with delight. The final result was even sweeter.

The shell shock, giddiness and confusion continued in the days that followed. Several senior Labour MPs didn't bother answering their phones when a 'withheld number' called on the morning after the election. It was No. 10 summoning them to meet the new Prime Minister so he could appoint them to the Cabinet.

Rachel Reeves was stuck in traffic and running late, which made her already frayed nerves even worse. She was trying to prepare herself for the long walk up Downing Street in front of the world's media to be appointed Britain's first female Chancellor. But her driver was playing some intense R&B music on the car radio. It was a bit much for Reeves, who asked for something calmer.

'Smooth Radio?' the driver offered. 'Yes,' she said. 'Smooth Radio.'[2]

• • •

This book is an attempt to understand the forces that dramatically recast British politics in 2024.

Labour won its first election in nineteen years, with 411 seats. The Tories fell to just 121 MPs, while the Liberal Democrats leapt

INTRODUCTION

to seventy-two. In Scotland, the SNP collapsed, losing thirty-nine seats. Nigel Farage powered back into the political front line and into Parliament for the first time. His late entry into the contest as leader of Reform UK blew up the Tory campaign and cost Rishi Sunak's party dozens of MPs. Even though Farage's team only secured five seats, they won more than 4 million votes and have changed the dynamic in ways that may not be clear for some time.

Why was it that nothing the Conservatives tried ever seemed to work? How could the country's most successful political party finally lose its winning touch so spectacularly? Was there anything Sunak could have done? What did Labour do this time that was different to the previous four elections that the party lost? What kind of a leader is Keir Starmer and how did his character shape the end result?

Morgan McSweeney, Labour's campaign director – who was later promoted to be Starmer's chief of staff in No. 10 – ran a highly disciplined operation. His team delivered the most efficient vote-to-seat ratio in history. How did McSweeney do it? What role did tactical voting play? What do the results say about the state of British politics and how will they shape what comes next?

Did the public even care? At 59.7 per cent, turnout was lower than at any election since 2001. It was generally lower in seats won by Labour than in seats won by the Tories.[3] The pollsters – and the obsessive way the media reported every one of their surveys and seat projections – may partly be to blame. Before a single ballot had been cast, most voters felt certain that a big Labour win was inevitable. How did that affect the outcome?

In order to answer some of these questions, and others, this book draws on more than 100 interviews, private conversations, official documents, text messages, emails, Zoom calls, strategic memos, presentations and other information from people involved at all levels of the national campaigns in Westminster and in Whitehall. The vast majority of those who provided information and detailed first-hand accounts wished to remain anonymous to give their candid views on what worked and what did not. Many now work at the highest levels inside the new government and are not authorised to speak publicly. Others used to sit at the same desks and are now licking their wounds and trying to rebuild their careers outside politics.

Politicians and their aides watch their words carefully in public, but when speaking in private, as many have done for this book, some tend to pepper their language with profanities. We have chosen to retain their original language in direct quotations in the interests of authenticity. There were also moments in the campaign when racist language was aired that some readers may find upsetting.

• • •

The focus of this book is on the battle for power, and that was always only a contest between Starmer and Sunak. It was a contest fought mainly in England, although Labour's resurgence in Scotland swelled Starmer's majority.

The first part of the book deals with the build-up to the election, tracing the impact of the toxic legacies that both party leaders inherited on their preparations for the campaign. That political baggage – and how Starmer and Sunak dealt with it – had a huge influence on the results in 2024. The second part explains the Labour and Tory election plans and how the campaign directors prepared their activists for the so-called 'ground war'. In the short campaign, rival parties compete to define the contest at national level in the media

INTRODUCTION

through policy pledges, speeches, manifestos and TV debates. The digital campaign, fought via social media channels on smartphones and websites, is now a central part of every election.

The third part deals with the campaign events that unfolded in the six weeks before polling day, including Sunak's D-Day debacle, the election betting scandal and the remarkably effective performances of Ed Davey's Liberal Democrats and Nigel Farage's Reform UK. It also takes a hard look at the polling industry in 2024. The fourth tells the dramatic story of the night of unprecedented upheaval that followed the exit poll on 4 July. The final chapters reflect on what the outcome means.

• • •

Elections are the moments when millions of citizens living in democracies exercise their muscle. Frontline politicians are the ones who get crunched or, if they're lucky, crowned winners. The story that unfolds in these pages sometimes reveals a picture of professional politics that is not flattering. The UK has suffered repeated bouts of turmoil over the past decade, with senior figures in both main Westminster parties guilty of failures of leadership, backroom plotting and feuds that have little to do with voters' priorities.

Despite that history, most people working in British politics do not primarily seek fame or personal advancement. They want to contribute to making the country a better place to live and work, often holding strong convictions over how best to achieve this. Elections are the moments when they get their chance. It is a high-risk business, and the rewards are rare and temporary. Most people lose, most of the time.

The two leaders vying for power in 2024 were unusual. They were classic mainstream centrist politicians of the type the UK has not had a chance to choose between for almost a decade. The transfer of power between Sunak and Starmer was smooth, courteous and good-natured. But a radical anti-politics mood is not far away, as the riots that swept the UK after the Southport stabbings in the summer of 2024 showed.

At the time of writing, the Conservatives are choosing a new leader. It will be either Robert Jenrick or Kemi Badenoch, both of whom hail from the right wing of the party, economically and socially. Nigel Farage's already powerful influence is likely to weigh heavily on whatever His Majesty's new-look opposition does in the years ahead.

Labour's landslide buried the Tories in 2024. But the ground is still unstable. If Starmer's opponents find a new figurehead who can connect with the public, as Boris Johnson did only five years earlier, another seismic change could soon follow.

PART I

THE LEGACIES

CHAPTER 1

KING BORIS

SHUFFLING

It was meant to be routine.

Boris Johnson, the Conservative Party's blond, bomb-proof, election-winning machine, had decided two months into his first full term in office to reshuffle his Cabinet. The truth was that Dominic Cummings, Johnson's subversive chief adviser, was the one doing most of the hiring and firing, and that was always liable to be explosive.

It was 13 February 2020 and Johnson was all-powerful. He had just led the Tories to their biggest election victory since Margaret Thatcher's landslide in 1987. Cummings, whose menacing utterances gripped most government colleagues with fear, was also at the height of his maverick influence. Bald, thin and prone to volatile outbursts, his shadow loomed over Westminster. He had a plan to remake the centre of government to consolidate Johnson's (or rather his own) authority, while ripping up what he derisively called the 'blob' of established Whitehall orthodoxy in order to reform the entire country. Central to that mission, and not for the last time in this story, was an attempt to tame the most powerful government department, the Treasury.

It is an unwritten rule of British politics that tensions are intrinsic to relations between the Prime Minister and the Chancellor of the Exchequer. A dynamic of conflict is almost built into the structure of the two roles: the PM is the figurehead, the leader with (usually) a popular mandate direct from voters to deliver on election promises and spend taxpayers' money on the country's priorities. The Chancellor, however, is the bank manager who is constantly being asked to stump up the cash. More often than is comfortable, it falls to the top minister at the Treasury to say 'No.'

In the case of Gordon Brown and Tony Blair, Labour's longest-serving double act, relations between the two were disastrously toxic. Wary of the risks, David Cameron and George Osborne consciously worked to maintain their exceptionally close partnership during the Conservative–Liberal Democrat coalition of 2010–15, even redesigning the interior layout of 10 and 11 Downing Street – where the PM and Chancellor had their respective offices – to ensure a free flow of staff, ideas and goodwill.

When Chancellor Sajid Javid wandered up the most famous street in London for Johnson's reshuffle, he was expecting to be confirmed in his role in a matter of a few seconds and to leave again to resume preparations for his first Budget.

Instead, he was ambushed. Johnson congratulated Javid on his reappointment but issued a condition. The Chancellor must fire his six top Treasury advisers – effectively neutering his ability to choose his own team – and allow Cummings to appoint their replacements, who would all report to No. 10.

A stunned Javid could not believe what he was hearing. When it became clear that Johnson was not, for once, joking, he quit. 'They wanted his balls in a jar,' one ally recalled later. 'He is rather attached to his balls.'[1]

Javid himself later described Cummings's sway over Johnson's government as far too powerful. Often, Johnson would have no knowledge of decisions being taken by Cummings in his name, which Javid objected to, saying later, 'At best, it was like having two Prime Ministers and sometimes they agreed and sometimes they didn't. At worst, you had one Prime Minister, it just wasn't the elected one.'[2]

Javid's dramatic departure opened the door to No. 11 for one of his friends – the diminutive, self-effacing, always-smiling young MP for Richmond in Yorkshire. At thirty-nine, Rishi Sunak became Johnson's Chancellor, one of the youngest holders of the second-biggest job in government.

Javid and Sunak were friends. They shared a background in investment banking (which made them both a lot of money) and a love of *Star Wars* films. A week after winning the 2019 election, Sunak, who was Chief Secretary to the Treasury at the time, tweeted a picture of himself with Javid at the cinema where they had just watched *The Rise of Skywalker*. 'Great night out with the boss – Jedi Master @sajidjavid,' he said. Javid responded with his own tweet that, looking back, reads more like a warning to Johnson about what was to come: 'The Force is strong in young Sunak.'

It was a rapid rise for the Cabinet's apprentice. Barely seven months earlier, Sunak had been a junior minister in the local government department. Newly installed at the Treasury, he had to contend with the small matter of a Budget due in three weeks.

Sunak's appointment as Chancellor came a fortnight after the UK had formally left the European Union, and most of Westminster believed his biggest task would be getting the country ready for life outside the single market and customs union. Under the terms of Johnson's bare-bones EU exit deal, the British had been given a 'transition period' lasting until the end of 2020 in which to prepare for the economic shock of severing ties with their closest and biggest trading partners. In the meantime, existing EU rules would continue to apply to the UK until that grace period expired.

Johnson had won his eighty-seat majority in December 2019 on a simple promise: after three years of chaos, with a paralysed Parliament refusing to endorse Theresa May's EU withdrawal plan, and with Labour proposing to rerun the referendum campaign, voters should give him a decisive mandate to 'get Brexit done'. The electorate agreed and the UK duly left the EU at 11 p.m. on 31 January 2020. Amid celebrations inside No. 10, Johnson made a characteristically idiosyncratic speech to his aides and supporters, celebrating the fact that 'French knickers' would now be 'made in this country'. Dominic Cummings, who had masterminded the 2016 Vote Leave campaign, also had the chance to speak. But the occasion was too much for him: overcome by the scale of the Brexiteers' achievement, he wept.

Sunak was an enthusiastic Brexit supporter and an early backer of Johnson's leadership campaign after May resigned the previous summer. He had good reason to be looking forward to a long partnership with the new PM, making Brexit a success and fulfilling the Tories' 2019 election pledge to 'unleash Britain's potential'.

Indeed, in the first weeks of 2020, Johnson was in the rare position of having brought together a Conservative Party that had spent the previous four years ripping itself to pieces over Europe – a civil war that had already claimed the scalps of his two predecessors as Prime Minister, along with multiple other senior Tory figures and former members of the Cabinet.

The official mission of Johnson's new administration was to 'level up' the UK, bringing a boost to regional economies in parts of the country that had been neglected for investment and had fallen into decline. Many of these were fervently Brexit-supporting areas, such as in the Midlands and the north-east, districts which had formed part of Labour's so-called 'red wall' heartlands but had voted decisively for Johnson in 2019.

In one Conservative Party broadcast in February 2020, Johnson personally thanked a voter referred to only as David from Bolton, who worked in highway maintenance. Over some acoustic guitar music, the caption told viewers that David, who previously backed Labour, had voted Tory for the first time in 2019. 'We wanted to thank him for placing his trust in us,' it said.

After a brief shot of Johnson being prepared backstage, David described how his parents were both Labour voters and he'd always believed Labour were 'the party for the working man' but was excited now because voters had 'given Boris a chance and I want to see how he takes that chance and runs with it'.

Then came the theatrical moment of surprise, in which Johnson walked on set and shook his shocked and grinning voter by the hand. But David recovered his poise to give the Prime Minister what amounted to a serious warning: 'The thing that I liked that you said, I think it was your first speech after winning the election, you said you're almost treating it as like you'd rented our vote, you're not going to take that for granted. That was important for me to hear.'

Johnson replied that this was his message to Tory MPs, too. 'We have to repay the trust of the electorate,' he said.

SHAKING HANDS

Those who have worked closely with Johnson describe a leader who has a rare ability to communicate and connect with the public. He inspires loyalty bordering on adoration among a few people who get close to him. In No. 10 he was addicted to a level of organisational chaos that made administering the affairs of the state a task far beyond his own abilities. That significantly complicated matters for those whose job it was to try to make things work. Boring meetings bored him and he was liable to change his views frequently.

Around the same time the video of David from Bolton was released, reports began to filter through to Whitehall of an outbreak of an unknown, flu-like illness in China's Wuhan province. Government officials decided to do what they do best and convene some meetings, including meetings of the Whitehall emergency committee known as COBRA. These gatherings are often technical affairs, bringing together senior figures in the UK's scientific and medical establishment with communications officers and ministers. Johnson, though he could have attended, decided to skip them.

Like many of the stickiest situations Johnson has found himself in over the years, the Covid crisis did not evaporate when he ignored it. By early March 2020, it was consuming virtually all the government's attention. Thanks to the prevalence of cheap air travel, the virus had spread fast and far beyond China. It was overwhelming the healthcare system in northern Italy, where hospitals were running out of beds, ventilators and intensive care space at frightening speed. One after another, governments in the west took the unthinkable decision to order their citizens to stay at home in an attempt to slow the dispersal of the disease. A new word entered public consciousness: lockdown.

Johnson came to power as a popular libertarian who rarely allowed himself to be constrained by convention and delighted in behaving as if the usual rules of politics and public life did not apply to him. Rule-breaking worked well for his brand and voters responded warmly to a candidate they saw as engagingly different from the slickly produced cut-out of a typical politician. He initially regarded the coronavirus scare as something to make light of, boasting to reporters of having visited a hospital where he 'shook hands with everybody, you'll be pleased to know,' when asked if members of the public should stop using handshakes as greetings.

Cummings, by his own incendiary and colourful account, was horrified at his boss's attitude. Then, on Saturday 14 March, a crucial meeting took place in Downing Street at which Johnson was for the first time receptive to the idea of imposing severe restrictions on the public to help slow the spread of disease. Cummings was particularly vocal in his support for restrictions. Yet it took nine more days for the Prime Minister to act.

On 23 March, Johnson finally ordered the first national lockdown, asking the public to stay at home in order to protect the NHS and save lives. 'You should not be meeting friends,' he said. 'You should not be meeting family members who do not live in your home. You should not be going shopping except for essentials like food and medicine – and you should do this as little as you can.' Anyone who disobeyed these instructions would find themselves in trouble with the law. 'If you don't follow the rules, the police will have the powers to enforce them, including through fines and dispersing gatherings.'

LOCKDOWN

The first Covid lockdown of 2020 wrought an unimaginable change on the nation.

For those not working in the NHS, daily life stopped. The warm, sun-filled days in March and April unfolded in an eerie stillness, filled with an absence of noise. Shops and offices stood shuttered, roads lay empty of traffic, even the sky, unendingly blue, was free of planes. In place of the usual clamour of city life came the sound of birdsong and the breeze, animating spring leaves and scraps of litter on empty streets.

For the Tory government, and its new Thatcherite Chancellor in particular, the change in economic outlook that the pandemic required was no less disorienting. The novice at the helm of the Treasury found himself designing a programme of what he would later proudly boast of as £400 billion worth of government spending on Covid-19 support measures. Chief among them was the vast furlough scheme, under which the state paid the bulk of the wages of people whose workplaces had been ordered to close.

'Today I can announce that, for the first time in our history, the government is going to step in and help to pay people's wages,' Sunak said on 20 March. In a mark of how quickly the pandemic was taking over, Sunak made this historic intervention only three days after he had delivered a full Budget. He returned to Parliament multiple times to announce extensions of the furlough and business-loan schemes and came forwards with other forms of support, including 'Eat Out to Help Out' subsidies to encourage people to go to restaurants and cafes for meals, in order to help revive the hammered food and drink industry.

For the low-tax, small-state advocate Sunak, along with many of his Tory colleagues, it was a jarringly uncomfortable position to be in. One Cabinet minister, stunned by the scale of public spending, privately joked that the reason voters rejected the unreconstructed socialist Jeremy Corbyn's Labour Party in 2019 was because 'he wasn't left-wing enough' for them.

During the pandemic, Sunak was hugely popular with the public, thanks to the fact that, in the words of one aide, 'he nationalised payroll'. By the summer of 2020, his ratings were the highest of all politicians who were scored for their handling of the pandemic: according to Ipsos, 60 per cent of the public thought the Chancellor was handling Covid well, compared to 43 per cent for Boris Johnson and 31 per cent for the newly elected Labour leader, Keir Starmer. Only Chris Whitty, England's chief medical officer, who was revered and relied upon as the nation's doctor during daily televised press conferences, scored slightly higher than Sunak, with 62 per cent approval.

But not everyone was happy with the government's willingness to shut down economic activity. Soon, cracks began to emerge in the Conservative Party's consensus, with vocal libertarian MPs such as Steve Baker and others objecting to the freedom-limiting Covid restrictions and the impact they were having on the economy. Over the next year or so – as curbs were imposed, lifted and then reintroduced – the dissent spread to the Cabinet. Sunak was on the side of easing the rules, while others were persuaded by the need to lock down hard, as expressed by Chris Whitty.

'People like Rishi, [and Cabinet members] Alok Sharma and Jacob Rees-Mogg were pushing back on Covid restrictions,' said one senior government figure. They argued that ministers should 'give people information and let them take their own choice. The government shouldn't be locking down, it shouldn't be restricting freedom. It shouldn't be killing off the economy.'[3]

But the reality of the medical emergency gripping the country was horrifying – as was the government's apparently poor record at dealing with it. In November 2020, the UK passed the landmark of 50,000 Covid deaths (a figure which would eventually rise well above 200,000). Only the US, Brazil, Mexico and India had passed 50,000 deaths by the same point – all countries with far larger populations than the UK.

As a classic libertarian himself, Johnson wrestled with the arguments for and against lockdown, changing his mind frequently on policy and earning from the acerbic Cummings (and apparently others) the contemptuous nickname of 'Trolley', a reference to the fact that he would change direction unpredictably, like a shopping trolley with a wonky wheel.

In one sense, the turmoil within the PM's own mind embodied the party's wider divisions over the right way to run the country in general. One striking thing about the way the Tories went to war with themselves over Covid was how closely the factions mirrored the groups that fought each other on Brexit. 'The issues that blew the party apart over Covid were exactly the same,' a senior official recalled. 'The ERG [the hardline Eurosceptic European Research Group of Tory MPs] just turned into the Covid Recovery Group.'[4]

For Steve Baker, who was a driving force behind the Brexit campaign in Parliament and within the Covid Recovery Group, lockdowns offended the animating philosophy of his politics: 'If the Conservative Party does not stand for freedom, it stands for nothing.'[5]

KING BORIS

Only a few months after Johnson won his eighty-seat majority, his authority suddenly seemed to be on shaky ground. Rebellion was in fashion. Splits, negative briefings and backbiting were rife. 'They had about six months when King Boris was able to unite the warring tribes,' the same senior official said. 'But the pandemic comes along and just creates another lightning rod for these quite fundamentally different views in the Conservative Party of how you're supposed to govern this country.'[6]

Some who were working closely with Johnson's top team at the time blame the cruel timing of the pandemic lockdown for robbing new MPs of the chance to feel part of a bigger party in Parliament. If the 2019 intake of Tory MPs had been able to rub along together in the bars of Westminster, the Tories in the Commons might have gelled into more of a team. 'I don't think that sense of unity ever existed,' one former Cabinet aide recalls. 'The 2019 intake arrived and all of a sudden the pandemic hit and they all dispersed around the country. It was never really a single party – they were all on their separate WhatsApp groups winding each other up.'[7]

Even while tens of thousands were dying in care homes and hospitals, Johnson displayed at best an ambivalent attitude toward Covid restrictions. On 27 March 2020, it was announced that he had caught the disease himself. Colleagues in No. 10 at the time privately blamed Johnson's reluctance to follow doctors' advice – he had carried on working, refusing to give an inch to the virus, and became progressively more unwell, they said.

Ten days later, Johnson was in hospital in intensive care, from where news filtered out to a shocked country that the PM was on oxygen to help him breathe. Inside No. 10, some officials began to panic, genuinely believing he would die. Foreign Secretary Dominic Raab, grey-faced and worried, was asked to step in and deputise.

Johnson survived and credited the NHS with saving his life. Clearly weak and still short of breath, he gradually returned to work, praising the healthcare he had received and renewing his calls for the public to obey lockdown and follow social distancing rules when taking exercise outside once a day or buying food or medical supplies.

On 13 April 2020, a day after Johnson left hospital, YouGov polling gave him the highest rating of his entire premiership, with 66 per cent of adults saying they believed he was doing 'well' as PM. This frightening virus had made the public want to believe in their leaders, to put their trust in the figures of authority responsible for keeping them safe and follow the rules.

Six weeks later, that faith was shattered.

On 22 May, the *Daily Mirror* and *The Guardian* reported that Cummings had been investigated by police for allegedly breaking lockdown after he was seen at his parents' home in Durham, some 260 miles from his normal place of residence in London. He was also spotted on his wife's birthday at Barnard Castle, a beauty spot.

At the time, during the UK's first national lockdown, the government was telling the public to stay at home and all non-essential travel was banned. On the face of it, this was an appalling betrayal, the most grotesque hypocrisy by a powerful official who seemed not to believe that the usual rules applied to him.

Two days after the first reports, Cummings held a press conference in the Downing Street garden to explain himself to the country. He feared he and his wife were becoming ill, he said, and worried how their four-year-old son would be cared for, so went in search of a childcare back-up plan to stay at his parents' property. Cummings was ridiculed after he tried to explain the trip to Barnard Castle as necessary to test his eyesight. BrewDog produced a new IPA beer called 'Barnard Castle Eye Test' to mark the scandal, while one well-known high street optician recorded a 6,000 per cent increase in online mentions of their advertising slogan: 'Should have gone to Specsavers'. The firm also placed a free eye-test voucher on the back of parking tickets in the County Durham town.

Johnson himself defended Cummings, saying he 'at all times behaved responsibly and legally' and had followed the instincts of every parent. But the relationship between the Prime Minister and his aide did not recover after the Barnard Castle incident, according to Downing Street colleagues. Later in the summer of 2020, Cummings urged Johnson privately to carry out a radical Cabinet reshuffle to focus minds amid headlines suggesting the government had no grip on the Covid crisis. Johnson, he said, looked like he was happy to have a Cabinet of 'useless fuckpigs' in charge, identifying Gavin Williamson, the Education Secretary, and Matt Hancock, the Health Secretary, as among the least capable ministers who were letting the country down. Johnson rejected Cummings's plan. It was a sign that the two were no longer on the same page.

One senior Tory still cannot believe how much political capital Johnson blew on defending his adviser:

> When you win a big mandate like Boris did, with 43 per cent of the vote, you feel it on the ground. Everyone who wins that big a vote share gets one 'mea culpa' moment. He used his defending Dominic Cummings's hypocrisy. He burnt all his capital on Cummings. It was absurd.[8]

Johnson himself recovered from his illness, but it took time. During his repeated defences of Cummings, he would occasionally be hit by a bout of coughing. On his birthday in June, his wife Carrie – herself a former Tory Party adviser and a powerful influence on his decisions – organised a celebration in the office with a cake. Up to thirty guests sang him happy birthday. There was just one flaw in the plan: such gatherings were prohibited under Johnson's own Covid rules at the time.

Conor Burns, a longstanding ally of the Prime Minister, tried to explain that the event was not a 'premeditated' party, though his choice of analogy didn't help. 'He was, in a sense, ambushed with a cake,' Burns suggested. The idea of the British Prime Minister falling victim to a stealth attack by an aggressive teatime treat piled ridicule on top of the government's attempts to explain Johnson's actions, further undermining his credibility.

Although the gathering was reported soon after it happened, the story was merely tucked away in an article in *The Times* and no mention of lockdown-breaching scandal was made. It wasn't until two years later that the country came to understand the full scale of rule-breaking behaviour that went on inside Johnson's Downing Street. The so-called Partygate news reporting – led by the *Daily Mirror*'s political editor Pippa Crerar and added to by others across the media, including ITV's Paul Brand – revealed a sordid portrait of debauchery in Downing Street.

One celebration in April 2021, in which two leaving parties – for one of Johnson's photographers and for James Slack, who had been the PM's communications director – joined up later in the night in the No. 10 garden was particularly wild. According to one witness, a staff member was sent out to a local shop to return with a suitcase full of wine. The event happened on the eve of the Duke of Edinburgh's funeral. The next day, the Queen was seen mourning her husband of seventy-three years at Windsor Chapel alone.

According to a senior Labour strategist, it was this event above all others that destroyed voters' faith in Johnson. Partygate had been 'a slow-burn' issue for voters, even though the Westminster bubble was 'way more excited about it'. However, images of 'the Queen sitting on her own' at Prince Philip's funeral, just as No. 10 staffers were nursing their illegal hangovers from the night before, was 'the thing that really hit home', the source said. 'People still talk about it now.'[9]

Helen MacNamara, a top civil servant who worked as Deputy Cabinet Secretary and as a senior ethics official, even brought a karaoke machine to a leaving party for a No. 10 staffer at an event held in the Cabinet Office next door. 'There was quite clearly stuff going on in No. 10 that was completely fucking unacceptable,' one senior Tory recalls.[10]

As the torrent of revelations continued, the police launched an investigation – as did Sue Gray, the civil service's go-to ethics guru. Her inquiry dealt with a succession of gatherings that took place over a twenty-month period, a number of which should never have been allowed to happen, she said. 'There were failures of leadership and judgement,' Gray wrote in her report.

> At least some of the gatherings in question represent a serious failure to observe not just the high standards expected of those working at the heart of Government but also of the standards expected of the entire British population at the time ... The excessive consumption of alcohol is not appropriate in a professional workplace at any time.[11]

Johnson, his wife, Carrie, and Sunak were among those who received fines in April 2022 for attending lockdown-breaking parties in Downing Street. Sunak thought seriously about resigning but was talked out of it, surprisingly for some, on the basis that quitting would put Johnson in an impossible position and potentially force the PM to go too. At that point, at least, Sunak didn't want to bring down the Prime Minister.

LOYALTY

In an interview with Laura Kuenssberg, Sajid Javid spoke about how Johnson is incredibly loyal but that loyalty is conditional: 'Do you back him in everything that he says and does? That's the basis that you win that loyalty.'[12]

Johnson is unusually vulnerable to criticism. His thin skin, combined with an apparently uncontrollable impulse to try to charm anyone and everyone he meets, made life difficult in government for those whose job it was to implement policy. Civil servants and political advisers alike complained that he would change his mind, often repeatedly, and didn't like to say 'No' to people. According to Cummings, Johnson once remarked that he liked the chaos that engulfed Downing Street because if nobody knew what they were doing, everyone would have to look to him for the answers.

Often, Johnson's inconsistency was the trigger for relationships breaking up in his personal life. Carrie is his third wife and he has at least eight known children (four from his second marriage, one from an affair and three from his third marriage to Carrie. He declines to tell interviewers how many others there might be). In his political alliances, too, the pattern for Johnson has been one in which his allies often walk away, unable to tolerate the stress of working for him any longer. Those breakups are often kept quiet but sometimes burst spectacularly into the open.

One famous example is Michael Gove, who was Johnson's campaign manager for the Tory leadership election in 2016. On the morning Boris was due to hold his launch event for the campaign, Gove announced he was running himself because he had concluded Boris was not up to the job. Years later, Johnson appointed Gove to the Cabinet, but when Gove joined the chorus of ministers advising Johnson to quit in July 2022, the Prime Minister angrily fired him instead.

When Dominic Cummings was thrown out of No. 10 in November 2020 after losing an ill-judged power struggle with Carrie over the appointment of an adviser, it was the final straw. After leaving government, Cummings made lurid claims about the scale of the dysfunction within Johnson's Downing Street, turning from the PM's chief ally to his most powerful and damaging enemy in the process. In one famous select committee hearing in May 2021, lasting more than six hours, Cummings called Johnson 'unfit for the job' and alleged that he had treated the pandemic as a 'scare story'. In an interview with BBC journalist Laura Kuenssberg, Cummings disclosed that he and other former colleagues from the Vote Leave Brexit campaign had begun plotting to remove Johnson within days of winning the 2019 election. 'He doesn't know how to be Prime Minister, and we'd only got him in there because we had to solve a certain problem, not because we thought that he was the right person to be running the country,' Cummings said.[13]

BETRAYAL

Johnson's relationship with his party followed a similar trajectory, from veneration to repulsion. After the 2019 election victory, Tories feted him as the greatest political campaigner of the age, with even his one-time leadership rival George Osborne declaring that politics was entering the Johnson era.

By the first half of 2022, however, what little faith Conservative MPs had left in his leadership was evaporating in the heat of the spiralling scandal over lockdown-breaking parties in Downing Street. In June, he survived the test of a confidence vote, but it was a close call: 148 Tory MPs voted that they had no confidence in his leadership of the party, with 211 supporting him to stay on.

A month later, when Johnson could not get his story straight about what he knew of allegations of sexual misconduct against

Chris Pincher, a government colleague and ally, a tipping point was reached. First, the civil service launched an attack, via Simon McDonald, the former top mandarin at the Foreign Office, who said No. 10 had not been telling the truth. For a former civil servant boss to accuse the Prime Minister of lying was an extraordinary moment. Some in Whitehall cheered McDonald, but others worried that a line had been crossed and reprisals against officials would follow. Then the resignations began.

At 6.02 p.m. on 5 July 2022, Health Secretary Sajid Javid quit, telling Johnson he'd lost confidence in his leadership. 'I am instinctively a team player,' Javid wrote in his resignation letter. 'But the British people also rightly expect integrity from their Government.' Later, in an interview with Laura Kuenssberg for the TV programme *State of Chaos*, Javid added, 'I knew someone at No. 10 has been lying, again.'[14]

At 6.11 p.m., Chancellor Rishi Sunak announced on Twitter that he was also leaving, delivering a hammer blow to the PM's authority. 'The public rightly expect government to be conducted properly, competently and seriously,' Sunak wrote in his resignation letter. 'I recognise this may be my last ministerial job, but I believe these standards are worth fighting for and that is why I am resigning.'

At the time, Sunak's shock decision was overshadowed by the drama of a government in disarray. But later it would be held against him by embittered Johnson fans in the party and the country, who blamed him for deposing their hero.

One after another, a succession of ministers followed Javid and Sunak out of government, most urging the PM to quit for the sake of the party and the country. For two days he refused, but the stream of resignations became a tsunami, with ministers quitting faster than Johnson could replace them.

During the messy, drawn-out endgame of his premiership, aides toyed with the idea of calling a snap election, to bully rebellious MPs back into line with the threat of punishment at the ballot box. But Cabinet Secretary Simon Case made clear to them that the Queen would be within her rights to refuse any request to dissolve Parliament to prolong the career of a Prime Minister who has lost the confidence of the House of Commons. The election threat melted away.

Reluctantly, on 7 July 2022, Johnson faced up to defeat and announced he would stand down, in a classically belligerent statement outside No. 10. 'In the last few days, I have tried to persuade my colleagues that it would be eccentric to change governments when we are delivering so much,' Johnson said. 'But as we've seen at Westminster, the herd is powerful and when the herd moves, it moves.' He added, 'To you the British people, I know that there will be many who are relieved but perhaps quite a few who will be disappointed, and I want you to know how sad I am to give up the best job in the world. But them's the breaks.'

For the third time in six years, the Conservative Party was thrown into the upheaval of a leadership election, while the country looked on once again at a government in chaos.

Four years and three Prime Ministers after the pandemic struck, it is clear that the Conservatives were never able to put themselves back together again and regain that elusive unity of spirit or the discipline required to deliver on a shared agenda for the country. Civil war inside the ruling Tory tribe had become a way of life.

Boris Johnson could have been Prime Minister for a long time. After winning a majority of eighty, he and his team were eyeing up at least a decade in power. But led by him, the Conservative government earned an unwanted reputation for callous hypocrisy during the pandemic, as well as for infighting and, perhaps most damagingly of all, for telling lies.

CHAPTER 2

TRUSSONOMICS

BALI

Liz Truss was on the beach.

The Foreign Secretary had not joined in the rush of resignations that triggered Johnson's exit. She was staying at a villa in Bali, preparing for a G20 meeting that was expected to feature a showdown with her Russian counterpart, Sergey Lavrov. Walking up and down the shore, she held anguished phone calls with allies in London about whether to return to the UK or stay to finish the meeting. Eventually, her adviser Adam Jones had to tell her, 'Liz, wake the fuck up and get back here.'[1]

In the leadership campaign that followed Johnson's resignation, MPs whittled down a long list of candidates to a final two who would go to a run-off vote among Conservative Party members. After a slow start, Truss made it through to take on the ex-Chancellor, and the man seen to have 'knifed' Johnson, Rishi Sunak. She was an early favourite and consciously encouraged comparisons with Margaret Thatcher, both in her presentational style – including the white blouses and blue jackets she wore – and her agenda for unleashing growth with a slash-and-burn approach to taxes and regulation.

Up against that, Sunak – who is, in reality, a classic, small-state Thatcherite Tory by instinct – was always likely to seem cautiously centrist. Such was the transformation of the Truss brand since the 2016 EU referendum that she appeared the more strident Brexiteer, despite having campaigned for Remain. Sunak looked like a product of the pro-European elite, even though he had voted Leave. 'Rishi didn't offer anything to the membership for the future, except for credibility,' according to one person who worked on his campaign. Credibility, it would turn out, can be an underrated quality, until it's gone.

The summer leadership campaign was hot-tempered. Both sides traded insults and played dirty as they competed for the votes of thousands of Conservative Party grassroots members. Sunak repeatedly interrupted Truss during televised debates and was hit with the toxic charge of 'mansplaining' by her allies as a result. Polling, always a tricky business among the Tory membership, predicted a two-to-one victory for Truss, overturning the preference of Conservative MPs, who had backed Sunak.* In the end it was much closer than that, at 57 per cent to Sunak's 43 per cent.

When Graham Brady, the chair of the backbench 1922 Committee of MPs, and the party's chief election officer, declared Truss the new leader at an event on 5 September, she displayed what was to become a trademark of her short time in office and its aftermath: a blunt and stubborn refusal to accommodate those who see the world differently, including her defeated rival. Although Rishi Sunak was sitting only two seats away from her, separated by a single empty

---

* In the final round of voting among Tory MPs, Sunak won 137 votes to Truss's 113. As the two candidates with the most votes, they then went to a run-off contest among the party membership, held over the summer.

chair, Truss didn't even acknowledge him, never mind shake hands for the cameras, as she strode up to the stage to claim her crown.

Truss's decision in the days that followed to appoint a Cabinet drawn largely from her long-trusted loyalists and backers did nothing to win her new friends in the parliamentary party – which had preferred Sunak, after all – or to heal the divisions of a particularly nasty contest. 'Liz only won 57–43 and yet she picked people for jobs only from her side,' one MP recalls.[2] When she needed their support a few short weeks later, it wasn't available.

The calibre of those who found themselves around the Cabinet table was also questionable, Conservative MPs felt. One MP says, 'She got in and appointed a whole load of people with minimal or no experience.' Other senior politicians who had been top ministers suddenly found themselves out of a job, feeling isolated and disgruntled on the back benches.

Inside No. 10, Truss's approach to hiring and firing and her combative, uncompromising style were given free rein. These qualities, which she had long displayed, contributed to her most devastating mistake: the so-called 'mini-Budget' package of unfunded tax cuts, which caused a market crash that almost brought the economy to its knees.

MORE HASTE

'She is always in such a rush.' If Liz Truss is one thing, it is 'impatient', according to one person who has worked closely with her: 'She has always been like that. Everyone always says that about her.'[3] Even the Queen advised Truss to pace herself, a suggestion the former PM has said she should have taken on board.

Truss's fundamental economic analysis was that the UK, since the financial crisis of 2007–08, had suffered a decade and a half of anaemic growth. She came into office believing, according to aides, that the nation needed aggressive and potentially unpopular measures to revive stagnant growth rates and put the economy back on the right track. These included dramatically scaling back fiscal policy, with cuts to both taxes and spending on public services, and liberalising planning laws to get the country building again. Such medicine would not be popular, but the payoff, Truss believed, would be to recharge economic activity, return people to work and deliver what she promised during her leadership campaign: 'Growth, growth, growth.'

It didn't matter to Truss or her aides that she had no mandate from the wider electorate to deliver such a radical economic revolution. She'd won the party leadership; this was her chance and she had been planning to take it for some time.

CHEVENING

In the late 1950s, the 7th Earl Stanhope, who lacked an heir, was contemplating what he would leave behind at the end of his life. He resolved to make a gift to the nation of Chevening House, the estate near Sevenoaks in Kent that had been in his family's ownership since 1717. Set in 3,500 acres of parkland, the 115-room stately home was built in 1630, reputedly to a design by Inigo Jones, and is now a Grade I listed building.

For the past forty years or so, the house has become the de facto country residence of the Foreign Secretary.* Truss had use of Chevening for government business and she chose to base herself there

---

* Lord Carrington, who set the precedent of using the house as Foreign Secretary while serving in Thatcher's government, recalled Stanhope as someone who was not 'at all interested in his own advancement or, in the modern jargon, the sort of image that he created'. Speaking in the House of Lords, as peers paid tribute after Stanhope's death in 1967, Carrington went on: 'He seemed to be, and I am sure he was, a man who by tradition served his country, and not for the rewards that he was likely to get, but regardless of the political misfortunes which might from time to time befall him and intent only on doing his job as best he might.'

as she finalised her plans for power. In the three weeks before entering Downing Street, she gathered her team of advisers to plan a fiscal event, which quickly became known as the 'mini-Budget', that would serve as the big-bang moment to supercharge her growth strategy. Along with her political advisers, senior civil servants, including Cabinet Secretary Simon Case, were regular visitors, as Chevening became the Truss transition headquarters.[4]

Among the economic brains brought in to give the soon-to-be premier advice on her fiscal statement were veterans of the Vote Leave Brexit campaign and right-wing academics in the orbit of the Thatcherite think tank, the Institute of Economic Affairs (IEA). They included IEA fellows Julian Jessop and Andrew Lilico, as well as Gerard Lyons, who was Boris Johnson's former economic adviser. Matt Sinclair, who cut his teeth at the Taxpayers' Alliance, another free-market campaign group in Westminster, had become Truss's principal economic adviser.

Lyons and Jessop wrote a paper for Truss aimed at supporting her growth agenda. It also contained a warning that would come to look prescient. 'The markets are nervous about the UK and about policy options,' they wrote. 'If immediate economic policy announcements are handled badly then a market crash is possible.'[5]

THE STORM

On 6 September, Truss met the Queen and 'kissed hands' in front of a roaring log fire in Balmoral, the monarch's estate in Scotland. Truss flew back to London and spent some time being driven around in her prime ministerial Jaguar, waiting for a break in the rain in order to arrive dry at Downing Street and make her first statement to the nation.

When the moment came, she declared her mission to deliver 'growth' via tax cuts and reform – her slogan during the campaign. 'I am confident that together we can ride out the storm, we can rebuild our economy, and we can become the modern, brilliant Britain that I know we can be,' she said. 'I am determined to deliver.'

Two days later, she unveiled the biggest state intervention in the energy market ever seen in the UK. With prices skyrocketing due to the war in Ukraine and global economic aftershocks from the pandemic, household bills were forecast to reach punitive levels the following month. Ofgem, the energy regulator, was preparing to raise the level of the energy price cap by 80 per cent from 1 October. It had already pushed the cap up by 54 per cent in April. Truss said she had to act, with typical household costs forecast to be £5,000 to £6,000 a year. On 8 September, the government announced the Energy Price Guarantee, worth an estimated £120 billion over the next two years. It was a vast commitment that would put a significant drain on public finances.

The energy policy was almost instantly forgotten. Later that day, Queen Elizabeth II died at the age of ninety-six.

It is hard to overstate the impact of the death of the Queen, after seventy years on the throne, on the functioning of the British state. While formally the sovereign has no power to determine the policies enacted by the government in their name, they remain the focal point of leadership for both elected members of Parliament and the permanent civil service, not to mention the criminal justice system and the armed forces.

It is central to the UK's constitution, which relies largely on politicians behaving honourably, for there to be a figurehead at the top of it all to set the tone. The Queen was – and had to be – above politics. Politicians could never afford to try to be above the Queen.

Johnson and Cummings, at various points, tried to play fast and loose with the convention that the sovereign must not be dragged into political games and found that the established way of doing things still had enough buy-in from MPs, and within the structures of Whitehall and the courts, to defeat them.

In the period of national mourning that followed the Queen's death, all politics ceased, along with any discussion of economic policy. Whatever political dividend Truss might have hoped for from her truly radical measures to help families pay their energy bills was stifled at birth.

Truss has admitted struggling to meet the moment as a national leader. (Boris Johnson chipped in with his own video address to the nation via social media.) She has described feeling an overwhelming sense of grief at the death of the Queen and recalled asking herself, 'Why me, why now?'

• • •

Truss always disliked big meetings. She preferred to hold working sessions with small groups of trusted aides. In her view, larger meetings tended to degenerate into performance art, with individuals taking their time to grandstand. When she took office, she tended to shut out most of her team, including some advisers she'd worked with for a long time. She did not even want to have a formal morning meeting each day, something that had been a Downing Street fixture for as long as anyone could remember. 'After things went wrong, the meetings got bigger,' one adviser recalls.[6]

Some of those around Truss believe the combined effect of her jetting around the country during the period of national mourning and preparing for the funeral, with the Queen lying in state, added to her isolation, leaving key advisers in the dark about the full extent of her mini-Budget plans.[7]

One person who felt invincible was Kwasi Kwarteng. He and Truss had been the closest of political friends and allies for more than a decade, ever since they both entered Parliament together in 2010. They had a shared economic outlook as free-market libertarians and had both been members of the Free Enterprise Group of Tory MPs during the Cameron–Clegg coalition. Neither had made much of a secret of their pro-growth, tax-cutting desires. But they did hold different views about how far to go and how fast.

TREASURY ORTHODOXY

One of Truss's first acts, via her new Chancellor Kwarteng, was to fire the most senior civil servant in the Treasury, permanent secretary Tom Scholar. A highly experienced and respected official, Scholar found himself the wrong fit for Truss's new agenda. Kwarteng immediately began looking for a replacement to deliver on her plan to rip up decades of what was disparagingly termed 'Treasury orthodoxy'.

Scholar's exit, which later saw him rewarded with a £335,000 payoff, robbed the Treasury of experienced leadership at a critical moment. Not only had the government just pledged a £120 billion intervention in the energy market but Kwarteng and Truss were at that very moment writing their 'mini-Budget'. In preparation for their big-bang, go-for-growth moment, Truss also decided to shun the services of the Treasury's independent forecasters, the Office for Budget Responsibility – another move that raised eyebrows (and government borrowing costs) in the City of London.

One person involved in the plan at the time describes the Energy

Price Guarantee as 'a masterful decision', with the country on the path to soaring household power bills amid a cost-of-living crisis. 'That would have destroyed the economy,' they say.[8] The problem was coupling such a vast package of relief for households with what would turn out to be a shock package of tax cuts, including for the very top earners in society.

Truss and Kwarteng apparently thought the bond markets would be fine. 'Because they managed to announce the energy scheme and effectively borrow money to fund it, there was a view that there was a lot more tolerance in the bond markets to turn on the taps even further,' one person involved recalls.[9]

'The fiscal cost of the energy package combined with the tax-cut package – I think the market would have bought one or the other but the market wouldn't buy both,' another former adviser argues. No one in the Treasury warned Truss and Kwarteng that combining these two huge commitments would be a problem, they added. The Bank of England later hit back, insisting that Truss hadn't briefed them about her tax-cut plans in advance.[10]

Truss's view was nobody should have been surprised that her first priority was to 'deliver' on her promise to fire up the economy, with a shot of neat tax cuts straight into the main artery of the nation's wealth creators, because she'd said she would do so during her leadership campaign. 'People were just not paying attention,' was how one adviser summarised the response to Truss's actions.[11]

In all, economists estimated that Kwarteng's mini-Budget of 23 September 2022 included £45 billion of unfunded tax-cut commitments. One of the most contentious plans was to abolish the 45p top rate of income tax for people earning more than £150,000 a year.

According to one senior official who was involved, the real flaw was not the scale of the cut to the top rate of tax. Abolishing the 45p rate would cost about £1.8 billion – not a trifling amount but not enough to spook the markets on its own. What made the difference to currency and bond market traders was the political significance of the move.

For years, centrist political leaders – including Cameron, May and Johnson – had all been wary of delivering sweeping tax cuts weighted so heavily toward the richest in society. Such a move was seen as politically toxic, especially for a Conservative Party frequently caricatured as relying on Eton and Oxford for its leaders and billionaires and bankers for its funds. 'What 45p signalled was the unpredictability of her premiership,' the senior official says. 'If she's willing to do that and bulldoze through established norms, what else is she capable of doing?'[12]

MELTDOWN

Sir Robert Stheeman has the air of a career diplomat. Balding, bespectacled and rarely seen out of a dark suit, he's known in the rarified world of the City for his immaculate manners and mischievous sense of humour. He exudes an air of droll serenity, which is just as well given that he's been responsible for arranging more than £3 trillion worth of government borrowing since 2003.

In order to raise money to pay for the things they want to do, governments have three main options: one is cutting spending on lesser priorities, another is raising taxes and the third is increasing borrowing. The Debt Management Office (DMO), the Treasury agency which Stheeman ran for more than two decades, manages the sale of government debt in the form of bonds, known as 'gilts', on the market. These bonds are a sort of 'IOU' that governments issue in order to raise the money they need for public spending. Traders and investors who buy the bonds charge the government a fee via the market for lending it money. The riskier the government, the higher the fee.

A banker himself by training, Stheeman would use the DMO's open-plan office in the heart of the City, close to the Tower of London, as a base from which to hold meetings with traders and investors as he drew up plans for gilt sales to meet the government's spending needs. As the chief government bond salesman, his role was to make managing the state's debts as smoothly as his own urbane demeanour. Keep borrowing calm and carry on.[13]

'This is, for anyone who works in markets, arguably just about the most interesting job around,' Stheeman dryly told MPs on the Public Accounts Committee in 2023. After Kwarteng and Truss unveiled their mini-Budget the previous year, his job was certainly more interesting than it might have been.

In the hours after Kwarteng's statement announcing the mini-Budget, the bond markets central to Stheeman's work went haywire, demanding a much higher price for taking on the UK government's debt. It was a clear sign that trouble was brewing, with the financial world deeply worried about what the Truss government would do next. A devastating set of factors combined to push Britain into a critical, self-induced financial crisis – Truss's free-enterprise economics running wild, bond markets freaking out and the failure of the Bank of England to anticipate this huge risk to pension funds.[*]

• • •

As bond markets recoiled, believing that Truss and Kwarteng had gone too far to be reliable customers to lend money to, the knock-on

---

[*] In their excellent three-part series 'Who Killed Liz Truss', on *The Rest Is Money* podcast, journalists Robert Peston and Steph McGovern describe how the new PM's perfect storm blew up.

impact was dramatic for other investors who held gilts. Suddenly, those bonds were worth less than they had been before. The biggest losers were huge pension funds, which had made use of a particular type of investment called liability-driven investments (LDIs). As the value of government bonds fell, these LDI funds, which invested heavily in gilts, got squeezed and then passed that on to the pension funds, which were suddenly then in huge trouble themselves. Investors sold off their UK bonds, driving the price even lower and making the problem still worse again.

Soon the Bank of England had to step in to promise to buy up to an astonishing £65 billion of government bonds in an attempt to stabilise the markets and protect pension funds. Multiple sources in government, including allies of Truss, believe the Bank of England messed up by failing to spot the risk posed by LDIs to pensions until the crisis was well advanced. Certainly, at the heart of Whitehall, in the Treasury and in Downing Street, no one saw the danger.

'None of us had ever heard of [LDIs] including at the Bank of England,' one senior government official recalled. Another said, 'The Bank of England weren't fully aware of the LDI issue and they didn't brief Treasury officials, so Treasury officials never briefed Liz or Kwasi.' A third says, 'The LDI thing was as much of a surprise to [the bank] as it was to us. There may have been a failure of regulation there.'[14]

The costs were huge, politically and economically. Interest rates stayed high and the Tories reaped the blame for millions of mortgage-holders moving off fixed-term deals onto eye-watering rates in the run-up to the election. International investors looked at Britain differently after the mini-Budget.

---

* The Bank of England argued in 2022 that it had identified risks related to LDI funds four years earlier but said most of these funds were based outside the UK, meaning more international work was needed. In a letter to MPs, the bank also argued that the 'scale and speed' of the price moves 'far exceeded' what had happened in the past.

For years, Cameron, May and Johnson had outshone their Labour opponents when it came to who voters trusted to manage the economy. But thanks to Truss and Kwarteng, the party had trashed its reputation even for basic competence. 'It felt like we were in the middle of a very serious, self-harmed economic collapse,' one senior official recalled.[15]

MORE TO COME

Two days after the mini-Budget, on Sunday 25 September 2022, Kwarteng gave an interview to the BBC's former political editor, Laura Kuenssberg. Despite the markets recoiling, he defended his tax cuts and insisted he was going to keep prioritising measures to deliver economic growth. 'There's more to come,' he declared.

But investors had had enough already. It was a Sunday, so markets were closed in London. Later that night, however, trading began again in Asia – and the instant reaction to Kwarteng's promise was 'panic', in the words of one Treasury official at the time.

'The final straw that broke the camel's back – and the thing nobody knew he was going to do – was Kwasi going on the Sunday [TV show with Kuenssberg] indicating that there were further tax cuts to come,' a separate senior official recalls. 'I don't know who he discussed that with. It was just something he said. That's the thing that tipped the markets over the edge. The recklessness was unbelievable.'[16]

There was indeed no plan to announce that more tax cuts were coming on Kuenssberg's Sunday show. So why did Kwarteng say it? 'Because I think they had every intention of doing that,' one aide recalls.

Politicians do mess up in interviews, of course, but they had every intention of going further. The prevailing view at the time was, 'We need to crack on, this is the right thing to do and it will stabilise. But this is needed for economic growth – that's the big prize and if we have to face people down to get there, we will.'[17]

But the situation didn't stabilise. The market panic had set in. TV news channels were a rolling horror show of doom graphs charting the demise of the UK's economic credibility in the form of a falling pound and rising borrowing costs. Images of stressed-out traders with their hands in their hair filled the screens. It was like the 2008 financial crash all over again.

The Conservative Party conference was about to begin. In chaotic and humiliating scenes, Kwarteng was forced to announce that his flagship tax cut – abolishing the 45p higher rate – had become 'a distraction' and would be cancelled. It wasn't enough to stabilise the markets.

By this point, there was only one thing on the minds of those working inside No. 10: stopping the market sell-off. While gilts tumbled and Tory MPs started to panic, the atmosphere inside Truss's Downing Street bunker took on an air of surreal detachment.

'It was actually quite calm and orderly, which felt odd,' one person involved recalls.

> When things are going crazy you would think it's going to be chaos. But that's not how it felt. At that point you're so boxed in that there is a very clear order to the decisions you have to make. Everything gets smaller and narrower so it gets calmer and more orderly. Eventually everything became about what's going to happen when the markets open in the morning. Everything revolved around the markets.[18]

Alongside Truss were her political aides Mark Fullbrook, Jason Stein, Jamie Hope and Ruth Porter. Nick Catsaras, a civil servant, had become her most trusted official and, along with Cabinet Secretary Simon Case, was highly influential. These two civil servants – each the product of the establishment infrastructure Truss has railed against – were trying to keep the show on the road, after the politicians had driven the economy to the cliff edge.

When all other options had been tried, the really painful questions began to be asked. Might Kwarteng need to be sacrificed to show markets that the government had turned the page on the mini-Budget disaster? Case was among those arguing behind the scenes that Kwarteng may need to be moved, according to sources. Kwarteng told his team he didn't believe Truss would dare to fire him and warned her directly that doing so would be a mistake for her, as she would be next in line for the axe. 'I'm her stab vest,' he told his team.

He was wrong. On Friday 14 October, Truss summoned Kwarteng back from the US, where he had been attending the International Monetary Fund meeting. After he landed, as he was being driven from the airport to No. 10, he learned via Twitter that his closest political friend was about to sack him.

'The focus was about how to reassure the markets,' one aide says. 'That was the main goal in No. 10 at that point,' another former official recalls. Truss was 'hugely conflicted' about the idea of sacking her friend, but 'she practically felt like she had no choice.'[19]

It is as well that neither Truss nor Kwarteng is prone to sentimentality. They remained friends and he rejects the idea that she betrayed him, though he has admitted to feeling a little let down.[20] As she weighed up the mess they had created together, Truss tried to set aside her emotions, one adviser says. When she finally resolved he had to go, however, 'it all spilled out – she was hugely upset. It was an awful thing to have to do.'[21]

Although he was forcibly removed, Kwarteng still ended up writing a sort of resignation letter to Truss, which was made public. In it, he defended their joint approach to tax cuts. 'As I said many times in the past weeks, following the status quo was simply not an option,' he wrote. 'For too long this country has been dogged by low growth rates and high taxation – that must change if this country is to succeed.' In her reply, Truss said she was 'deeply sorry' to lose him. 'We share the same vision for our country and the same firm conviction to go for growth.'

CHEQUERS

Jeremy Hunt had initially thought it was a prank when he received a text from a number he didn't recognise while on holiday with his family in Belgium. He laughed out loud as he read it to his wife: 'Jeremy, it's Liz Truss, please call urgently.' In the end, Downing Street's legendary switchboard had to find one of Hunt's former aides to contact him and persuade him that he really did need to call No. 10 back, and it really was urgent.

After Hunt accepted Truss's offer of the role of Chancellor – capping a long career in senior ministerial roles with his biggest job of all – he set about trying to dig the government and the country out of the mess she had made. At this point, he was as powerful as anyone in government and arguably more so even than Truss herself. International financial markets, the whole of Westminster, the Bank of England and the civil service were all looking to Hunt to reassure them.

If seventeenth-century Chevening House in rural Kent was where Truss's doomed economic masterplan was born, Chequers, the Prime Minister's sixteenth-century country residence, was where it finally died. It was here, forty miles north-west of London in the Buckinghamshire countryside, that Truss herself also began to confront the beginning of the end.

She had already announced some major U-turns, including scrapping her plan to reverse Sunak's increase in corporation tax to 25 per cent from 19 per cent, when she fired Kwarteng on Friday 14 October. But it hadn't been enough to quell the market turmoil. Hunt got back from his Belgian holiday and spent the evening of Saturday 15 October locked away inside the Treasury with permanent secretary James Bowler and Clare Lombardelli, the top economic adviser. Together they worked up an action plan to reassure the rattled markets.

The following day, Sunday 16 October, Truss hosted Hunt and his family at Chequers for lunch with her, her husband Hugh and their children. Hunt brought a clutch of Treasury officials along too, while Truss brought Case, the Cabinet Secretary, and political aides including Fullbrook, Porter, Stein and Catsaras, the civil servant she trusted the most.

The children went out to play in the extensive Chequers gardens, while Hunt, Truss and a few officials went upstairs for a crunch meeting. It was then that he told her he was going to scrap almost everything she and Kwarteng had announced in the mini-Budget, including all the key tax cuts. Truss must have known it was coming, but it was still a devastating blow.[22]

Truss sat down with Hunt and their families, along with some long-serving political aides, to a lunch of roast chicken. During a walk in the garden, she chatted with her husband Hugh, who asked the big question: since she'd been forced to ditch her most cherished policies, should she continue as Prime Minister?[23]

Truss then openly began courting views, pondering aloud among her key advisers whether she should give up the job she'd worked so hard to secure. It wasn't clear yet to her that it was finally over, but in the words of one of those present, this was the moment when she first asked, 'What's the point?'[24]

The next day, Truss sat on the government front bench while Hunt systematically dismantled her growth plan, piece by piece. 'It was uniquely painful,' she said later. Listening to Hunt 'shredding the platform on which I had won the leadership election', she recalled, was 'something of an out-of-body experience'.[25]

The *Daily Star* newspaper had been running a cruelly satirical live stream of an iceberg lettuce, asking the question whether Truss's premiership would be over before the salad started to wilt. After Hunt's statement, the *Star* warned that Truss's leadership was on 'leaf support'.

FRACTURED

The final act arrived surprisingly fast. On Wednesday 19 October, the government was facing an awkward vote in the Commons on a Labour motion on fracking, the contentious method of extracting gas from underground reservoirs by fracturing the rock in which it is stored. Tory MPs were initially told the motion was being treated as a 'confidence' vote, making supporting the government position a matter of the utmost importance. The whips, who are in charge of maintaining party discipline during parliamentary votes, gave the message out to Conservatives that they must do as they are told or face the consequences.

But shortly before voting began, Graham Stuart, the junior minister speaking for the government during the debate, announced that the vote would not amount to a confidence motion after all. His last-minute intervention apparently followed an instruction from Truss's team, who feared she would suffer a humiliating rebellion and it would therefore be better to look like she didn't care what happened. Stuart's intervention created chaos among MPs, who now did not know what to do with just moments to spare before the vote. Was it a confidence motion or not?

Witnesses reported seeing Tories manhandled through the Commons voting lobby by angry government ministers trying to make sure Truss did not lose. Amid the mayhem, one Tory MP asked Deputy Chief Whip Craig Whittaker if it was a confidence motion and which way they should go. Whittaker replied, 'Don't ask me, I've resigned.' Another MP asked the same question to the Chief Whip, Wendy Morton, and got the same answer: 'I've resigned.'[26] Amid the chaotic scenes, Morton was later persuaded to 'unresign' after Truss chased her down the corridor. But the little credibility the PM still had with her party had been irreparably destroyed.[27]

Sir Charles Walker, the veteran Tory MP, spoke for many of his colleagues when he declared on TV in the minutes after the debacle:

> I think it is utterly appalling. I'm livid and, you know, I really shouldn't say this, but I hope all those people that put Liz Truss in No. 10 – I hope it was worth it. I hope it was worth it for the ministerial red box. I hope it was worth it to sit around the Cabinet table. Because the damage they've done to our party is extraordinary. I've had enough.

One senior Tory who witnessed the scenes recalls, 'It was just a farce.' A senior official who was working on the rescue package says that after the 'bizarre' fracking vote, 'the game was up' for Truss. It was obvious to all that her government was 'imploding'.[28]

Truss knew it too. That night, she went back to the Downing Street flat to talk to her husband. Over a bottle of Sauvignon Blanc and a pork pie, they discussed the inevitability of her resignation.[29]

• • •

She took soundings from her senior team. In one awkward exchange, she even asked Simon Case, the politically neutral head of the civil service, what he thought she should do. Case attempted, carefully, to be helpful and told the PM that the question for her to consider was whether she had the confidence of her party. 'I'd better speak to Graham Brady,' the PM replied.[30]

Brady was the man who just six weeks earlier had announced to the world that Truss had won the leadership. Often referred to as the 'shop steward' of Tory MPs, he was chair of the 1922 Committee, representing backbench politicians in the parliamentary Conservative Party. In the end, Truss called him to ask for a meeting just as he was picking up his phone to dial Downing Street to request one.[31]

On 20 October, Truss walked out of the famous black door, with her husband to support her, and announced she was bringing an end to the shortest premiership in British political history. She looked shattered, but there was no emotion in her voice as she delivered her short statement. There were no thanks for officials, her team, party colleagues or her family either.

'We set out a vision for a low-tax, high-growth economy that would take advantage of the freedoms of Brexit,' Truss said, with a rueful half-smile on her lips.

I recognise though, given the situation, I cannot deliver the mandate on which I was elected by the Conservative Party. I have therefore spoken to His Majesty the King to notify him that I am resigning as leader of the Conservative Party. This morning I met the chair of the 1922 Committee, Sir Graham Brady. We have agreed there will be a leadership election to be completed in the next week. This will ensure we remain on a path to deliver our fiscal plans and maintain our country's economic stability and national security. I will remain as Prime Minister until a successor has been chosen. Thank you.

A former Cabinet minister says Truss, more so than Johnson, toxified the party in the eyes of voters for the contest to come. 'The worst thing about it was that it wasn't just about Liz. It was that Tory members had voted for her, so the toxicity bled across to the whole party. With Boris, it was restricted to Boris.'[32]

REVENGE OF THE GNOMES

Since leaving office, Truss has complained that dark forces of the British establishment and the global elite thwarted her reforms and forced her from office. This might play well in certain corners of conspiracy Twitter, but in Westminster and Whitehall it doesn't. If the 2024 election is any guide, voters in Truss's seat and around the country didn't buy her version of events either.

'For as long as the government runs a deficit, the people we borrow money from have a great say in economic policy, of course they do,' a senior Truss-era adviser says. 'It's our choice to run a deficit and we have effectively abdicated control to those we borrow from. It's not as if the market is some kind of evil, controlling beast.

Our country has depended on them. If you're borrowing from people, they have a say.'[33]

Government officials are still clearly stung by the experience of working through Truss's self-inflicted maelstrom, trying to save the country from collapse. One summarised Truss as 'someone who came in on the attack, really wasn't interested in listening to any notes and sounds of caution on anything, blew up so quickly, and then totally had to rely on us to undo her mistake'.[34]

Looking back, a senior Whitehall official dismisses Truss's attempts to blame, in their words, the 'gnomes of Zurich' and the Bank of England for her own failures. While it is certainly true that top Whitehall mandarins such as Case, James Bowler and Beth Russell at the Treasury, and Bank of England governor Andrew Bailey were in regular contact during the crisis, that does not amount to a plot. 'You might be right, Liz, it was markets,' the senior official says.

> You might want to blame these faceless financiers and the global elite – yep, it may well be. But they are the people who have been investing and therefore funding the UK economy for quite a long time now, in fact probably largely since the 1980s. And they're not people who like reckless [actions]. They're like bank managers – they like steady, sure management of their money and investments. It's that classic childish thing that's both very Boris and very Liz to blame all these other things. Well, they were fine before your mini-Budget. And it's kind of what your Chancellor said that caused them to say they're not fine any more. I don't think it was a global conspiracy to take down Liz, I just think the people who fund and pay for this country thought you'd gone mad.[35]

CHAPTER 3

THE LAWYER

MR METHODICAL

'He thinks step by step,' said Shabana Mahmood, who became Labour's Justice Secretary after the election. 'I've not met anyone quite so methodical in politics.'[1]

From day one as an MP in 2015, Sir Keir Starmer never behaved like an ordinary backbencher. His colleagues noticed how he rarely drank in Parliament's bars or shared the latest gossip, and never joined in the chat in MPs' WhatsApp groups.

Starmer was always fiercely competitive. Those closest to him underlined how he despised the impotence of being on the losing side in politics. 'Keir hated opposition,' says one former aide. 'He didn't get into politics to stand up in the Commons and just talk.'[2]

Despite his intimidating CV – which included a knighthood, a string of landmark cases, and a stint leading the Crown Prosecution Service – Starmer's family background was distinctly ordinary. According to those who know him and have studied his rise, it is his working-class roots that drove his ferocious work ethic and made him so determined to win.

Starmer grew up in a semi-detached home in a small town on the Kent–Surrey border, the second of four children. His father, Rodney, worked in a factory (he was a toolmaker, as Starmer never stopped reminding the public later in life). His mother Josephine, a nurse, struggled with Still's disease, a rare form of inflammatory arthritis. Cash was so tight at home in the 1970s that the telephone was cut off when his parents could not pay the bill.

As a teenager, he dabbled in left-wing activism, joining the Surrey Young Socialists – a somewhat niche group in the affluent commuter belt, which numbered only a handful of members. 'We marched around East Surrey up long drives telling people we thought nationalisation was the answer,' Starmer has recalled. 'There weren't so many that were persuaded.'[3] He excelled academically at school – his siblings gave him the nickname 'superboy' – but arrived to study law at Leeds University in 1982 not even knowing the difference between a solicitor and a barrister.

Starmer has described feeling 'imposter syndrome' and has argued that this is something working-class people experience particularly sharply. Tom Baldwin, his biographer, has explained, 'He doesn't have that swaggering entitlement that some people in politics have. He feels he has to work harder to prove himself every time.'[4]

In the late 1980s, after completing postgraduate studies at Oxford, Starmer moved to a grotty flat in Highgate, now one of north London's most expensive suburbs. While his friends partied hard, he was 'so obsessed by his books' that on one occasion he 'didn't notice two burglars walking round the house, helping themselves to our stuff', one friend recalled.[5]

As a lawyer, he made his name representing underdogs and slaying giants. He defended people facing the death penalty abroad and worked on the 'McLibel' defamation case, in which his team partially defeated the global restaurant behemoth.

Starmer rose to be Director of Public Prosecutions and made several key changes while in the role, including new guidelines on when not to bring charges in cases of assisted suicide. One of his proudest achievements at the Crown Prosecution Service was more modest: moving paper files onto a digital system. It was, those close to him concede, a particularly 'Starmerish' triumph – methodical and more than a little dull.

His most obvious obsession, however, wasn't political at all. 'In the main,' says one colleague, 'he likes talking about football.'[6]

Starmer's beloved Arsenal was often derided as 'boring' in the 1990s, the era when the student Rishi Sunak was nurturing his own passion for Southampton FC. Their political fortunes at the top of their respective parties mirrored those of the teams they support. Starmer rarely set pulses racing but ground his opponents down and got the job done, eventually taking the biggest trophy of all. For Sunak, it was always a relegation battle, a fight for survival, not silverware.

Before Starmer got the chance to reshape his party for an election, however, he first had to watch it descend into disarray and despair.

VICTORY ALE

It was a painful verdict for Jeremy Corbyn.

At 10 p.m. on 12 December 2019, Big Ben chimed and the national broadcaster's exit poll confirmed the worst: his Labour Party was heading for its heaviest election defeat since the 1930s.

That vote resoundingly humiliated Labour's socialist left. Since Corbyn won the leadership in 2015, repeated attempts by centrists in the party to oust him had failed. This time, there was no escape. At the election night party at Labour headquarters, more than 100 bottles of specially branded 'Corbynista Victory Ale' went unopened as the scale of the defeat became clear. Later that night, Corbyn announced he would resign.

Watching the exit poll on TV, Morgan McSweeney, a long-suffering activist from the moderate wing of the party, barely shrugged. He had ignored the entire campaign. Instead of joining the Labour masses knocking on doors trying to oust Boris Johnson, he had spent every spare moment of the previous six weeks working on Keir Starmer's leadership bid, so it would be ready in the event that Corbyn fell on his sword.

When the exit poll confirmed Johnson had crushed Labour, McSweeney felt a sense of release: the Corbyn wilderness era was finally over. Then he got straight back to work, hitting the phones, determined that Labour's moderates must not miss this chance to retake control of their party.

MORGAN'S MISSION

A fast-talking ball of energy with reddish-brown hair and a neatly trimmed beard, Morgan McSweeney is an Irishman who began his working life as a builder. He joined Labour in 1997 and had his first taste of electoral politics as part of the 2001 general election campaign, feeding data into Peter Mandelson's famous rapid rebuttal machine, the 'Excalibur'.[*]

As a campaigner, McSweeney had success in helping to lead Labour's efforts to kick the BNP out of Dagenham, after the far-right

---

[*] The two grew to know and trust each other, and Mandelson remained a key influence on McSweeney's thinking.

group won seats on the council. But he also failed to get Labour MP Liz Kendall off the floor as a leadership candidate in 2015. She won just 4.5 per cent of the vote.

When McSweeney was introduced to Starmer in north London before the 2017 general election, his first impressions were relatively neutral. The distinguished lawyer was clearly smart and seemed relatable, but there was no blinding moment of revelation for McSweeney.

Then, one day, as the pair walked to the underground station together, Starmer burst into a passionate discussion of knife crime in his London constituency. Corbyn and his team, Starmer said, were totally failing to notice the importance of this basic law-and-order issue and just did not understand how vital it was to tackle street crime in Britain's cities.

McSweeney was struck by how serious Starmer was about the issues that Labour had ignored under Corbyn and about the party's failure to connect with working-class voters. 'He gets angry at the right things,' McSweeney told a friend later.[7]

• • •

Corbyn's failure in 2019 had been forecast for years, but his internal opponents could not prise the leadership from his grip. Moderate centrists like Starmer, McSweeney and former frontbenchers including Rachel Reeves and Yvette Cooper had no way to take back power. The problem was the membership, which had overwhelmingly backed Corbyn when MPs tried to replace him.

Unsure of the road ahead, some moderates quit. Those who stayed resolved to keep fighting to stop Labour sliding further to the left. McSweeney had been running the think tank Labour Together, which battled the more toxic elements of the Corbyn project. For him, as for others, Corbyn's defeat came years too late. But at least it had finally arrived. Now, they needed a candidate to steer the battered party back onto the centre ground.

McSweeney had decided who it would have to be.

A few months before the 2019 catastrophe, he told Starmer that of all the potential candidates he'd ever met, the former chief prosecutor would make the best Prime Minister. The pair knew a leadership bid would be a long shot. Corbyn's hard left still had a complete grip on the grassroots members. And privately, McSweeney wasn't sure if Starmer even knew enough about Labour to be able to win the contest.

But he decided they had to try. Phone banks staffed by moderate activists were swiftly up and running, canvassing views among Labour members and circulating Starmer's name. A campaign team was assembled with leaflets, a website and strategy. Once the 2019 election crash destroyed Corbyn's project, McSweeney's greatest mission began.

• • •

The leadership election of 2019–20 opened with six candidates but entered its closing stages with just three: Starmer, Lisa Nandy, who was running on a soft-left platform, and Rebecca Long-Bailey, who had served on Corbyn's front bench. Early opinion polls, which hold great influence in leadership elections, showed a clear lead for McSweeney's man.

In large part this was due to ten pledges Starmer had made, many of which seem radical in retrospect. They included preserving the free movement of people between the UK and the EU, scrapping punitive state benefit sanctions, hiking taxes for high earners and the re-nationalisation of rail, mail, energy and water.

The pledges could have been written by Corbyn. They certainly helped Starmer convince the bruised socialists in the party membership that he could be trusted to carry forward their stuttering flame. Starmer won easily. He secured more than 56 per cent of the vote, double the tally of Rebecca Long-Bailey, his nearest rival.

By the time of the 2024 election, however, Labour's leader had shown just how ruthless he really was. He junked almost all those original ten pledges and repeatedly ruled out any return to joining the EU single market or customs union. Rather than apologise for ditching the last vestiges of Corbynism, he would proudly embrace the charge that he played hardball in his quest to take over and then overhaul the Labour Party. Before then, however, he nearly lost everything.

FAILING

In 2019, Boris Johnson had humiliated Labour. He stormed their strongholds in the so-called 'red wall' of Brexit-backing, economically depressed, former industrial towns in the north of England. But there was one prize that had not fallen to the Tories: the seat of Hartlepool, once held by Tony Blair's close ally, Peter Mandelson. It had been Labour's since 1974.

In 2021, Mike Hill, the incumbent MP, had triggered a by-election after quitting amid allegations that he had sexually harassed a member of staff. The special vote came on a packed day for democracy which the media had dubbed 'Super Thursday' – it was the biggest set of local and devolved parliament elections since 1973.

The outlook for the 6 May elections was dire for Starmer's

fledgling leadership. Internal polling based on surveys of around 10,000 people suggested Labour's support in the seaside town had almost halved since the 2019 election. Johnson, meanwhile, was mobbed like a rock star. Residents surrounded him asking for selfies as he strolled along the beach.

Locals were hostile to Labour, not just because the toxic Corbyn era was still fresh in their memories but also due to a succession of errors by Starmer's new team. It emerged that Labour's candidate Paul Williams, a Teesside doctor, was part of a clinical commissioning group that had backed the closure of Hartlepool's A&E. To top it off, old social media posts emerged, showing he had made off-colour remarks about women.

Labour tumbled to a miserable defeat, with a 16 per cent swing to the Conservatives. The gloom did not end there. In the local elections held that day, once-safe Labour territory turned blue all over the country. The party lost eight councils, including Durham. Johnson's Tories were rampant. Conservative Ben Houchen kept the Tees Valley mayoralty, with 73 per cent of the vote.

Starmer's authority had been severely damaged and rumours swirled of a leadership challenge. The defeat prompted soul-searching about the scale of the mountain Labour had to climb.

Criticism came from all sides of the party. Lord Adonis, a Blairite adviser and former minister, described him as a 'transitional leader' and said Labour was in 'no-man's land' under his leadership. Diane Abbott, on the left of the party, tweeted: 'Crushing defeat for Labour in Hartlepool. Not possible to blame Jeremy Corbyn for this result. Labour won the seat twice under his leadership. Keir Starmer must think again about his strategy.'

Starmer was deeply downcast. After just a year in the job, he wondered if he should quit.

FIGHTING

The Hartlepool defeat confirmed what the Labour leader already suspected: he was failing and something had to change.

After trying in his first year to accommodate the Corbynite left of his party, he concluded this was no longer possible. It was time to launch a major escalation in his mission to wrench Labour back to the centre ground, detoxify the brand and get the party up to match fitness for the general election. Having resolved not to resign, Starmer had no choice but to go into battle head on. Thanks to Morgan McSweeney, he had a blueprint ready and waiting.*

McSweeney had written a critical analysis of the party's desperate condition earlier in the spring of 2021 and sent it to Starmer. It was agreed as a way forward in April, shortly before the Hartlepool defeat. In the memo 'Labour for the Country', McSweeney predicted the local election failures and got straight to the point: 'Labour suffers from a lack of trust to govern that is potentially catastrophic,' he wrote.

> The damage to the Labour Party brand has been such that we must change more profoundly than we have accepted until now, we must embrace the conflict that is inevitable, and we must show the public that our vision is something worth fighting for.

McSweeney proposed a two-phase plan. On 7 May, the day after the Hartlepool and local council elections, Starmer must 'come out of

---

* Two factions on the right of the party, Progress and Labour First, had joined forces under an umbrella organisation called Labour To Win. Its express purpose was supporting Starmer's leadership when it came to internal battles. Matt Pound, one of McSweeney's closest allies, and Matthew Faulding, now secretary of the Parliamentary Labour Party, were at the helm. Pound helped Starmer secure a majority on the party's ruling National Executive Committee.

the traps quickly and seize the initiative', saying the results showed the party had not done enough to show the public it was different from the Corbyn years. Staff roles at Labour HQ should be aligned properly with Starmer's priorities and the shadow Cabinet should be overhauled and professionalised. Core team members must '[get] off Twitter'. This phase would last until the party conference on 25 September.

The second phase was focused on the conference itself. That gathering, when the media would be giving Starmer's team far more extensive coverage than usual, must include a leader's speech that makes 'the case for a different post-Covid country', he wrote. It should highlight Labour's 'patriotic' achievements under Tony Blair and Gordon Brown. 'Labour is the party with a plan to make Britain great again,' McSweeney wrote, echoing Donald Trump.

He was unambiguous in his view that party 'unity' was overrated. 'Voters prize unity not as something to be valued in itself but because they want to know that a party can follow through on its statements and promises and will not be diverted by internal squabbles and dispute,' he wrote. 'Prizing unity above all else leads us to look inwards and away from our voters. We over value its importance and this narrows our thinking and shrinks our electoral appeal.'

Labour's leader must show he understands the scale of voters' dislike and distrust of Corbynism and prove to the country that he is moving the party into a new phase, McSweeney argued:

> This lack of trust we inherited is a long way from being repaired. The British people will not listen to Keir until he shows he has heard them and their clear and repeated verdict on Labour's leadership since we left office in 2010. Parties that go from opposition to power first go through a visible transformation. The nature

of the transformation is often about issues that are unimportant to everyday voters (Clause 4, huskies etc.) – but the process of change, and the demonstrable struggle are an indication to the country that the party has listened, it is no longer focused only on itself, and it is ready to govern. It is only when they do this that they can win again.

It was time, in other words, for a fight.

• • •

Starmer began with an overhaul of his back office and his shadow Cabinet team. That led to a clash with deputy leader Angela Rayner. She had been national campaign coordinator but had delivered only failures. When he gave that job to Shabana Mahmood, Starmer had to find a way to mollify a furious Rayner. She got two more jobs in addition to her deputy leader role: shadow Cabinet Office minister and shadow Secretary of State for the Future of Work, with control over Labour's plans for new employment rights.

In that sweeping reshuffle, Starmer demoted his shadow Chancellor, Anneliese Dodds. In her place he put Rachel Reeves, a promising member of Ed Miliband's frontbench team who had been in the wilderness for four years under Corbyn. Reeves was given one crucial mission: rebuild Labour's wrecked relationship with businesses. From that moment on, she was at Starmer's side whenever he made strategic decisions. Regaining voters' trust on the economy became central to Starmer's mission.

There were more changes inside his own top team of staff. McSweeney moved from his position as Starmer's chief of staff to the critical role of campaign director. Starmer also hired the respected pollster Deborah Mattinson, a former adviser to Gordon Brown, as his director of strategy. Others came and went. It was a destabilising and emotional period, but the Labour leader felt it was necessary.

Around this time, Starmer's team decided Labour's internal party rules and structures needed reform too. And this was where the public fight that McSweeney regarded as both inevitable and vital would come.

The days of trying to placate the hard left were over. The party's ruling National Executive Committee, packed with Starmer's allies, banned four groups that had claimed antisemitism allegations were politically motivated. Accusations of antisemitism had become a racist stain on Labour's name that had grown into a full-blown disaster under Corbyn. Hundreds of party members were expelled as a result of their links to the four groups.

But Starmer could not make progress if his MPs were against him. Nor could he possibly win over wavering voters if they were being asked to back candidates for Parliament who were maverick Corbynites. He decided to shake up the rules governing the selection of would-be MPs.

The key was to strip local constituency branches of the Labour Party of the power to draw up their own longlists. Potential contenders were instead assigned to constituencies by the party centrally before local members voted on a shortlist. This selection process became the front line of the battle between Labour's hard left and its leadership. But the losers were angry. Starmer repeatedly faced furious accusations that he was unfairly gaming the system.

Sam Tarry, a sitting MP who led Corbyn's leadership campaign, was deselected in a ballot in Ilford South in 2022. He went further than others, submitting an official complaint about 'procedural irregularities' in the online voting system to the party's general secretary, David Evans.

Labour has always maintained that its selection process has been put in place to ensure high-quality candidates and has denied interfering in selections for political reasons. The clear impact of the process, however, was to sideline the hard left and create a model army of MPs from the liberal and social democratic mainstream. Starmer had secured his people.

STALINGRAD

The dust had not yet settled on Starmer's post-Hartlepool shake-up when yet another potential electoral disaster loomed.

On 1 July 2021, two months after that fateful defeat in the northeast, a by-election was due to be held in Batley & Spen, West Yorkshire. The seat was made up of relatively affluent villages and post-industrial towns. For Starmer's badly beaten party, it looked out of reach, but not putting up a fight was never an option.

Batley & Spen held a symbolic power in Labour circles that was unlike any other constituency. It had been held by Jo Cox, the Labour MP who was murdered by a far-right terrorist at the height of the Brexit referendum campaign in 2016. Her sister, Kim Leadbeater, was selected as Labour's candidate in the by-election.

The contest quickly became a circus. Alongside some thirteen candidates from smaller or independent parties and the Conservative contender, the far-left firebrand George Galloway was also running. The Workers Party leader, a Corbyn ally exiled from the Labour Party years ago, relished his role as the bogeyman of his former comrades.

For Starmer, with his leadership on the line, the vote meant everything. He waited up all night for the results. Labour won but by just 323 votes. It had been perilously close, but Starmer was delighted and hugely relieved. He picked up the phone and called Deborah Mattinson in the small hours of the morning to tell her. 'I don't think that's really where the turnaround started,' Mattinson recalls. 'It was where the rot stopped. That result could have been awful and it wasn't.'[8]

Many insiders look back on the by-election as Starmer's Stalingrad, the moment when the tide began to turn for him. 'If Batley & Spen had been when Hartlepool was and we had lost it, Starmer would not have survived,' one Labour source adds. 'I don't think he would have been able to overcome that narrative.'[9]

HERO VOTERS

Red-haired, formidably intelligent and not known for her patience with fools, Deborah Mattinson had only been in her job as Starmer's strategy director for four weeks when she delivered a blunt assessment of Labour's standing.

Six in ten voters did not know what the party stood for, she told the shadow Cabinet in August 2021. Labour's 'central problem', she said, was a 'lack of clarity'. But this, she said, was fixable and Labour would get its chance in the months ahead. Mattinson predicted a national appetite for change as the country emerged from the pandemic. Events would prove her right.

A former pollster to Gordon Brown as PM and at the Treasury before that, Mattinson later set up her own research business, BritainThinks. She quickly became one of the country's leading strategic consultants. Shadow Chancellor Rachel Reeves was impressed and approached her to become Starmer's director of strategy. She started work in July 2021, after an interview with the Labour leader on Zoom.

Over the next three years, Mattinson drove her agenda with colleagues in ways that sometimes made her unpopular. She didn't care. She refused to compromise in her demand for message discipline and her relentless focus on the critical group of voters who held the election in their hands.

'Everybody talked grandly about our "electoral coalition", the electoral coalition that we had to win,' Mattinson says. 'It was very broad and basically, people were focusing on whatever bit of that coalition they felt most comfortable with, which was too often not the bit that we really needed to win.'[10]

Her central diagnosis was that Labour had been casting the net too widely and needed to single-mindedly target one section of the electorate: what Mattinson termed 'hero voters'. These were the estimated two in five people who did not vote Labour in 2019 but would consider it and those who voted Labour but had doubts. A significant proportion of this group had at some time in the past been Tory supporters.

These 'hero voters' were usually homeowners, working-class, middle-aged or older, more likely to have voted for Brexit and less likely to be university-educated. They were patriotic, proud of Britain and family-oriented. They tended to feel neglected – that their hard work was not paying off and their local area had been left behind. They were broadly split, Mattinson assessed, between 'competence-driven Conservatives', who cared most about the economy and the country being well run, and 'culture-driven Conservatives', who prioritised action to tackle crime and immigration.

Policy solutions were not enough, Mattinson argued. Labour

also needed to find 'punchy, memorable language' for the party's messages and be disciplined in delivering them, again and again. 'In opposition, communication is our only weapon,' she said in one presentation. 'And, of course, we should stop talking to – and about – ourselves.'

Her 'hero voters' rarely bothered paying attention to politics in the news, so the party's MPs and spokespeople must at all times remain on-script. Any deviation from the agreed lines, even internally, was likely to result in a pointed rebuke. The party also had to work harder to find its target voters – for example, by giving interviews to wider-interest magazines and daytime TV and engaging with social media.

There were challengers to Mattinson's plan. Labour Together, an organisation that McSweeney had previously led as a refuge for moderates in the Corbyn era, had also presented findings to Starmer's team about a particular target voter group. They came up with a different name: 'Stevenage woman'.

Such terms can seem ridiculous to those working outside politics and are often a source of mockery in the media. But having an image in mind can focus the efforts of MPs and political aides, who need to think constantly about the target audience for their messages. Companies often come up with target customer persona profiles. These are the political equivalents.

Stevenage woman was a suburban mother in her forties, sceptical about politics and struggling with the cost of living. She was also deeply frustrating to Mattinson. Having a rival voter type on the scene could confuse the Labour election team. If party officials and MPs saw a new voter type to target, they might just ignore them both and revert to doing their own thing, she thought. Discipline – that crucial precondition for success – would break down.

Mattinson was 'evangelical' in her relentless focus on 'hero voters', which irritated some colleagues, but she apparently didn't mind. 'Giving those voters a name – hero voters – really mattered,' she explains. 'I know it was corny. I know people would roll their eyes. But it helped us all focus on this group of people.'[11]

BRIGHTON

It was the autumn of 2021 and Morgan McSweeney, Starmer's most trusted aide, had barely slept for days. The Labour Party conference was about to begin on the seafront in Brighton, but the first in-person gathering since the pandemic was shaping up to be a showdown. That wasn't an accident.

In his influential memo 'Labour for the Country', McSweeney had argued that a public fight with the party's Corbynite left was inevitable and important to signal to voters that Starmer was different. He explicitly called for 'a conference that illustrates the struggle to change the party for the country'.

Starmer's aides had drawn up a plan for contentious reforms they knew would trigger an outburst of rage from those in the party whose loyalties still lay with Corbynism. It was crucial that the new leader, who was still weak, fought this battle and won. He needed to show a sceptical public that he was in charge and he was changing Labour.

The aim of the proposals was to lock the socialist left out of power for a generation by changing the leadership election rules to bombproof the party against a Corbynite fightback, regardless of whether Starmer himself survived. Delegates were preparing to vote on the rule changes in Brighton, after Starmer's team sprang them on the conference at the last minute.

In 2015, Corbyn only needed the backing of 10 per cent of MPs to make it onto the ballot for the party leadership election. None of them thought he would win – and he didn't want to – but he did, surviving for four years and leading the party to two election defeats. Starmer and McSweeney were determined to prevent a repeat. They proposed raising the MP threshold to 20 per cent, alongside other rule tweaks that empowered senior politicians over the grassroots members.

It was a high-risk move. Should it backfire, the entire Starmer project would be thrown into jeopardy again. Some in the Labour leader's top team thought it was reckless and argued against taking the gamble. Voters would see him as weak and his internal rivals would see him as beatable if he lost. McSweeney knew that he, personally, would be finished if they failed.[12]

Trade unions banded together to fight the plan, watering down the most radical options. It looked disastrous for Starmer's chances of getting the main bulk of his reforms approved. The critical vote on his rule changes went down to the wire, but in the end it passed by 53.67 per cent to 46.33 per cent.

Luke Akehurst, a Starmer backer who is now an MP, had been a scourge of the socialist left for years. He was responsible for drawing up the plan earlier that year, alongside McSweeney, the Labour peer Roy Kennedy and Matt Pound, a senior adviser to the party's general secretary. All were instrumental in trying to marshal delegates to back the leadership in the knife-edge vote.

That evening, Akehurst could not resist the opportunity to gloat, posting on social media, 'Nice glass of pinot grigio at the Regency Cafe, with a chaser of salty Trot tears.' McSweeney, meanwhile, saved his celebration for another time.

A storm blew in. Wind and horizontal rain lashed Brighton's pebble beach and the hotels lined up along the seafront. The Labour Party conference would close that week with a keynote speech from the leader. All signs pointed to the left staging a disruptive protest.

Andy McDonald, one of the few frontbenchers remaining in the shadow Cabinet from the Corbyn era, had been agitating for a £15-an-hour minimum wage. He quit Starmer's team by letter – telling him the party was 'more divided than ever' under his leadership – at the most damaging moment, with the full media glare on Labour's conference. Starmer battled on.

He began his big speech on the afternoon of Wednesday 29 September by saying to Dame Louise Ellman, a former MP and chair of Labour Friends of Israel, with a wide smile, 'Welcome home.' She had rejoined Labour after leaving in 2019 over allegations of antisemitism in the party. Since Starmer took over, Jeremy Corbyn himself had been thrown out after stating that the scale of Labour's antisemitism problem had been 'dramatically overstated for political reasons'.

Moments later, the hard-left heckling began. When the protesting reached fever pitch, Starmer addressed it directly and appeared to offer his party an ultimatum: 'Shouting slogans or changing lives, conference?'

His aides were pleased that he had won the stand-off with the Corbynite left. As one source put it, 'The change needed to be real, and it needed conflict to ensure the country knew it was real.'[13]

A few weeks afterwards, the four architects of the leadership rules showdown met for dinner. McSweeney had a surprise. He had brought gifts to mark their historic triumph and to thank his allies – Pound, Kennedy and Akehurst – for their hard work. A pair of cufflinks each, engraved with the winning percentage on one side and the loser's result the other. Their greater victory – over the Conservatives – was still far off. But Starmer's leadership team had passed their most important internal test, imposing his authority on an unruly and unpredictable party.

Three years later, McSweeney put on those cufflinks, dressed up in a suit and walked into No. 10.

SUE

By early 2023, with Boris Johnson's administration having imploded over Partygate and Liz Truss having quit after crashing the economy, the polls were consistently showing Labour was in with a chance of taking power just one term after its devastating 2019 defeat.

As he prepared to challenge Rishi Sunak, Starmer needed to make sure his party looked like a credible government-in-waiting. He needed a fixer who knew the workings of Whitehall and could command instant respect from his troops. He needed someone like Sue Gray.

In football terms, it was a spectacular star signing. Gray, a long-serving civil servant who had earned a fearsome reputation as head of propriety and ethics, had shot to prominence as the chief investigator into Johnson's lockdown-breaking parties inside Downing Street at the height of the pandemic.

Her 'Partygate' report had attained near-scriptural status before it was even published. For months, Johnson's government would urge people to 'wait for Sue Gray's report' to deflect questions over just how many members of his team got drunk together while the rest of the country stayed at home to protect the NHS and save lives.

When Gray published her findings on 25 May 2022, they made sober reading for the revellers of Whitehall and its environs. She found there had been 'failures of leadership and judgment in No. 10 and the Cabinet Office' for which 'the senior leadership at the centre, both political and official, must bear responsibility'. Johnson was among those who were fined by police for breaking his own lockdown rules. Within two months of Gray's final report, he was forced out.

Less than a year later, Labour announced that Gray had accepted Starmer's offer of a job as his chief of staff. Her move enraged the Tories and dismayed senior civil servants. Labour loved it.

When she arrived at the party's Southworks HQ in September 2023, Gray immediately impressed, and terrified, the staff. Coming from the vast bureaucracy of the civil service into the relatively small Labour campaign team was a jolt. But most were pleased to have her on board. 'We could ideally have done with her six months earlier,' one Labour official says.

> Her very presence is a reminder that you have to implement your policies, your plans. She has a massive presence, and she walks with the authority of the leader, but she also walks with the authority of somebody who knows how to make things happen. She's a big hitter.[14]

Gray gave Labour officials confidence. They could trust that she was on top of what they would need to do to make policy ready for government. The division of responsibilities in Starmer's top team was always easy for staffers to understand, as one recalls: 'Morgan was responsible for everything up to polling day and Sue was responsible for everything after polling day.'[15]

They didn't agree on everything, but McSweeney and Gray were two of the most effective backroom operators any opposition could wish for in the run-up to what would be a long and punishing election campaign.

Keir Starmer is not a politician by training. He is a methodical, meticulous lawyer. Like a barrister taking instruction from solicitors, he had no hang-ups about delegating crucial tasks and gave his trusted lieutenants plenty of freedom. But first he had to assemble a team that could shake up the shambles of a party he had inherited. In doing so, he picked people who were every bit as relentless and focused in their pursuit of power as he turned out to be.

CHAPTER 4

THE BANKER

COMEBACK KIDS

When Liz Truss announced her resignation outside No. 10 on 20 October 2022, Rishi Sunak was enjoying half term with his daughters, eating lunch at a TGI Friday's restaurant in Teesside.[1]

Although he had spent the previous summer warning her plans were folly, he was as shocked as the rest of the country that Truss's government had disintegrated quite so fast. That night, he sped back to London and began reassembling his leadership campaign team. Plenty of MPs – including those who had not backed him previously – were telling him he was the right person to take over now. Sunak believed it too, though he knew winning the leadership and doing the job of PM in the circumstances would be daunting work.[2]

In Downing Street, the Treasury and the Bank of England, officials were still trying to steady the ship amid an ongoing financial and political earthquake. Simon Case, the Cabinet Secretary, told Graham Brady, the Tory MP in charge of the leadership election, that the contest must be quick because a drawn-out campaign would do nothing to reassure the markets. Brady agreed – the party did not need another long and bloody battle any more than the country did.

Sunak's rivals, however, had other ideas.

Boris Johnson always had his eye on a comeback and saw his opportunity. The former Prime Minister was on holiday in the Caribbean when Truss resigned, and he flew home on the first available flight. His team then posted a photo showing their would-be candidate in a makeshift campaign office, looking carefully dishevelled in an open-necked shirt and a suit with a Union Jack behind him. Pressing a phone to his ear with one hand and giving a thumbs-up to the camera with the other, the message was unmistakable: brand Boris was back in business.

There was a high hurdle to clear, however. Under the rules designed by Brady, candidates needed a minimum of 100 nominations from Conservative MPs in order to make it onto the ballot. That decision, which fitted with Case's requirement for a speedy process, dramatically shortened the likely list of contenders. If MPs couldn't agree on a single candidate, the final two would hold hustings with the party membership, who would be given a vote online, and the new leader would be announced by Friday 28 October.

Sunak had all the early momentum. He benefited from his prior warnings about Truss's economic recklessness during the summer leadership contest and MPs piled in to back him. His aides announced on Saturday 22 October that even before he had formally declared his candidacy, he had already met the threshold of 100 backers he needed to get onto the ballot. Johnson's team also briefed that their man had the numbers to make the cut. Penny Mordaunt was the third big Cabinet name in the running. Suella Braverman, the ambitious, right-wing former Home Secretary, thought about standing but cut a deal to back Sunak. After winning, he restored her to the Home Office and made tackling small boats carrying migrants from France to British shores a top priority.

But increasingly, the contest looked like it would deliver what all sides knew was the worst outcome for the country: a vicious fight between Johnson, hungry to regain his old job, and the man his allies blamed for ousting him.

In an effort to thrash out a peace deal (and secure the prize for himself), Johnson invited Sunak to a meeting. It took place amid the utmost secrecy in Millbank Tower, a 1960s skyscraper in Westminster which had once been Tony Blair's Labour Party HQ. They spent forty-five minutes alone together in their first face-to-face conversation since Sunak had quit three months earlier, triggering the wave of resignations that brought Johnson down. While the conversation was apparently polite, no agreement was possible. Sunak felt he had the better chance of being able to deliver the stable economic leadership that the country had been lacking.[3]

Other MPs agreed. One recalls, 'I wasn't averse to Boris coming back, but it just felt like it was the wrong time, after the Liz debacle. The whole thing was completely mad. What we needed was a firm hand on the economic tiller so we could try to rebuild our credibility.'[4]

Steve Baker, who had served in government alongside Johnson and Sunak, was vocal in urging colleagues not to give him the reins of power again because a second term was always doomed. 'It was very clear to me that Boris would be chaos if he was back. But crucially, the biggest element of that chaos would be the unresolved problem of the privileges committee inquiry,' Baker says. 'He was not going to survive that.'[5]

The House of Commons privileges committee had been

investigating whether Johnson deliberately misled Parliament over the rule-breaking parties in Downing Street during lockdown. Baker's message in a TV interview was that if Johnson stood and won the leadership again, it was a 'nailed-on' certainty that he'd be forced out a second time once the committee had completed its inquiry: therefore, Johnson must not be allowed to stand.

'What I think most of us would have wanted was Boris at his best, complying with his own rules, charismatically leading people forwards and actually delivering on the more free-market things he said – we would have all loved that,' Baker says. 'But I'm afraid "best Boris" wasn't actually available.' In June 2023, the privileges panel did find against the former PM, just as Baker had predicted, and Johnson subsequently quit in disgrace – and in a rage – as an MP.

It was never completely clear whether Johnson truthfully had the numbers he needed to challenge Sunak in a run-off vote among the Tory membership. In the end, he withdrew rather than force the point. Johnson was typically triumphalist, even in retreat:

> There is a very good chance that I would be successful in the election with Conservative Party members – and that I could indeed be back in Downing Street on Friday. But in the course of the last days I have sadly come to the conclusion that this would simply not be the right thing to do. You can't govern effectively unless you have a united party in parliament. And though I have reached out to both Rishi and Penny – because I hoped that we could come together in the national interest – we have sadly not been able to work out a way of doing this. Therefore I am afraid the best thing is that I do not allow my nomination to go forward and commit my support to whoever succeeds.

Not for the first time or the last, Johnson made clear this was an intermission, not an ending: 'I believe I have much to offer but I am afraid that this is simply not the right time,' he said.

When Penny Mordaunt bowed out as nominations closed at 2 p.m. on Monday, Sunak was set for Downing Street as the sole candidate left. The following day, Tuesday 25 October 2022, the 42-year-old MP for Richmond in Yorkshire became Britain's youngest Prime Minister in more than 200 years and the first British Asian to hold the highest office in the land.

In his speech outside No. 10, after being appointed by the King, Sunak chose to pay tribute to both his predecessors. Some colleagues now think it was a mistake not to have distanced himself as far as possible from two toxic leaders that the public were never likely to forgive. But that's not Sunak's style.

Truss, he said, 'was not wrong to want to improve growth in this country, it is a noble aim. And I admired her restlessness to create change.' 'But', he added, 'some mistakes were made, not borne of ill will or bad intentions – quite the opposite, in fact. But mistakes nonetheless and I have been elected as leader of my party, and your Prime Minister, in part, to fix them.'

Sunak did not refer directly to the scandals and lies of Johnson's era but promised: 'This government will have integrity, professionalism and accountability at every level. Trust is earned, and I will earn yours.' Johnson, he said, had delivered a historic majority in 2019, but his mandate belonged not to a single person but to the whole party. The 2019 manifesto must be delivered. 'I will always be grateful to Boris Johnson for his incredible achievements as Prime Minister, and I treasure his warmth and generosity of spirit.'

Then Sunak turned to the work ahead. He promised to bring the same compassion to Downing Street as he showed in the Treasury as the author of the Covid furlough scheme (though he did not mention the contentious 'Eat Out to Help Out' programme):

> I understand too that I have work to do to restore trust after all that has happened. All I can say is that I am not daunted. I know the high office I have accepted and I hope to live up to its demands. But when the opportunity to serve comes along, you cannot question the moment, only your willingness. So, I stand here before you ready to lead our country into the future. To put your needs above politics. To reach out and build a government that represents the very best traditions of my party. Together we can achieve incredible things. We will create a future worthy of the sacrifices so many have made and fill tomorrow and everyday thereafter with hope.[6]

ADULTS IN THE ROOM

Simon Case had got what he believed the country needed – a quick resolution to the Tory leadership crisis. The appointment of an economically literate and reliable Prime Minister suggested that Tory MPs, at least, had rediscovered their senses. Jeremy Hunt, who had sat out the leadership campaign, was immediately reappointed Chancellor amid wide acceptance that markets wanted some continuity at the Treasury.

Over the preceding four months, Case had been in an awkward position at the centre as the Tory Party melted down around him. Throughout multiple crises during 2022, he was the only senior figure constantly present at the top of the British state's decision-making machinery, while political, constitutional and financial turmoil swept normality aside. He was burnt in the Johnson-era Partygate scandal, though did not receive a police fine for attending events. The fact that some junior colleagues did was a reason others briefed against him. He was also blamed for not doing more to restrain Johnson and stop Truss and Kwarteng ousting Tom Scholar from the Treasury.

Now another rookie Prime Minister, this time without even a mandate from Conservative members, was stepping through the front door of No. 10, shaking Case by the hand, eagerly trying to learn the routines of office. And the markets were still a mess.

For officials in Whitehall and at the Treasury in particular – as well as for Sunak – those early days in October and November 2022 were still entirely about stabilising the economy. Reappointing Hunt as Chancellor was key. Sunak's new team urgently needed to repair the damage Truss had done to investors' confidence in the UK with an autumn Budget that would include real spending cuts to most departments to put the public finances back into order.

'It was still incredibly precarious,' one person involved recalls. 'We said that our only goal here was to get to Christmas. That is our objective. If we're still here at Christmas, that will be success.' It was not clear even that modest aim was achievable for Sunak. 'It was all incredibly fractious amongst the party, so it was very much not sure how long this was going to last,' the person said.[7]

When Hunt delivered his autumn statement on 17 November, the Office for Budget Responsibility (OBR) finally had its say. After Kwarteng and Truss had shunned consulting the OBR before announcing their mini-Budget in September, the body delivered a withering verdict on the state the pair had left the British economy in. The OBR predicted that instead of growing, the economy would nosedive into a recession; real household disposable income would fall 7 per cent over two years in the sharpest hit to living standards since the Second Word War; and unemployment would rise to almost 5 per cent.

That was the fraught backdrop against which the fresh-faced new Prime Minister would have to try to resell his battered party to the electorate. 'There was a huge amount of pressure on him,' one Cabinet minister recalls. It was as well that Sunak liked hard work.

CHILDHOOD

As a boy growing up in Southampton, Sunak had always impressed his teachers with his conscientiousness and his neighbours with his unfailing politeness. His parents were born in Africa, from families who emigrated from India. He liked cricket and was good at it, but he also loved studying. With state schools in Southampton not offering middle-class parents much of a choice at the time, Sunak's father, a family GP, and his mother, who ran a chemist, worked long hours to raise enough money to put him through fee-paying schools. Conscious of his exceptional academic abilities, they entered him for a scholarship exam at Winchester College, one of the best public schools in the country.

He won a regular place and attended as a day pupil, though not on a scholarship. As noted in Michael Ashcroft's biography of Sunak, *All to Play For*, the culture of intellectual superiority at Winchester probably helped forge Sunak's formidable work ethic as he realised how hard he would need to study to succeed.

Sunak loved his own schooling and that passion fed into some of his policy priorities as Prime Minister, notably his plan to make studying maths to the age of eighteen compulsory. His own A-level choices were eclectic: English literature, maths and economics, with AS-levels in biology and French. His true love was economics and he went on to study the subject at Oxford University, along with politics (and philosophy, for a year).

As far as teenage schoolboy misbehaviour goes, Sunak tried alcohol along with most of his peers, but he never enjoyed it. As an adult he is a confirmed teetotaller: instead of waxing lyrical about particular vintages of Bordeaux or Burgundy, as Boris Johnson or David Cameron might, Sunak's taste has led him to proclaim the virtues of full-strength Coca-Cola, especially the Mexican version.

'I am a total Coke addict,' Sunak told two school pupils in an interview, several years before he became PM, before awkwardly clarifying that he wasn't referring to the Class A drug. 'I collect Coca-Cola things,' he added, aware this wouldn't help him shed his geeky image. After confessing to having 'seven fillings' as a result of his unquenchable thirst for the drink, he revealed he only allows himself one can a week these days. He had more to say: 'Actually my favourite drink is not even Coke, it's called Mexican Coke – it's special Coke because it's the only place in the world where it's made with cane sugar rather than high fructose corn syrup.'

Growing up, Sunak became an avid fan of Southampton Football Club. His hero during the 1990s was the languid but brilliant midfielder, Matt Le Tissier. Saints were Sunak's local team and therefore a perfectly natural choice (his father was a regular at The Dell). But this authenticity and loyalty came with a price – not for the last time in Sunak's story.

Southampton has never been a cool team to support and generally struggled for results. Most of the club's best players left for bigger things as soon as they could. Le Tissier was unique in loyally staying at Southampton for his whole career and making his home in the city, which loved him back and gave him the nickname 'Le God'. Young Rishi even owned a Le Tissier No. 7 shirt.

If there's one thing that supporting the Southampton team of the 1990s would have given Sunak, it is an appreciation of the status of the underdog. Each victory was a minor miracle and more often than not, fans spent their time expecting the worst – defeats and disappointments and a nerve-shredding relegation battle at the end of every season.

'As a longstanding Saints fan, particularly one who had to go through all those relegation battles of the late '90s, I can tell you, it is not over until the final whistle blows,' Sunak said in his final campaign speech of 2024. 'And I can also tell you that this underdog will fight to that final whistle with your support.'

Sport can be powerfully formative, particularly for children and teenagers as they grow up. The psychology of the underdog could have played a part in forging Sunak's outlook, as well as his approach to the challenges he would face later in life – maybe even including his own party's ultimately doomed relegation battle in 2024.

RICH MAN

Sunak's route into politics was in many ways a conventional story for a Conservative: public school, Oxford University, a career in investment banking and then launching his own businesses. Sunak's first boss at Goldman Sachs was Richard Sharp, who later went on to chair the BBC. 'He came there very bright, very willing, very eager, and he had this mentality of flawless execution,' Sharp later recalled.[8]

In 2004, Sunak left Goldman Sachs to study for an MBA at Stanford University in California. He has described his time surrounded by clever, creative people in the US as hugely exciting. It was also where he met his wife, Akshata Murty, the daughter of a billionaire

Indian businessman, and went on to run his own hedge fund. Sunak returned to the UK to fight the 2015 election but still has a home in the golden state. His $7.2 million apartment is a short walk from Muscle Beach in Santa Monica, where bodybuilders work out in the sand and a crab eggs benedict with wasabi hollandaise will set you back $34 for brunch.[9]

Sunak entered Parliament for the safe Yorkshire seat of Richmond in 2015. The vacancy arose when William Hague stood down after a long career at the top of politics. As a rookie MP, Sunak was instantly tipped in the media as a future Cabinet minister or PM, impressing everywhere he went with his eloquence, intelligence and energy. A Cabinet colleague, who is on some matters highly critical of Sunak's leadership, praises his 'enormous' abilities. 'He is genuinely the most exceptional answerer of questions I have ever seen,' the minister says.[10]

Sunak's decision to snub Cameron on Brexit and campaign to leave the EU showed an independent spirit that many more experienced Westminster operators lack. As well as being true to his beliefs, it was a shrewd career move.

Some MPs, especially, it must be said, on the Conservative side, are independently very wealthy. But Rishi Sunak is staggeringly rich. Thanks to his career in investment banking and in two hedge funds, including one he co-founded in California, he would have been rich even before his marriage to a billionaire's daughter. But with Akshata Murty, who owns a 0.91 per cent stake in her father's company, global technology giant Infosys, the couple had an estimated net worth of £651 million in 2024, according to data compiled by the *Sunday Times* Rich List.

During his tenure as Chancellor and then Prime Minister, however hard he tried, Sunak could not hide the fact that he enjoys the kind of lifestyle and resources that the vast majority of his colleagues in Westminster, never mind the country at large, could not begin to comprehend. He isn't just the first British Asian in No. 10, he is by far the wealthiest person ever to be Prime Minister.

At times, it was painfully obvious that he lived in a different world from most of the country. As Chancellor, he was in the headlines for being a fan of Peloton, the high-end fitness brand, working out at 6 a.m. to a Britney Spears soundtrack on one of the company's £1,750 exercise bikes. He also posed for a pre-Budget photo in 2020 with a 'smart' coffee mug that retailed at £180 (it keeps coffee warm at the precise temperature users set for it for up to three hours). These are not the sort of choices that most voters can afford.

Sunak's response to criticism over his wealth, and especially his wife's financial decisions, has been to dig in, sometimes angrily. When it emerged in 2022 that Murty had claimed non-domicile tax status, triggering a wave of public criticism and political flak, Sunak responded with barely suppressed fury.

When the BBC's Laura Kuenssberg showed him a 'word cloud' of terms that voters associated with him, it included the descriptions: 'rich', 'elite', 'rich people', 'wealthy', 'money', 'himself', 'upper class' and 'greed'. Initially, Sunak didn't take the bait, remaining calm as he tried to move the topic on. But he was visibly annoyed in some of the exchanges about net-zero climate policy that followed.

His team have never attempted to explain or apologise for the PM's use of private air travel, including helicopters. And he himself has said he welcomes the interest in his finances. During the election campaign, however, some Conservative MPs worried their leader's ostentatious wealth would put voters off. Their anxieties were well founded.

During the infamous ITV interview with Paul Brand, for which

Sunak left the D-Day commemorations, he was asked about the cost-of-living crisis affecting millions of families. He blustered a bit and when pressed for an example from his own life, eventually said: 'There are all sorts of things that I wanted as a kid that I couldn't have. Famously, Sky TV! That was something that we never had growing up.' It wasn't the kind of comment that would resonate well with millions of voters who had been struggling with the cost of living or relying on food banks in recent years.

STARTUP

Political advisers are endlessly fascinating characters to Westminster obsessives. They usually remain hidden from view, whispering advice – and in some cases, instructions – into the Prime Minister's ear while avoiding interviews themselves. The more intriguing characters attract (and sometimes encourage) a mythology about the extent of their unelected power and unaccountable influence. Perhaps because these secretive advisers rarely speak in public, the media tends to focus on their appearance, though they are often conspicuous specimens too.

David Cameron had Steve Hilton, who padded around No. 10 in bare feet and a T-shirt and even took his shoes and jacket off in sub-zero Stockholm during one summit. Theresa May had Nick Timothy, who grew a full beard that earned him the nickname 'Rasputin', which seemed to fit the mesmerising influence he had over the premier at the time. Dominic Cummings was rarely out of a T-shirt and jeans, even daring to appear at a parliamentary select committee without a tie (or many of his shirt buttons done up).

Liam Booth-Smith, Sunak's chief adviser since his time as Chancellor, fitted the pattern, too. Pictured in an unbuttoned shirt, revealing a portion of chest under a black leather jacket, he was known as the 'Travolta of the Treasury'. As well as looking the part, he was also an indie music fan and singer, recording an EP entitled 'August Varlet' in 2007 and touring pubs. When a video of a solo gig emerged, he quipped to the Guido Fawkes website, 'It was the least embarrassing thing I did at nineteen.'

The pair first worked together when Sunak was a junior minister in the housing department, before collaborating again after Cummings picked Booth-Smith to be the top economic adviser in Johnson's beefed-up Downing Street operation in 2020. Although he was clearly bright and talented, Booth-Smith, in his mid-thirties, was relatively inexperienced compared to others who have taken on the role of Downing Street chief of staff.

Booth-Smith was brought up in a single-parent household in Stoke-on-Trent, took a degree at Loughborough University and then went to work for a think tank before entering government as an adviser. 'I really rate him,' says one source who is generally critical of Sunak's team. 'He brings a dollop of common sense and is a normal person from a normal upbringing on a council estate in Stoke-on-Trent. You can see that feed through into a no-nonsense, straightforward approach.'[11]

In 2023, Booth-Smith brought his close friend Jamie Njoku-Goodwin back into government as Downing Street's director of strategy. The two shared a flat together and worked as special advisers in Johnson's administration during the pandemic, with Njoku-Goodwin taking on an unenviable role in the Department of Health at the height of the pandemic. As well as sharing a commitment to Tory politics, both are music lovers – Njoku-Goodwin is an accomplished musician and has worked as chief executive of

UK Music. In Sunak's Downing Street, he held the pivotal role running the government 'grid' – the schedule of announcements and ministerial activity designed to make sure policy priorities got the focus and media attention they needed.

Perhaps the most interesting appointment to Sunak's core team was that of James Forsyth as political secretary, a crucial position for liaising with MPs and ministers. Sunak and Forsyth have been close ever since their schooldays together at Winchester. Sunak was best man at Forsyth's wedding. That kind of friendship comes as close as possible to unconditional love in politics.

Forsyth – a cerebral writer and scrupulously polite, even in the aggressive environment of Westminster – was a formidable figure in political journalism for over a decade. As political editor of *The Spectator* and a columnist at the *Mail on Sunday* during the Cameron era, his dispatches were weekly must-reads for what was coming up on the agenda, as well as for understanding the thinking inside No. 10.

It was Forsyth's wife, Allegra Stratton, who first worked for Sunak as a key adviser during the pandemic, helping to add polish to his image and turning the new-boy Chancellor into a powerful and popular political figure. Stratton then went to work for Johnson before resigning in tears over a leaked video of her joking about Christmas parties in Downing Street during a rehearsal for a press conference.

Forsyth knew everyone at Westminster and, like Njoku-Goodwin, was popular with the political correspondents based in Parliament, known collectively as 'the lobby', as well as with Conservative MPs and aides. That was a valuable set of attributes for a party leadership adrift in the polls.

Yet despite being internally popular and clearly trusted by their boss as loyalists and friends, Sunak's team suffered from one persistent complaint: they seemed a little too green in the ways of frontline party politics. Inexperience among key aides is a serious gap at any time for a Prime Minister, but it becomes critical during the run-up to an election. All the key advisers were around Sunak's age or younger, including Nerissa 'Nissy' Chesterfield, who went with him from the Treasury to No. 10 as communications director. Rupert Yorke, who is now Chesterfield's partner, was among the more experienced of the aides in Sunak's team, having worked as a special adviser in government for much of the past decade, and took on the role of deputy chief of staff.

Some ministers looked on aghast as the team took shape, hoping that the new PM would see the problem and hire some old hands to bolster the Downing Street operation. It never happened.

'It's like he went into No. 10 as if it was a start-up, rather than a senior management buyout,' one senior Tory recalled. 'If it's a senior management buyout, you get a senior team in there who you know are good – a great CFO, a great CEO. Rishi went in as if it was a start-up and these people would learn the job. You had eighteen months to two years before the election – they did not have time to learn.'[12]

A senior Conservative adviser saw a different problem – Sunak's inner team were starry-eyed fans who 'couldn't see his flaws' and were stuck on the view that he had been popular during the pandemic, believing he still should be. 'You need to speak truth to power, that's what any good adviser does,' the aide says. 'But if you think your boss walks on water, you can't give frank advice.'

> He valued loyalty and those around him were fiercely loyal. But remember, they'd just come out of the Treasury where Rishi was the most popular politician in the country. And that probably

deluded them into thinking that was sustainable. He was loved and revered. He was absolutely loved across the country. He was the Tory politician in Scotland with a net positive score because of his actions in the pandemic so that probably deludes you into thinking he's omnipotent.

But I think they probably kept that delusion and were quite emotional about it. They couldn't understand why that didn't translate into him being PM. For them it was just unfair. It was, 'hang on, he didn't put a foot wrong in the pandemic, he had to come in and clean up the mess and stabilise the party and the country, and he's got no thanks for it. That's not fair.' It is deeply unfair, but so is politics, right?[13]

DELIVERY

After becoming PM in October 2022, Sunak did not have much time to make an impression with the electorate before he'd be asking them to give him another five years in power. The question was how to focus the government's energies in a way that got things done and showed voters that they should give the Tories another chance. Sunak had ticked the first crucial box by preventing a full-blown economic collapse.

With the new year came the chance for a clean start. On 4 January 2023, Sunak set out his stall to the country, announcing five key goals he would prioritise immediately. These were: halve inflation to help with the cost of living; grow the economy to deliver more jobs; make sure national debt is falling; reduce NHS waiting lists; and pass new laws to stop the boats carrying illegal migrants to Britain and remove those who arrive.

The hope in Downing Street and Conservative Campaign

Headquarters (CCHQ) was that by showing the government was focused on the public's priorities and delivering on them, Sunak would earn back the trust of voters that Johnson and Truss had squandered. 'These are five pledges to deliver peace of mind, so that you know things are getting better, that they are actually changing, that you have a government working in your interests, focused on your priorities, putting your needs first,' Sunak said. 'And I fully expect you to hold my government and I to account on delivering those goals.'

The following month he had a breakthrough, sealing a new deal with the European Union to resolve the long-running sore point of post-Brexit trade rules for Northern Ireland. It was a significant achievement, and Sunak cleverly leveraged the caché of the new King to add some sparkle to the occasion, welcoming European Commission President Ursula von der Leyen to Windsor to mark the deal. The agreement with the EU – duly named the Windsor Framework – wasn't just crucial to resolving difficulties for businesses in Northern Ireland. It would prepare the ground for eventually restoring the region's power-sharing administration.

Privately, Tory aides dared to hope that whatever Sunakism was – and it had started to look something like unflashy competence – it was working. The party's internal polling gave him a chance against a Labour leader who had yet to convince voters that he was a better alternative.

The reckoning, though, would come. Inflation did fall, but that merely meant prices were not surging up as fast as they had been, while interest rates remained high by recent standards. The picture on NHS waiting lists was far from positive, and there's no way any Tory could claim success on 'stopping the boats'. Judges repeatedly blocked government efforts to deport illegal migrants to Rwanda, to the fury of Home Secretary Suella Braverman and the right-wing press.

Sunak joined in the outcry and drafted a new law declaring Rwanda a safe place to receive migrants, in an effort to beat the Supreme Court, which had ruled it was not. The issue became more known for the government's ongoing struggles and failures than for any success at actually bringing down the number of arrivals, though ministers claimed a 'deterrent' effect could be seen.

Sunak was not alone in struggling with global migration trends. The mass movement of people fleeing conflict and poverty had contributed to a surge in support for far-right parties across Europe, including in Italy, Germany and the Netherlands. Despite the lack of success with the Rwanda plan, Sunak's offshore immigration processing policy sparked a trend overseas, with hard-right Italian leader Giorgia Meloni – Sunak's friendliest ally in the EU – aiming to send migrants to Albania. Germany also started looking into copying the policy.

It wasn't that the Rwanda policy didn't get an enthusiastic reception from some people. They just weren't in Britain.

TETCHY

'I don't understand that,' said Rishi Sunak. 'I am fighting for the things I believe in. There's nothing tetchy.'

It was December 2023 and the Prime Minister had just been asked in an interview with the loyally Tory *Spectator* magazine if he was prone to irritability. 'I am passionate. When things are not working the way I want them to work, of course I'm going to be frustrated.'

A stubborn poll deficit and the government's inability to get the Rwanda immigration policy through the courts may have taken their toll. But in truth, Sunak has always been given to flashes of emotion, which have sometimes come through as disparaging to those on the receiving end. In some ways, it's not surprising. The job of Prime Minister is obviously among the most stressful in politics. When your party is heading for electoral disaster and nothing you do seems to make a difference, it must be a particular kind of torture.

'Nobody really knows what somebody is going to be like as Prime Minister until they're Prime Minister – I don't think any individual knows what they will be like either,' according to one senior official. 'Even people who have seen Prime Ministers up close – Theresa May, Boris Johnson, Rishi Sunak – even they really don't know how to do it.'[14]

Part of that pressure comes from Parliament, which is set up as a shouting contest between the government on one side and the opposition on the other, especially during the weekly sessions of Prime Minister's Questions. Around the same time as his *Spectator* denial, the PM was pictured at the dispatch box with his face contorted in an angry snarl, as he responded to a question from Keir Starmer about 140,000 children who would be homeless at Christmas. The image went viral on social media in a gift to Labour spin doctors, who then picked it up and posted it themselves with the caption, 'When you ask the Prime Minister about homeless children at Christmas.'

It was a harsh piece of editing, taking a video and isolating a still image, but that isn't rare in politics. And the attack hit home, reinforcing the public perception of Sunak as 'rich' and out of touch with ordinary voters' lives and struggles.

• • •

Sunak works hard and has sought out environments that require him to do so. His early career at Goldman Sachs was built on long hours. As Prime Minister, he would often be up working until 10 p.m. or later, after rising early. During the years of Brexit mayhem in Parliament under Theresa May, he was one of the few MPs who could be seen with plenty of energy, immaculately turned out, and a smile on his face despite brutally stressful sittings of the Commons that frequently ended in knife-edge votes late at night (or early in the morning). He is unfailingly considerate to colleagues and retains the politeness that won him approval as a schoolboy in Southampton.

But colleagues, including many who support him, like him and rate him highly, frequently say one of Sunak's biggest flaws is that he struggles to delegate. He would always want to get into the fine print of policies crossing his desk and would frequently demand briefings from relatively junior officials if they were the people inside Whitehall departments who knew the details better than their bosses. Cabinet meetings were also pointless, according to one minister who attended. Clearly 'pre-scripted' affairs, there was never any meaningful discussion: 'It was just "show-and-tell" day.'[15]

Another senior colleague says, 'Rishi is incredibly thoughtful. But he finds it impossible to delegate and micromanages a lot. He just gets into the weeds of everything – whatever he's involved in.'[16]

A Tory aide says:

Rishi is unbelievably diligent – he knows the issues back to front. He didn't dither, believe it or not. He was quite firm about what he wanted, and his views, and quite direct with people, challenging his ministers to get the best. You had to come prepared to meetings otherwise he would run rings around you. He was a very good administrator in that respect. But to be PM you need a lot more on top of that.

Boris was a horrendous administrator – he couldn't give two hoots about it. He was of the view that if he asks for something it happens. It doesn't work like that. But he had qualities that Rishi didn't have. He was a figurehead, a leader, a visionary. He brought people with him. He was a leader in that respect. And the two of them combined were actually quite a force to be reckoned with, until the relationship didn't work.[17]

Sunak's focus on the detail is a trait that may have equipped him well for the role of Chief Secretary to the Treasury, responsible for trimming cash from government spending in departments. His diligence and drive as an administrator no doubt also helped him force through unprecedented peacetime state interventions, such as the furlough scheme. But Prime Ministers need to be able to inspire their troops and their voters with a vision too. By the time the election was called, even members of his own Cabinet were still wondering what Sunak stood for.

'We never set out a vision for the country,' one Cabinet minister says.

Another agrees: 'Boris constantly gave you a vision and came up with the policy afterwards. With Rishi it was the other way around. He'd give you a policy and then be unable or unwilling to share his vision.'[18]

Steve Baker, another minister in Sunak's government who lost his seat on 4 July, agrees that voters did not know what the party's mission was and that the biggest problem with the Tory campaign was 'a lack of reason to vote Conservative'.

Baker describes Sunak as 'well meaning' but not political enough.

He's got a heart of gold and a very strong moral compass, which I've seen for myself. He's an absolute gentleman with an exemplary character. You know, the sort of person who would be a managing director at an investment bank. You could absolutely see a real professional. But for various reasons, I would say it was not a sufficiently political premiership. I think, possibly, Rishi expected the world to work in politics with him as Prime Minister in the way that a big corporate would work, with followers following and the leader taking decisions and being adhered to and just not needing to do as much in the way of media and politics.[19]

TRIGGERED

The new year of 2024 began with a flurry of questions from journalists about when Sunak would call the election. In order to avoid endless repeats, No. 10 decided the best answer would be to signal that a working assumption was that the election would be called in the second half of the year. That left the option of July – just – open.

Around the same time, Isaac Levido, the party's Australian-born election campaign director, hailed as a Tory hero for delivering Johnson's 2019 majority, moved into Conservative headquarters at 4 Matthew Parker Street in Westminster to get the party machine on a war footing. Once there, he began bluntly warning key figures just how bad the outlook was for election year.

Internal polling, based on seat-by-seat models, suggested the party could slump from 365 seats in 2019 to as low as seventy. If that happened, it would be an 'existential' risk, relegating the

Conservatives to potentially the third-largest party in British politics, behind the Liberal Democrats. The biggest fear in CCHQ was that the Tories would not even have enough MPs after the election to be the official opposition.

With that horror scenario haunting party bosses, Levido, Sunak and a handful of the Prime Minister's most trusted allies began discussing in earnest when the election should be called.

Officially, there was no hurry. By law, it could have waited until January 2025. Even as far back as 2020, in Johnson's time, Levido was keen on waiting for as long as possible: the pandemic had done such damage to the economy, it would take years for the public to begin to feel like life had returned to normal and their living standards were recovering.

Levido remained convinced that the Conservatives would do well to wait until autumn 2024 before going to the polls. The economy was showing signs of revival, with inflation heading back to normality, and wages were also rising. The drip-drip of good news on the economy would help boost the mood of the country as time went on, Levido believed.

More time would also allow the party election machine to get its necessary preparations done, such as selecting candidates, canvassing voters and drafting leaflets and social media adverts. Crucially, an election offer built on the message of 'stick with the plan' would be more effective if the Tories themselves stuck with their own plan and could point to evidence that it was working. Levido was clear what he wanted: a vote later in the autumn.[20]

But Sunak and some of his other allies felt there were more risks to waiting. First, immigration. A whole summer could pass with thousands of illegal migrants landing on English shores in small boats, with no flights taking them away again to Rwanda. Then, the economic news was not guaranteed to be good – growth was precarious and there was every chance voters would not be feeling the benefit of Sunak's rescue efforts even by October.

And 135,000 households every month were moving off fixed-term mortgages and onto loan deals that were far more costly, thanks in large part (in voters' eyes) to the damage done by Liz Truss. 'They blamed us for that, rightly or wrongly, arguably very unfairly,' one Tory strategist recalls:

> You've seen mortgage rates shoot up everywhere in the world. Liz Truss hasn't caused high mortgage rates in the US. But the narrative is set that she and the Conservative Party are responsible for high mortgage rates. We have lost that argument. And what that means is whenever someone moves off a fixed-term mortgage onto a higher-rate mortgage, they blame us for that. It was having a catastrophic impact on voting intention. One of the things we found was that every month there were 135,000 households who were finding themselves moving onto a higher rate and were going, 'You fuckers, we're never voting for you again.'[21]

Public services were also in a mess and in some cases reaching critical condition. Privately, the Ministry of Justice (MoJ) had been warning Downing Street for months that prisons were running out of space to dangerous degrees. There had been close calls before, but the MoJ was concerned that without action, prisons would no longer be able to accommodate any more criminals. No. 10 did not want to engage, but nor did they want to risk the headlines of releasing dangerous prisoners early, certainly not before an election they had planned.

In mid-May, Alex Chalk, the Justice Secretary, wrote Sunak a personal letter warning in the most dramatic terms that the prison system was in the 'endgame'. Although he was never explicit, it was clear that the minister was contemplating resignation if No. 10 refused to grip the crisis and authorise an early-release programme.

Chalk demanded a meeting with Sunak. Having repeatedly dodged such requests in past months, the Prime Minister finally agreed. On Monday 20 May, Chalk told the PM that there was no more room for manoeuvre, the prisons were full. The situation was so dire that there would be nothing the government could do to avoid the system collapsing within a month, other than hope.

He described mid-June as 'pray day', the point when ministers would have to start praying that things would be OK. If a riot broke out at a prison, meaning it needed to close temporarily, for example, there would be no space to re-house the inmates elsewhere by then. Even an outbreak of bedbugs at a facility could prove disastrous.[22]

Sunak was furious. He could not understand why this was his problem now.

One source on the other side of the debate said Chalk had stopped thinking about the politics of how to manage the crisis without turning it into a huge PR disaster. 'When Dominic Raab was Justice Secretary, he never once raised it because he understood that this was not where we were politically,' the source said.

> When you have a situation which is difficult but your political imperative is not to do something, then it just requires active management. You just have to go every day and find the places and work it out. On the day we left office, there were 700 [prison] places. The department always wanted more.[23]

If the Tories were still in power, the source added, they would likely not have done what Labour has done since and released 1,700 prisoners early. Instead, they would have kept 'sweating the system'.[24]

Chalk finally succeeded in persuading Sunak to embrace the need for an early-release scheme just two days before the PM called the election. The minister was reportedly 'very upset' when Sunak announced that the election campaign was starting, knowing that his emergency early-release plan was dead.[25]

• • •

The Conservatives, after fourteen years in power, a disastrous split over Brexit, four ousted leaders, a war and a pandemic, had lost any semblance of discipline they once had. The Chief Whip warned Sunak that the situation was not sustainable, as did others in Cabinet. MPs were so worried about losing their seats, so keen to look for other jobs or so uninspired by what the government was trying to do in Parliament that growing numbers asked to be excused from voting on laws in the House of Commons to go and do other things. Some weren't even asking permission any more, they were just going AWOL.

In one single day, the whips had 200 'slip' requests – meaning 200 MPs asked to be let off the need to show up in Parliament for a potential vote. 'The parliamentary party was becoming increasingly unmanageable,' one of Sunak's allies says. Some MPs were saying, 'I'm telling, not asking', another senior Tory outlines, adding that 'it just started to crumble'.[26]

Another source close to Sunak said:

> There was infighting in the parliamentary party, there were constant plots and Suella being Suella; people on our own side

shitbagging us again and again. It was coming up on the doorstep that we seemed very divided. This idea that if you wait until November, things were going to get better? It felt like things were getting worse and worse.[27]

The Prime Minister had grown increasingly frustrated that nothing he tried seemed to be making any difference to the party's position in the polls or its coverage in the media. Keir Starmer, Sunak felt, was getting an easy ride. The PM was 'getting impatient because things weren't working' and did not want to keep waiting for the right moment to call an election.[28]

From April, it was clear to a handful of trusted party officials close to Sunak that he would go for an election in July, technically just in the second half of the year, overruling Levido's concerns that the election-fighting machine would not be ready. 'There was a chance he would hold off until November, but lots of the prep we were doing was in the event he decides to have a July election,' one strategist recalls. 'When did I know? When was I certain? The morning he called the King. We were doing a whole lot of work to get ready, but ultimately it's the Prime Minister's call.'[29]

Sunak's mind was made up. Officials in No. 10 quietly enquired whether the sovereign might be available to grant the Prime Minister an audience. The wheels of the state began to turn.

PART II

THE STRATEGIES

CHAPTER 5

TEARS AND RAIN

It was the question that hung over every conversation in the bars and restaurants of Westminster. When would Rishi Sunak trigger the election?

The Prime Minister himself had been clear that a vote was coming in 2024 and had let it be known that it was likely to be in the second half of the year. Some in Labour suspected this was a weak attempt to lull them into relaxing for a few months, believing he would call a spring poll to try to catch them off guard. According to people who worked with Sunak, Labour's suspicions were correct. The Tories came 'much closer' than most Westminster observers realised to calling a vote earlier in the spring, to be held at the same time as the local elections on 2 May. In the end, Isaac Levido put his foot down and Sunak was talked out of it.[1]

On Wednesday 22 May, the Westminster rumour mill – fuelled by gossip in the corridors and cafes of the House of Commons – began churning again. This time it felt different. At Prime Minister's Questions, Sunak was challenged directly to reveal his plan.

'Speculation is rife, so I think the public deserve a clear answer to a simple question,' declared Stephen Flynn, the SNP's shaven-headed Westminster leader, who delights in peppering his interventions with Scottish slang. 'Does the Prime Minister intend to call a summer general election or is he feart?'

Sunak smiled. 'As I have said repeatedly to the right honourable gentleman, there is – spoiler alert – going to be a general election in the second half of this year,' the PM said, maintaining a decent poker face. Then he rehearsed an argument that would become familiar to voters over the six weeks that followed: the choice at the election, whenever it comes, will be between 'a party that is not able to say to the country what it would do' and 'the Conservatives, who are delivering a secure future for our United Kingdom'.

The PM's words did little to calm the nerves among anxious Conservative MPs. More than 20 points behind in the polls, Tories in Parliament dreaded the prospect of facing the electorate. MPs began texting their contacts in No. 10 to ask if there was going to be an election but could not get answers. In desperation, some Cabinet ministers turned into news hounds and frantically contacted as many senior aides and officials as they could. But when they were met with silence, they knew something was up. David Cameron, the Foreign Secretary, was ordered to return from Albania for an important Cabinet meeting. Defence Secretary Grant Shapps was asked to postpone a NATO visit to eastern Europe.

By 3 p.m., the social media platform X, formerly known as Twitter and still a driving force in the Westminster conversation, was ablaze with reports that Sunak was going to pull the trigger on a 4 July vote. That afternoon, the Prime Minister invited a handful of his most senior ministers to a private meeting in his No. 10 study to brief them all first. They included Cameron, Shapps, Chancellor Jeremy Hunt, Home Secretary James Cleverly, Levelling Up

Secretary Michael Gove and Kemi Badenoch, the Business and Trade Secretary.

'I hoped it was going to be a conversation about "Look, I've had this idea, I just want to run it past you,"' says one of those present. It wasn't. In his usual style, with a bounce and a smile, Sunak told his most senior ministers, 'I've just been to speak to the King and he has graciously agreed to dissolve Parliament for a general election on 4 July.'

Packed into that small, intimate room deep inside No. 10, most ministers put aside their reservations and gave Sunak their backing. Cameron told the PM it was a 'bold move' while Gove said words to the effect of 'fortune favours the brave'. Even Badenoch, who was said to be shocked and unhappy with the decision (and would later make her disquiet public), was 'totally supportive' of Sunak.[2]

Only Grant Shapps spoke against the decision. He had been Conservative Party chairman during the 2015 election campaign when Cameron won an unexpected majority. He had also studied Conservative leadership contests intensely, bringing his analysis to bear on a spreadsheet setting out where every Tory MP sat on the spectrum of support or hostility towards each candidate during the 2019 contest, which Johnson eventually won. A snap election now, he felt, would be a horrific mistake.

'Prime Minister, I just would not have done that,' he told Sunak. 'We are 21 points behind. We have got up to seven months to run. I really would not have done this.'

Sunak told Shapps there were a lot of things coming up that could go wrong and waiting for the economic data or political atmosphere to change wouldn't necessarily make anything better – in fact, it could make the Tories' task even harder, he said.

Shapps was not alone in worrying. Another senior minister

privately described Sunak at around this time as 'miserable and scratchy and fed up' that nothing they tried was working with voters, even a major cut to National Insurance bills. 'He was just exasperated. I just think that he had had enough,' the minister said.

'They were just punch drunk,' another Cabinet minister said. 'They had just been hit so many times that the only things they could imagine were things getting worse. They got themselves into a negative mindset where it could only ever be bad.'[3]

• • •

Soon afterwards, the rest of Sunak's Cabinet arrived. Sitting around the long, coffin-shaped table in the Cabinet Room, the Prime Minister spent the first five minutes going through routine matters. Then he announced that he'd just asked the King to dissolve Parliament for an election and wanted to discuss the campaign ahead. With the meeting turning political, Cabinet Secretary Simon Case tidied up his papers and left the politicians to discuss tactics. As Case crept out, Isaac Levido, the Tory campaign chief, walked in.

Most of the Cabinet made encouraging noises in response to Sunak's bombshell, though one or two spoke out against. Chris Heaton-Harris, the Northern Ireland Secretary, and Esther McVey, the Cabinet Office minister, both voiced reservations. The Chief Whip, Simon Hart, said he wasn't convinced initially but could see arguments in favour of a snap vote.

Sunak concluded the meeting and left to prepare his speech to the nation, announcing what by now was being widely reported following leaks to the media anyway. Shell-shocked ministers hung around in the Cabinet Room to watch their leader on TV screens. Many knew instantly that the decision was a disaster. Some knew that they were in the fight of their lives just to hold their own seats. Lucy Frazer, the Culture Secretary, was tearful and Attorney General Victoria Prentis was also visibly upset. Justice Secretary Alex Chalk was clearly deeply unhappy, according to witnesses. All three were rejected by the voters on 4 July.

'There was shock, and tears in quite a few places for those who, even before the polls got as bad as they got, probably thought they were going to lose their seats,' one of those present said. Ministers 'found it very hard to take'.

One minister recalls:

> I felt sick as a parrot, to the pit of my stomach. I absolutely knew that it was a crazy mistake: self-defeating, self-harming, bad for the party, bad for the country. I had that feeling in the pit of my stomach of what an unbelievable error this was, throwing away seven months of your premiership.

In the hour that followed, events turned from shock to shambles.

The sky had been threatening showers all day. Sunak's communications team, led by Nerissa Chesterfield, his long-serving adviser, were conscious that the world's media were waiting outside for a statement from the PM announcing the date of the poll. Against the backdrop of the famous black door of No. 10, speaking silently of power and authority, the open air of Downing Street is the traditional place for premiers to address the nation at set-piece moments such as this.

A lectern was set up on the tarmac without the government crest on – another signal that what the Prime Minister was about to say was a political matter rather than official state business. The sky darkened. A back-up plan was pulled together for the PM to make his announcement indoors in one of the state rooms upstairs in No. 10 if it rained. While ministers were nursing their misery in the Cabinet Room, Sunak's team debated what to do.

In the Prime Minister's office, a group of his most trusted aides had gathered to help him prepare to make the election announcement to the world. At around 4.50 p.m., Liam Booth-Smith, the PM's chief of staff, walked downstairs and went outside into the Downing Street garden at the back of the building to check the weather for himself. Looking back up at the PM's study window, he held out his hands and frowned to indicate that it was definitely raining. When he got back indoors, Booth-Smith told his colleagues, 'It doesn't look like it's going to stop. But if people feel like there's genuinely not an alternative, then fine.'

Eventually, Sunak made the call himself. 'Let's just crack on,' he said.

One source says, 'The PM had a bit of a sense that if you're going to announce an election, this is the way it's done. You usually do it on the step.'

The drizzle continued as Sunak walked out through the shiny black door of No. 10 to face the world's media. But what was more of a problem, to begin with at least, was not rainwater but noise.

• • •

Steve Bray is a veteran activist from south Wales who has made Westminster's grey pavements his workplace. For years, he trolled right wingers in the Tory government and Nigel Farage's party in his efforts to humiliate those he believed had stupidly driven the UK out of the European Union. His signature move was to shout 'Stop Brexit!' at Parliament through a megaphone at least once a day during the Theresa May era, when MPs were unable to agree on a deal to leave the EU. Having seen, like the rest of the Westminster village, that Sunak was about to announce an election, Bray relocated his megaphone to a point outside the Downing Street security gates.

About two minutes into Sunak's speech, just as the PM was getting to his point, Bray decided it was time for a song. He began playing 'Things Can Only Get Better', a 1990s pop tune by D:Ream, at top volume. The hit is now famous in political circles for one thing above all: it was the anthem for Tony Blair's 1997 Labour landslide victory. It could not have been a more embarrassing soundtrack for the beleaguered Sunak. Broadcast microphones are usually good at cutting out extraneous sound, but Bray had cranked up the volume so high that it was almost impossible to hear the Prime Minister's words, even filtered via television.

'Watching it in the Cabinet Room, it wasn't the rain,' said one person present.

> He'd gone quite a long way through [his speech] before the rain was the issue. It was more Steve Bray. He was being drowned out by the megaphone. And then the whole Cabinet could just see this disaster unfolding. It did seem to be a harbinger of doom for the whole campaign.[4]

It started with a few flecks of drizzle catching the light on Sunak's suit. But by the time he announced the election date, his jacket was visibly wet. He still had another four minutes to go.

'This election will take place at a time when the world is more dangerous than it has been since the end of the Cold War,' he said, gripping the lectern with both hands.

In the Cabinet Room, Tories were furious that the megaphone was winning the battle with Sunak's voice. James Forsyth, the PM's political secretary, observed to Simon Case, who had returned to watch the statement, that this kind of unjustifiably noisy disruption was likely to be against a controversial new protest law passed in 2022, prompting the Cabinet Secretary to take steps to contact Downing Street security.

Six minutes into Sunak's speech, Bray's musical trolling finally stopped. The rain did not. Having listed his work so far as PM and promised to keep delivering on his 'bold plan', he turned to Labour:

> I can't say the same thing for the Labour Party. Because I don't know what they offer. And in truth, I don't think you know either. And that's because they have no plan, there is no bold action and as a result the future can only be uncertain with them.

With a minute still to go, the Downing Street downpour intensified. Rivulets of rainwater ran from Sunak's shoulders down the front of his jacket, which glistened in the bright lighting from the TV cameras. Here was a Prime Minister making his pitch for five more years in power, unable even to call his own election without fate intervening to humiliate him. It was a public-relations fiasco for the ages.

A Conservative source explains how the luckless leader ended up soaked:

> Everyone now acts as if the whole day it had been tipping it down. The forecast was sort of unclear. There was a back-up plan to do it in the Pillared Room. I think one of the problems was it wasn't raining until [just] before he went outside and it started very

lightly drizzling. He'd done a speech outside in similar rain on extremism three weeks before and it had been fine. If they'd wanted to move it inside they'd then have had to move a whole load of cameras, journalists – it would have been a bit of a mess, so I think the call was taken, go ahead with it. Then it started. Whatever had happened, if we had done it indoors, everyone would have said that he ran away from the rain. If they'd done it with an umbrella outside, they'd have said, 'Oh, the wally with a brolly.'[5]

Once back inside, Sunak tried to repair some of the damage. Taking off his drenched suit jacket, he sat down to record a video for use on social media, rehashing some of the points he'd made in his speech.

Conservative strategists insist the images of the soggy PM that dominated media coverage over the next twenty-four hours did not significantly damage his campaign or make voters change their minds. That may just be because most had already decided what they thought of Rishi Sunak and the party he led.

DRESS REHEARSAL

On Tuesday 21 May, the Liberal Democrats' campaign team went out on the town to say goodbye to one of their colleagues. They had decided to go to the Market Halls close to Oxford Circus, where nine food stalls offered options ranging from modern gourmet kebabs to Malaysian street food and 'fried chicken done right'. One of those present explains: 'It's really handy because everyone can have the cuisine they want and no one falls out about choosing a restaurant.' It was an admirably Lib Dem compromise.

The following day, Dave McCobb, the party's campaign director, was due to bring his senior team together for a routine day of general election planning. Once Sunak had decided not to go for an election in May, the general assumption was that he was holding out for better economic data and would call a poll for November or possibly December. When his team met at 9.30 a.m. in the party's offices in Vincent Square, McCobb set out the agenda for the morning – planning through what a November campaign would look like, week by week.

Then the rumours began. 'As the day went on, more and more news dripped out,' McCobb says. By late morning, they decided to scrap their planned agenda for the day and instead have a dress rehearsal for what they would do if Sunak did call the vote.

McCobb says:

> So from about 10.30 a.m. we were basically behaving as if it had been called. I took the view that it was either a really useful dry run for a general election that was going to be called later in the year or we were going to be quite grateful we'd done it.

The campaign team plotted all the things they would need to do hour by hour over the next forty-eight hours and then day by day for the first ten days of any campaign. Party staffers calculated during the course of the day that they needed to send to print eight different pieces of literature to voters in every seat in the first three days of campaigning. 'We had printers lined up, we were speaking to volunteers in the seats who were providing photographs and artwork, fixing leaflets that weren't quite right – it was a really intense first day,' says McCobb.

When the weight of media reporting pointing to a 4 July poll became overwhelming, McCobb knew it was on. Watching Sunak get soaked in the rain, however, was mystifying.

The immediate response from everyone in the room was the one thing the Tories had left was power over how to call the election in a manner of their choosing. So why would they do it in such a terrible way? Why would they choose to make the defining image at the start of the election one of you looking bedraggled and hopeless and lost?

There is an old bell fixed to the wall in the office of Lib Dem HQ at 1 Vincent Square in Westminster. It has been in the party's possession for many years and nobody quite knows why. When the party downsized its offices from Great George Street in 2021, they saved about £1 million, bolstering their campaign war chest. They also saved the bell and brought it with them. Once Sunak had finished, McCobb spoke to his team: 'I went out and rang the bell and called everyone around and said, "Right, we have been planning for this for four years. Everyone in the team has got this. Everyone knows what they need to do. Just go to it."'

The party had done a huge amount of work preparing for the election they expected to come in May. This included designing and printing thousands of 'flying start' leaflets, which would be the first communication from the Lib Dems hitting doormats after the campaign began. These leaflets are vital to make a first impression, introducing voters to their local Lib Dem candidate. They were all printed in March and then distributed around the country to a network of local people, who each deliver 150 copies in their own streets.

'We had all this stuff boxed and batched,' McCobb says. 'So within an hour we had people standing with open car boots of pre-bundled "flying start" leaflets that we printed in March, and we had tens of thousands out across our target seats the day the general election was called.'

In the party's target seats, too, almost all candidates were selected and ready to go – and had been since the spring.

BE PREPARED

If he can help it, Morgan McSweeney doesn't like to leave things to chance. As leader of the team running Keir Starmer's election campaign, he had expected Sunak to go to the country on 2 May. Early in 2024, he told Starmer that he was going to order every member of Labour's election campaign squad to get ready to go for an election on that date. Starmer agreed. 'We were ready. We had agreed our line. All the candidates had little films, absolutely everything was ready – the manifesto was ready. The "first steps" stuff was all ready; we had booked a venue for a speech,' one senior source recalls.

When Sunak let March slide into April with no election called for May, most staffers breathed a sigh of relief and recalibrated their expectations for a vote in November. McSweeney did not relax at all.

'Morgan and the core group was basically prepared for every single day it could have been,' said another senior Labour source. 'There was zero complacency whatsoever.' With the threat of an imminent vote hanging over Starmer's team, McSweeney and Pat McFadden, the shadow minister in charge of the political side of the national campaign, were relentless in the discipline they demanded from the party headquarters team.

Labour staffers were effectively banned from taking holiday. 'There was a state of permanent vigilance,' an insider said. Maintaining that level of alertness, waiting for the moment Sunak pulled the trigger 'can be quite stressful', the source added. 'It wasn't without a price.'

During the previous weekend of 18–19 May, a few of what seemed like the usual noises had reached Labour HQ about Sunak calling an election in the week ahead, but party bosses didn't take them too seriously. 'We had all heard rumours over the weekend, and we were still dismissing them because we'd had so many rumours,' one senior party source said.

On Wednesday 22 May, however, it was clearly different: the 'chatter' was 'growing'. McSweeney had been told that the betting markets showed a surge in backing for a July vote, which made him believe Sunak was going to pull the trigger.

'We had the plans all ready for whenever it was going to be,' another person involved said. 'It was just a case of when do we hit send?'

The wait wasn't long. When Sunak made his announcement, looking like 'a drowned rat, with Labour's biggest election-winning anthem blasting in the background', it felt to Starmer's team like they had won the lottery. The official continued:

> It was just extraordinary. I nearly dislocated my jaw. You have these dreams about the most excruciating thing that could ever happen to you, often when you're younger – you go to school and realise you're not wearing any trousers. This was every political operator and politicians' worst nightmare, being played at the time on TV. It was like we had hit the jackpot because it was just ridiculous in the extreme.[6]

McSweeney had planned a speech himself to rev up his troops. He was supposed to say to all staff, 'This is the most unstoppable, unbeatable campaign machine in the history of world politics.' But the image of the Prime Minister on the TV 'getting drowned wet almost took away the threat of it', one source recalls.[7]

Labour's election machine swung into action. In the first twenty-four hours, headquarters was full of people and there was a business-like hubbub. Decisions were being taken rapidly and everyone knew what they needed to do. McSweeney was in his element and would later tell colleagues that day one was his favourite moment of the campaign.

Practical matters needed to be dealt with, such as MPs clearing out their offices in Parliament before the dissolution and making sure they didn't leave anything behind. Leaflets were printed; social media ads were prepared and released. A grid of events was drafted and preparations were made for finalising Labour's manifesto.

But even months later, Starmer's aides still marvel at their luck on that first day. Having suffered demoralising defeats at the hands of superior Tory campaign machines since 2010, they couldn't quite believe Sunak was making such basic mistakes. One trusted member of Labour's top team says:

> People have said, how badly advised was he? I'm sorry, but if I'd told Keir to go out and stand in the pouring rain and make an announcement, he would have said, 'No, I'm not doing that.' I can't think what was in his head. In fact, I still can't think what was in his head going earlier. I'm still mystified. I just don't understand it.[8]

Rishi Sunak triggered an early election so he could get the country's attention. Unfortunately, what the country saw was a political leader getting drenched in the rain. He wanted to take his rivals by surprise. But both Labour and the Liberal Democrats were more than ready for the fight, with candidates selected, ground armies prepared and leaflets ready to go. The same wasn't true of the Conservatives' campaign.

Just as with Theresa May's disastrous decision to call a snap election in 2017, the element of surprise in the Prime Minister's gambit rebounded to hit the Tories hardest of all.

CHAPTER 6

ON THE GROUND

OH, ISAAC LEVIDO

On the night of 12 December 2019, Conservative activists, packed into the party's headquarters in Westminster, were ecstatic. They had just notched up their biggest election victory since the days of Margaret Thatcher.

Surrounded by bottles of wine, Prosecco and beer, they chanted the name of the man who had masterminded their all-conquering campaign. 'Oh, Isaac Levido!' they sang to the tune of 'Seven Nation Army' by the White Stripes. They were parading a musical scalp. Back in 2017, the song had been Labour's anthem during a far more successful election contest for the socialist left, when thousands of supporters would fill football grounds and chant 'Oh, Jeremy Corbyn!'

Softly spoken and slim, with a thick, black beard, Levido had become a widely liked and respected figure in charge of Conservative Campaign Headquarters (CCHQ) in the run-up to Boris Johnson's victory. 'He's reserved but he's confident. He knows what he knows,' says one Tory who has seen him in action.

Levido was credited, alongside others, with coming up with pithy slogans including Johnson's campaign-defining 'Get Brexit Done'. Johnson was so impressed he wanted to make Levido strategy director in No. 10 but instead kept him on as the party's election consultant. After being fired by Liz Truss, Levido returned under Sunak to run the 2024 Tory election campaign.

Levido is a protégé of the godfather of Conservative strategists, Sir Lynton Crosby. A fellow Aussie, Crosby initiated Levido in the Tory election battle that delivered victory for David Cameron in 2015. In that campaign, Cameron put Crosby firmly in charge and ordered all Tory MPs and aides to follow his instructions, which, by and large, they did. Crosby's relentless message discipline in 2015 – hammering home the party's commitment to its 'long-term economic plan' – alongside his rigorous analysis of hard data on voters and charismatic leadership of the operation, delivered Cameron a majority that nobody had predicted.

Levido was born in Maitland, New South Wales in August 1983 and grew up playing sport, including Sunak's beloved cricket. After a spell working as a consultant, he went to join Crosby's firm, where he met his wife.

He founded the political consultancy Fleetwood Strategy in 2020, along with Michael Brooks, another former colleague of Crosby's, and Peter Dominiczak, the *Telegraph*'s former political editor.

• • •

Levido took up permanent residence in CCHQ at 4 Matthew Parker Street in Westminster in January 2024, election year. His private polling did not give Sunak and his team a much brighter view than the polls in the media. Some Tories remember him warning at the start of the year that the party could find itself facing an existential crisis. It's possible, he told them, that the election would leave the Conservatives with as few as seventy MPs, a loss of almost 300 seats. That would potentially mean the Tories could not even form the official opposition in Parliament.[1]

For Levido, the crucial message to voters needed to be to stick with the Conservatives in order to consolidate the progress the government was making toward economic stability and prosperity. Sunak, he believed, would have a stronger story to tell the later he left the election and as the economic data improved, with interest rates coming down, wages rising and inflation back under control.

The party campaign machine would also have more time to prepare. Selecting candidates was a tricky business, especially with so many Conservative MPs announcing they would be standing down at the election, apparently unwilling to put themselves through a campaign that seemed doomed. In the end, seventy-five Conservative MPs had decided they would not be contesting their seats this time. There were also gaps in the ground operation, some Tories believe, and more time would allow canvassers to gather more data about who their potential voters were and what they wanted to hear.

Inside the Tory 'war room', Levido sought to emulate the working environment of past election successes, reviving the Crosby-era traditions of early starts and public praise for staffers who do good work.

As in the Crosby–Cameron 2015 campaign, the first call of the day with senior campaign aides began at 5.40 a.m. before the main morning news shows on radio and TV. Then at 6.30 a.m. another call was held, led by Jamie Njoku-Goodwin, Sunak's director of strategy, mapping out what needed to happen during the day and preparations for the following day's campaigning.

Levido also demanded high standards of professionalism. At the start of the short campaign, he made a speech in the main open-plan office telling his team what he expected of them. First, no drinking. 'This will be a dry campaign,' he said. While there might be exceptions to watch England in the Euros, consuming alcohol inside the office was forbidden. 'You can do whatever you like outside the building,' Levido said. 'But be warned: decisions are made very early in the morning and I'll have zero tolerance if I pick up the phone and call you and you're hungover.'[2]

Alongside the whipping, there was encouragement. Another import from the Crosby years was the award of soft cuddly toys to staffers who had done a particularly good job each day. And a 'campaign song' was played daily in the office – this time, it was DJ Junkie XL's remix of Elvis Presley's 'A Little Less Conversation', chosen via 'a democratic process'. These were lighter-hearted moments that helped lift the mood during what was inevitably a depressing period for the Tory workforce.[3]

Like Crosby, Levido is a firm believer in the virtue of message discipline – repeating what you want voters to hear until they remember it, even if it bores you to tears. He gave presentations to the Cabinet, MPs and peers in the months leading up to the election. He warned them that voters would be put off by a party that was seen to be divided. His warnings made sense, but according to some present, his sometimes quiet style risked underplaying the strength of his point.

Crosby didn't indulge in angry shouting either, but he was ready to make a noise and could be direct when he disagreed instantly with someone's unfounded opinion. One person who'd worked on the Tory campaign says:

Isaac is very different from Lynton. Lynton is very outgoing; Isaac is not. Isaac is softly spoken, organised. I don't think he's spontaneous. Lynton I can imagine being spontaneous in taking decisions.[4]

When the election date was being discussed earlier in the year, Levido was arguing hard in private for autumn or winter. At one point 12 December was considered, which would have been exactly five years to the day since the previous election, when Johnson won his majority.

But senior Tories were never sure if Sunak would comply with Levido's instructions or listen to his advice. The PM always found it hard to relinquish control and often got stuck into the details himself. Even Boris Johnson, infamously chaotic as an administrator, understood from Crosby how vital it was to maintain an iron discipline and do what you're told in an election campaign. Sunak, encouraged by some of his allies, rejected Levido's concerns about an early election and settled on 4 July.

'I like Isaac a lot,' one Cabinet minister says. 'He was placed in the impossible position of not wanting that date and being made to run a campaign on that date. That must never happen. Your campaign director must be totally in charge.'

There was only one person who was ultimately in charge of when to trigger the vote. Unfortunately for the Conservatives, it wasn't the person who knew how to win an election.

THE CELL

By early 2024, every poll put Keir Starmer's Labour on course to win. The expectation of success galvanised Labour staffers. As the party prepared to target the Conservatives in the contest for power, it was overrun with recruits.

In fact, bosses at Southworks, Labour's new headquarters in Southwark, south London, were starting to worry that too many people were showing up to work. The smart new-build office thirty minutes' walk across the River Thames from Westminster, which they had moved into in autumn 2023, had sensors installed to measure noise levels, air quality and, crucially, occupancy rate. 'They stopped handing out passes to people because they thought they were in danger of breaking fire regulations,' said one campaign official.[5]

The intensity of Labour workers' motivation was easy to understand. The party had been out of power for fourteen years. Staffers were desperate to make themselves useful to Morgan McSweeney, Labour's charismatic campaign director, who commanded operations from a desk in the centre of the room. 'They were turning away volunteers. You had to be picked,' one person recalls.

A digital clock counting down the days, hours and minutes left before the polls opened was displayed prominently. Inside the open-plan space, directing his troops, sat McSweeney and his core team. Pat McFadden, the MP and national campaign coordinator, was one of the party's most experienced hands and a regular spokesperson in the media. He provided political leadership on key decisions and gave reassurance to candidates and officials alike, as the trusted frontline politician in the heart of operations.

Alongside these two men were some hugely influential women: Hollie Ridley, the field teams director; Ellie Reeves, the shadow Chancellor's sister and McFadden's deputy; Marianna McFadden,

Pat's wife and McSweeney's deputy; and Deborah Mattinson, research expert and director of strategy.

Paul Ovenden, Labour's director of attack and rebuttal, had a team of seven on the hunt for news stories that could damage the Conservatives. In the months leading up to the campaign, Matthew Doyle, Starmer's communications director, would also be found at the hub of things. He had previously worked for Tony Blair. When the election was called, he spent his time on the road with Starmer, travelling thousands of miles on media visits up and down the country. Peter Hyman, who was Blair's speechwriter, was another veteran of the New Labour years. He took on a role advising Starmer on policy issues.

Their deep experience of both politics and governing, along with on-call advice from New Labour grandees Peter Mandelson and Alastair Campbell, was a vital foundation on which to build a campaign. It stood in contrast to Sunak's operation. The Tory leader had a young group of aides around him, and while there were a few old hands doing their bit in CCHQ, his inner circle lacked the years of experience at the top of politics that Starmer's team had.

• • •

With an election to win, a highly disciplined focus on the practicalities of campaigning dominated every meeting at Southworks. Behind the relentless drive towards the goal of winning a majority was one person, above all others. 'Undeniably, Morgan,' said a senior party figure, when asked who the boss was. 'There was one person in charge, and it worked effectively because it was one person – and because it was him.'

Since becoming a key figure in Starmer's inner circle, McSweeney has earned a reputation for ruthlessness, especially when it came to neutralising the threat from the party's far left. But those who worked closely with him during the election campaign also saw his effectiveness as a leader, identifying speedy problem-solving and strategic thinking among his most impressive skills.

McSweeney was a constant presence in the office. He was approachable, took decisions fast, could be funny, and inspired his team with praise for their work and his natural energetic authority. He speaks quickly but communicates with clarity.

The way he and McFadden ran the campaign war room was also key. The hours were long. The day started around 6.30 a.m., with McFadden's morning meeting. It had to be in-person, not on a call. Those meetings involved Doyle, Mattinson, Ridley, shadow minister Jonathan Ashworth and Ellie Reeves. They would run through plans for the day and look ahead to the next two or three days of campaigning.

For some, the day would often not finish until 11 p.m. or later, once reports had come in from teams campaigning in target seats around the country. Pizza was laid on sometimes for those still working late.

McSweeney thought how nice it was that people would bring food into the office during their long days. Then it dawned on him that he never left the building. It was becoming like a jail cell and this was 'prison food'. The team referred to their office as 'the cell' for the rest of the campaign.[6]

Mostly, Labour staffers fuelled themselves with strong coffee and sandwiches from the Pret around the corner. 'We all had a Pret subscription,' one member of the team recalls. 'So, because we were all living in HQ and getting our lunch there and starting so early in the morning, there was a queue outside Pret. It was like hard drinkers outside waiting for the pub in the morning.' Some liked to vary their diet. McFadden, however, had a favourite – the chicken Caesar and bacon baguette. It was the same sandwich of preference famously ordered by former Tory Cabinet minister Dominic Raab.[7]

TORY TARGETS

Every election is, in the end, fought on ground level.

For months beforehand, but most intensively during the short six-week campaign, political parties mount a massive, street-by-street operation to make their case directly to voters by dropping leaflets and mail through letterboxes and engaging them in doorstep conversations.

Through 'canvassing', parties gain vital information about which addresses house voters who are likely to support them and which do not. Then, on polling day, candidates and their teams return to knock on the doors of voters listed as supportive to make sure they exercise their democratic rights. This is the 'get out the vote' operation.

First, election campaign directors have to pick their targets. There is no point campaigning in safe seats for their party or in constituencies they have no chance of winning. The usual place to start identifying the key marginal seats that will be where the election is won and lost is by looking at what happened last time. In 2019, Boris Johnson's Conservatives won 365 seats and a majority of eighty. By the time Rishi Sunak called the election on 22 May 2024, Tory campaign chiefs had given up on any hope of holding onto half of them.

Levido's team had identified 100–120 'battleground' marginal seats. Tory HQ gave campaign teams in these constituencies the most intensive support they could, with more people and more money for leaflets, direct mail and Facebook ads. There was a smaller group of 'safe' seats that did not need much help, but they numbered only in the tens – far fewer than at past elections. And the party was not attacking any new seats to try to win them from other parties anywhere. As one source says, 'We were down to under 200 seats that we could possibly even campaign in.'[8]

The fact that Conservatives had decided there was no point throwing resources at so many seats was a sign that the data from those districts was deeply negative. Voters who had backed Johnson in 2019 were turning away from the party, though many more than usual were not sure who they would vote for – or if they would even bother at all.

In addition to the party's national unpopularity, Levido had two logistical problems – a lack of activists and a shortage of cash. 'The idea that there are tens of thousands of Tory volunteers is like Hitler in the bunker in 1945,' one party source explains. 'The armies don't exist.' Labour has always outnumbered the Conservatives in the number of activists available to pound the pavements up and down the land. 'It's getting worse,' the source says.

A clear signal that the Tories were fighting a predominantly defensive campaign came in the choice of seats Rishi Sunak spent time visiting before polling day. Instead of targeting new areas, which a confident party seeking to seize more territory would do, Sunak made 90 per cent of his visits to seats that Tories had won in 2019. These Conservative-held areas were the battleground – in England, at least.

The other parties agreed. According to analysis by the BBC on 26 June, with one week left of campaigning, 76 per cent of Keir Starmer's visits were to Conservative constituencies and 94 per cent of Lib Dem leader Ed Davey's visits were to Tory-held seats.[9]

Inside Tory headquarters, there were serious worries about whether a clutch of senior party figures, including half the Cabinet, would survive. Chancellor Jeremy Hunt, Defence Secretary Grant Shapps and Culture Secretary Lucy Frazer were among those deemed vulnerable. Jacob Rees-Mogg, the grandee Brexiteer who served in Johnson's Cabinet, and Liz Truss were also judged to be at risk. At one point, Tory high command urged Truss not to stand. The election in her South West Norfolk seat would be hard for her and if she lost it, would be terrible, her team was told. The request was ignored.

About two weeks into the campaign, candidates in some seats initially regarded as priorities for defending were told they wouldn't get any more resources. The data was showing they were lost causes. 'There was a big push to tell people it's over in your seat,' one senior campaign official said. The harsh decision to switch off their access to voter canvassing data and stop leafleting was in order to focus the Tories' limited resources on areas where MPs had a better chance of survival. 'Things that weren't realistic, they just switch the thing off,' another Conservative says.[10]

LABOUR TARGETS

With his strategy in place and the ground army tooled up and ready, it was time for McSweeney to pick his targets.

Working with Hollie Ridley, the field director, he split the country's constituencies into seven categories from zero to six. 'Zero' covered the seats that Labour were guaranteed to take. Seats classified as 'six' were those Labour had no hope of winning.

When Sunak named the date in May, McSweeney, Ridley,

Mattinson and McFadden met to finalise their ambitions. They felt confident. So much so that they opted to focus on some of the most ambitious Tory-held seats in the land in categories 'four' and 'five'. In all, they designated around 250 Parliamentary constituencies as 'battleground' target seats. Their selection took in huge swathes of Conservative heartlands in Yorkshire, the east of England and across the south. McSweeney was plotting an assault on Tory shires.

Seats such as Cannock Chase in Staffordshire, where the former Tory chair Amanda Milling had a 19,879 majority, Essex's Thurrock, where 72 per cent of people had voted Leave, and true-blue Banbury, deep in rural Oxfordshire, were on the list.* 'I was thinking "Oh my god, it's so brave,"' said one official. 'We were going for it. Normally the Labour Party would play it safe, but we had done a lot of work in those target seats. It blew my mind.'[11]

In these target constituencies, candidates would be prioritised for deliveries of leaflets and placards, while residents in the area would receive multiple digital ads via Facebook. High-profile Labour frontbenchers would visit the districts to boost the profile of the candidate in the local press. Mail would land on doormats, making sure nobody was in any doubt that Labour wanted to win their support.

After the May local elections, McSweeney added another eleven targets to the battleground list. Some of these required enormous swings in excess of 20 per cent, including Harlow, Essex; Redditch in Worcestershire; and Aldershot in Hampshire. Even North East Somerset & Hanham, where high-profile Brexiteer Jacob

---

* Bridget Phillipson, Labour's new Education Secretary, recalls campaigning in Banbury, in the final ten days of the election, as the moment she knew a big win was on the cards. 'It was very clear that something was happening,' she says in an interview for this book. 'Even with lifelong Tories, there was a clear appetite for change.'

Rees-Mogg was facing Labour's Dan Norris, became a target, along with Cabinet minister Penny Mordaunt's seat in Portsmouth North.

• • •

McSweeney still had one big problem. In past elections, the party's most vigorous campaigns were fought in constituencies that were already safe, piling up votes where they were not needed. He had to find a way to get door-knocking activists out of their home territory and into the marginal seats that would swing the election.

The answer was to 'twin' safe constituencies with priority target seats. Activists in solid Labour areas were told to leave their home territory and join the fight in the streets in the key marginal constituency they had been twinned with.*

While the Tories cut off access to data for candidates who had no hope of saving their seats, Labour had the opposite problem. In some cases, volunteers were practically forced to abandon door-knocking on home turf to travel to a neighbouring constituency, as McSweeney's team disabled their access to the centrally held data in Contact Creator, the party's canvassing software. This effectively blocked activists from finding potential Labour voters locally. It sometimes happened without warning after officials in the London office deemed that canvassers were knocking on too many unnecessary doors.

The system was not popular, even if the short-term logic made sense. The plan shredded the nerves of some candidates who feared

---

* According to a Labour source, McSweeney first deployed this ruthless targeting strategy while working with his friend Steve Reed, the new Environment Secretary, at Lambeth Council in 2006. Reed, who led the Labour group on the council, bucked the national trend, gaining eleven seats on what was a bad night for Blair's party nationally. Their secret was the targeting of 14,000 working-class voters in seven key wards in the borough.

they could lose. Ellie Reeves acted as one of the party's enforcers who could be heard 'all day on the phone telling people off' if they were failing to travel to their twinned seat, a colleague says.

One source recalls that a 'few people were naughty', disobeying HQ's orders, and Reeves would be asked to persuade them otherwise, adding, 'You would not have wanted to be on the receiving end of that call.' In one instance, when a candidate was attempting to wriggle out of canvassing, Reeves was overheard to have said, 'I know you have to pick your children up from school in the constituency. Maybe you should just get someone else to do that.'

McSweeney's command-and-control approach proved highly effective, but it ruffled feathers. 'There was a really un-nuanced view of it all,' said one Labour source. 'At times, Morgan will take a short-term view regardless of some huge implications in the medium and long term.' Some party officials worried that recruitment would be harder in future in those safe Labour seats that had been ignored because activists had felt badly treated.[12]

Ann Black, a member of Labour's National Executive Committee, would later accept that this led to some 'resentment' among grassroots members, some of whom were disabled or had family commitments. 'We are all volunteers, and punishing members will not move them en masse 50 miles down the road,' she wrote in a report to the party's ruling body. The same document acknowledged that McSweeney's ruthless approach, on this occasion, was devastatingly effective, with Labour winning 92 per cent of the party's targets.

The battleground list kept growing more ambitious as the campaign went on and more voters resolved to back him. Labour ended the general election with 33.7 per cent of the vote, up a mere 1.6 percentage points on its 2019 performance under Corbyn. But it won 63 per cent of the seats in the Commons – the biggest gap between those two measures on record. It underlined the extraordinary efficiency of the party's vote distribution and the genius of McSweeney's highly focused campaign.

FIELD OPERATIONS

Hollie Ridley joined the Labour Party in 2011 as a trainee organiser, after working on the campaign against the far-right BNP in east London. By 2024, she was commanding Labour's army of thousands of activists and organisers across the country. Many insiders credit her as the unsung hero who played a critical role in delivering victory for Starmer. A few weeks after the election, she was promoted to be Labour's general secretary, the party's most powerful official.

Ridley's background is unlike the 'metropolitan elite' image that has been attached to senior Labour politicians in the past. She worked cleaning toilets in McDonalds for a time, as well as in a branch of Mecca Bingo. She is also a committed and clearly resilient member of the Labour hierarchy, sticking around when many did not after the party's successive defeats in 2015, 2017 and 2019. In 2024, Ridley was the general marshalling Labour's forces and she left nothing to chance.

With McSweeney convinced that Sunak would go for a poll in May, Ridley made sure her field teams were ready. Every one of them had a 'break in case of emergency' box of materials delivered to them at the start of the year, to be opened when the moment came. It contained a plan for the first twenty-four hours of campaigning, including posters, leaflets and instructions for staging a launch event.

Ridley was also committed to exploiting the latest-available campaign technology. Canvassers on the doorstep followed a digital script called 'Persuasion Pathways'. Voters would be asked first what issues they cared about and then how likely they were to vote Labour, on a scale from one to ten. It helped the party to figure out how much of their support was soft, while also gathering detailed information on voters' concerns.

Ridley pioneered a system known internally as the 'feedback loop'. Party organisers on the ground would collect and submit comments from voters, stories from regional or local news outlets, and results from surveys. An AI tool would then collect this information into a written report. These reports would be poured over by campaign chiefs the next morning to help inform the orders McSweeney and his deputies would send back into the field that day.

Many insiders credit Ridley's innovation with helping Labour keep on top of what the Tories were doing and whether their actions were making any impact. The 'feedback loop' system alerted Ridley and McSweeney to how effective the Tories' attack on Labour's tax plans was and with which voters. It told them, for example, that while the election date betting scandal was splashed across the front pages of *The Times* and *The Guardian*, it was not gaining much traction with voters in their target seats.

Each morning, Ridley would speak to the party's eleven regional directors and guide them through priorities for door-knocking, leafleting and what to brief their local organisers. 'We had an extensive ground operation that was listening to voters every day,' a party official says.

McSweeney and others received regular updates from conventional focus groups conducted by Mattinson, as well as rolling seat projections. 'We were trying to get data from as many sources as possible,' a Labour staffer explains. 'You've got to listen to voters every way that you can.'[13]

Labour's approach – listen, reflect and persuade – recognised a structural shift in British politics. Voters are less loyal to traditional parties than they were twenty or even ten years ago and more sceptical about politicians. 'Elections have fundamentally changed,' says one senior official:

> In the 1990s, three-quarters of voters never changed which party they voted for. That's flipped completely. It's now probably only a quarter of voters that never change. So the electorate you're talking to is very different, their confidence and trust in politicians and in institutions is different.[14]

By the time the election was called, all of Labour's digital innovations had been fully integrated and tested in real life during local elections and by-elections. In May 2024, any remaining members of the party's old guard who doubted what such a data-driven approach could deliver were silenced. In the election for West Midlands mayor, Labour's Richard Parker succeeded in ousting the popular Tory Andy Street. The margin of victory was 225,590 votes to 224,082, a difference of just 1,508 votes across the entire region.

'We piled everybody into the West Midlands for that mayoral election, and we won by the equivalent of one extra vote per ballot box,' a senior Labour figure explained. 'That was very powerful. After that, people said the campaign seems to know what it's doing.'[15]

TECH FAIL

Getting good, quick data on what voters think is essential for campaign directors. Isaac Levido and his lead pollster, Zach Ward-Elms, ran a highly sophisticated polling operation, refined over many years and contests.

They questioned 600 people every night during the election campaign for a 'tracker' poll based on results taken across a three-day rolling period. It focused mainly on residents in key swing seats. The Tory team would ask potential voters who they preferred as Prime Minister and whether they thought Labour or the Tories best fitted descriptions such as: 'best to make people feel more secure'; 'share my values' and 'have a plan for the future', among many others. The data would then be fed through a 'regression' computer model to enable Ward-Elms and Levido to establish exactly why the party was winning or losing ground. Their model allowed them to track which messages or events – like the D-Day debacle or a TV debate – were affecting the campaign, for good or for bad, in the key swing seats. They also ran focus groups four times a week in marginal seats to provide qualitative data that would inform the results from the polls.

The canvassing operation on the ground, however, was a completely different matter.

The quality of information gathered from volunteers' conversations on doorsteps during the short contest and in the months and years beforehand is a huge contributor towards the success or failure of a campaign. Before the 2015 election, which the Conservatives unexpectedly won, a huge amount of time and money went into the party designing a new IT programme to harness the power of all the canvassing data, known as Vote Source.

When it worked well, it enabled 'central office', as CCHQ is still known to many Tories, to send detailed, personalised letters or leaflets to individual voters in key seats. That proved highly effective in 2015, although the programme was not without its problems. On polling day that year it crashed. Lynton Crosby, who was running the Tory election operation at the time, felt sick with worry as constituency activists stumbled around their local streets trying to get their voters out to polling stations but not knowing which doors to knock on.

Nine years later, problems struck again. Some candidates and their teams complained that the system was telling them to knock on the doors of people who fitted the profile of Tory voters – perhaps because they were in older age groups – but had in fact not voted for 'decades'. These were people who were not likely to vote anyway, a Conservative election adviser says. 'They were a waste of time.'[16]

Steve Baker, a minister who was defending the seat of Wycombe for the Conservatives, remembers how many of his colleagues in marginal seats had complained about Vote Source at previous elections. Now, under pressure from Labour and Reform UK, he needed the system to work on polling day.

'It's get-out-the-vote operation in Wycombe for the first time in a long time so we were literally [trying to] get as many activists [out knocking on doors] as possible in the morning,' Baker recalls.

> And we just went out with our clipboards and our lists and went knocking up people who told us they would vote Conservative. And, as usual, as always happens, the software was giving us lists of Labour voters. And for four general elections I'd heard my colleagues in marginal seats who'd been returned complaining about the inadequacies of this Vote Source programme. But because I'd

never been a target seat before I didn't have that problem. But as soon as I was a target seat, Vote Source was churning out lists, we were knocking up people who were going to vote Labour. Disaster. To find that the software – still – was giving us non-Conservative voters. How hard can that be? What was the point of collecting the data?'[17]

As a candidate for a nationally unpopular party, the worst thing you can do is knock on the doors of people who support your opponents and give them a reminder about why they should go and vote to get you out. The Vote Source error in Wycombe was electoral self-harm on polling day. Baker's team worked quickly to change the filters on the software to find voters who were truly open to backing the Conservatives.

Of course, Vote Source is only as good as the data that candidates and their teams put into it from years of canvassing in their constituencies. This, in many cases, was part of the problem for the Conservatives. Tory campaign chiefs in Westminster set local party associations targets for how many local residents they needed to get to complete voting intention surveys each month. Some do not take any notice, especially if they're in long-held seats sitting on fat majorities. After watching a procession of Conservative leaders win elections against lacklustre Labour opponents since 2010, some Tories had become complacent. 'We had lots of MPs who were very poor,' a senior campaign source recalls. 'Either they were new MPs over the last couple of years, or MPs who were vulnerable for the first time and were lazy and never spent time in their constituencies.'[18]

Another member of Sunak's team says, 'We got properly found out at this election. There's a culture around safe seats which is a very bad thing.'

There was a report that someone collected their first voting intention survey since 1997. They have a safe seat with a rock-solid Tory majority – with a 25,000 majority. The MP lives there in a nice country seat which they're never going to lose. So they don't bother campaigning, they don't bother knocking on doors, they don't bother going around. Suddenly they were finding actually 'we don't know where our voters are, we don't know what doors we knocked'. They just hadn't been doing the work.[19]

LISTENING

'Listening isn't passive, listening is powerful.'

David Evans, Labour's general secretary and its most senior official, was talking to party activists at a training bootcamp at the Progressive Britain conference on 11 May 2024. What nobody gathered at the stylish conference venue in the City of London knew was that eleven days later, Rishi Sunak would trigger the general election.

Evans's audience were Labour's ground team, the volunteers who would knock on doors and talk to voters to persuade them to back Keir Starmer in the campaign about to begin. He was trying to guide them through those crucial interactions. This insight on the power of listening was inspired by American academic Bernard Ferrari – his rule for effective communication was to spend 80 per cent of the time listening and only 20 per cent speaking.

'That might feel and sound a bit counterintuitive, given we are a political party that has a lot to say about our vision, our message and our story,' Evans went on. 'But it absolutely isn't, because if somebody hasn't been heard, they won't be in a place where they are ready to listen.'

Evans, who had set about modernising Labour's campaign

machine when he took over in 2020, drafted in teams of tech experts. One group built an AI bot to help train party volunteers in how to talk – and listen – to voters in the real world. Activists were given a 'score out of ten' for their performance.[20]

Evans stressed that these canvassers should only present the party's offer once the voter felt heard. The policies to emphasise should be Starmer's six 'first steps' for power: these promised 6,500 more teachers; 40,000 more GP appointments; economic stability; launching a new Border Security Command; a crackdown on anti-social behaviour; and setting up Great British Energy.

'We've got ourselves into a position where we have an opportunity to change the country, but it is only an opportunity,' Evans told the bootcamp. With an electorate that was fed up with the Tories but not yet sold on Labour, those doorstep conversations would be vital to securing victory. Volunteers must tell voters that Starmer has 'fundamentally changed the Labour Party', Evans said. 'He has, it's real, it's true.'

NOT LISTENING

Richard Holden's entire election campaign – and with it, perhaps his political career – was slipping from his grasp. And that was before he had even found a seat to stand in.

It was early evening on Wednesday 5 June and Holden was in his car, driving as fast as the speed limit would allow from London to Essex with an aide in the passenger seat beside him. After his own constituency in North West Durham had been abolished in routine boundary changes, party chiefs in Westminster parachuted him into the Essex seat of Basildon & Billericay. But the local party, which had not been consulted, was outraged.

Holden's mission was to try to win over officials in the Essex district who were 'apoplectic' that they had been given no choice over their candidate for Parliament. Amid the scramble to get organised for the snap election, party headquarters had bluntly told them that Holden was the only choice they would have.

It is easy to see why local officials would have been furious. Their long-serving MP John Baron had announced as long ago as October 2023 that he was standing down at the next election. They had expected to be given a choice of at least three potential candidates to interview before selecting the person they thought would be best to represent their local area. That is the normal procedure for selecting candidates when time is tight in an election campaign.

Holden, a loyal party servant and member for more than twenty years, had no say over which seat he would be given either. He was presented by Tory bosses on the selection committee with a decision that had already been taken. And given that it seemed to be blowing up in his face, he decided to try to do something about it. The Basildon & Billericay Conservative Association were so angry that they were holding a special meeting that same evening when they would decide whether to run independent candidates against him.

Holden knew he needed to speak to the local party as soon as he could. He rang the constituency association chairman, Richard Moore, and suggested he should drive down to meet them all. Moore replied that the local executive committee were due to meet in half an hour, but he'd speak to them to see if they could delay their decision.

A number of senior figures in the party's high command tried to stop Holden making his dash to Essex that night. One of them told him to ignore the local party. 'I don't think ignoring them is a very good idea,' he replied.

So, Holden jumped in his car with his chief of staff, Ryan Stinger, and hit the A13. While he was on the road, Downing Street called, also advising him not to go. 'You can advise me all you want,' Holden answered. 'I am going to try and undo some of the damage.'[21]

As Holden approached his destination, the phone rang again. This time it was Moore, asking how far away he was. When Holden told him he was only twenty minutes out, Moore said the committee would wait. By this time the media were all over the row and broadcasters had dispatched cameras to the town.

The Tory chairman walked into the meeting with a dozen or so local officials, two of whom were planning to stand as independents against him. He spent an hour and a half taking the heat, answering their questions and trying to convince them he would do a good job. And then he left them to make their decision.

Stopping for a drink in a pub before making his way home again with his chief of staff, Holden's phone rang, before he'd even had his first sip of beer. It was Moore, calling him back in. The association had unanimously decided to back Holden as their candidate but only after meeting him and seeing the effort he was prepared to make for the seat.

Holden's opponents unfairly characterised his search for a new seat as a 'chicken run'. The implication was that he was fleeing an area where he feared he was going to lose in search of somewhere safer. But in the end, Basildon & Billericay was not safe at all. Holden needed all the support he could get – including from his recent converts in the initially hostile local party – to make his case to voters. He ended up holding onto the seat for the Tories but only after a recount and by just twenty votes. It was the thinnest Conservative majority in the country.

Holden, a hard-working and committed Tory, has served the party in a range of roles including as a minister and special adviser in government. His experience of a shambolic selection process was not isolated. Some Tories believe the turnover of MPs who have held the role of party chairman is partly to blame for the fact that CCHQ was not in better shape as a fighting force.

Holden was the ninth person to serve as party chairman in the five years since Johnson won his majority in 2019, and when a new chairman moved in, they would often want to review party processes and election planning. The role is a critical one, especially in an election year. Their tasks include rallying troops and providing leadership to campaign staff in party headquarters, managing internal and HR matters, and supporting local Tory associations to prepare.

The churn at the top of the party also disrupted CCHQ's efforts to support candidates in seats that were at risk. A big push to shore up support in Tory-held marginal constituencies had been planned for the summer of 2022, but then Johnson was forced out and a leadership election was held, derailing that work.[22]

Candidate selections are almost always contentious. One of the biggest problems the Tories faced in 2024 was the fact that so many MPs were standing down – and that so many of them only announced their decisions late in the day and even after Sunak had called the election. CCHQ officials had tried hard to put pressure on MPs to decide early whether they were going to fight the next election. But even some who were telling their friends they were going to retire months earlier did not formally notify party headquarters until after the election was called. 'It was utterly unnecessary,' one party source said, clearly frustrated.

CCHQ also made some problematic decisions, including wanting to handle selections in 'batches'. The result was that a 'serious backlog' of candidate vacancies had built up by the spring, even in seats where it was well known in advance that the MP would be standing down. This was all in marked contrast to the Tories' rivals in the south of England, the Lib Dems, who had selected most of their target-seat candidates by March. They needed to, because, like Labour, they thought the election would be in May.

The other factor was the rise of localism. Conservative associations wanted local people to represent their area. This trend coincides with a marked decline in public backing for the main parties. In previous decades, voters would identify much more strongly as lifelong Labour or lifelong Tory supporters. In more recent campaigns, the electorate has been far more volatile. The scale of Starmer's success in 2024 illustrates the point: between one election and the next, Labour went from its worst defeat since the 1930s to the second-best result in the party's history, almost surpassing Tony Blair's historic 1997 landslide.

'Because people have no allegiance to politics in general, the one thing party workers could hang onto would be that he or she is a local man or woman,' according to a Tory involved in the selection of candidates. 'I have never known the obsession about local connections being so strong.'[23]

With voters no longer tethered to political parties, for anxious and embattled Tory associations at least, a local identity became a substitute for a political one.

• • •

Sunak ended his campaign with a final rally on 3 July at a rugby club in Romsey & Southampton North, where Caroline Nokes was defending a majority of more than 10,000. He appealed to Tories not to give up. As all Southampton FC fans know, especially if they have suffered season after season with knife-edge relegation battles, 'it is not over until the final whistle blows,' Sunak said. 'I can also tell you that this underdog will fight to that final whistle.'

Nokes held her seat, but nearby Ranil Jayawardena lost in North East Hampshire, despite defending a majority of more than 20,000.

LEFT OUT

Selections were also highly contentious for Labour.

The election gave Keir Starmer his chance to complete the job of transforming the Labour Party. Picking the right sort of candidates for Parliament was the final step Starmer needed to block out the hard left.

During the short campaign, members of the party's ruling National Executive Committee were in charge of the process of selections. The body was dominated by Starmer's allies. Among the candidates chosen were Josh Simons, director of McSweeney's former think tank Labour Together; Torsten Bell, a former Ed Miliband aide; and Georgia Gould, leader of Camden Council and daughter of the late New Labour adviser Philip Gould.

It was also the final chance for Starmer supporters to sideline left-wingers they believed could threaten the leader's authority. Faiza Shaheen, a Corbyn ally who had been selected to fight Iain Duncan Smith in Chingford & Woodford Green, was dropped for allegedly liking posts downplaying antisemitism allegations. The decision sparked outrage and the resignation of some fifty local members in the constituency. Lloyd Russell-Moyle, the Corbynite MP for Brighton Kemptown, was told he was subject to a complaint and ineligible to stand. He was replaced as a candidate with Starmer adviser Chris Ward.

Insiders believe party officials would have gone further were it not for an explosive row involving Diane Abbott that dominated the news cycle in the early days of the campaign. Abbott was the first Black woman to enter Parliament, doing so in 1987. She had been Corbyn's shadow Home Secretary and a vocal critic of the Starmer operation. Abbott was suspended as a Labour MP in April 2023 over a letter she penned in *The Observer* which stated that Jews, Irish and Traveller people 'undoubtedly experience prejudice' but were not subject to racism 'all their lives'. Jewish groups had claimed it established a hierarchy of racism and Abbott apologised.

By May 2024, the investigation into the matter had seemingly dragged on for more than a year. Party officials had attempted to broker a deal whereby she would regain the Labour whip but agree to stand down, allowing the 71-year-old to end her parliamentary career with dignity. But any hope of a deal was wrecked when an article appeared in *The Times* on 28 May suggesting Abbott would be barred from standing for re-election in her seat.

Abbott organised a rally in Hackney, telling supporters she would be the MP 'as long as it is possible'. Starmer was furious at the *Times* story and Morgan McSweeney knew how distracting the episode could be to Labour's campaign. He launched a frantic round of crisis meetings to work out how to fix it.

Meanwhile, BBC *Newsnight* broke the news that the investigation into Abbott's conduct had, in fact, concluded in December 2023 when she had been asked to complete an antisemitism awareness course. Starmer allies were subject to a torrent of criticism and accused of trying to edge out a trailblazing Black Labour MP, while Tories reacted with glee that Starmer appeared unable, after all, to deal with the left. Jeremy Hunt, the Tory Chancellor, jibed, 'If Keir Starmer can't deal with Diane Abbott, how on Earth is he going to deal with Vladimir Putin?'

Two days after the *Times* story, Labour's deputy leader Angela Rayner offered a fig leaf, telling Sky News she knew no reason why Abbott could not be the candidate. Rayner's intervention was discussed with Starmer first. The next day, the Labour leader followed suit, saying Abbott was 'free' to stand, after dodging questions over her status for days. It was an example of how slow Starmer and his team could be to act when faced with negative headlines – a weakness they would take into government. It was also a rare, if only symbolic, victory for Labour's socialist left faction during the Starmer era. Momentum, the organisation set up to support Corbynism, gloated in a post online, 'You come at the Queen, you best not miss.'

GAZA

Not all battleground seats were categorised as 'offensive' targets that Labour was aiming to win from its rivals. More than twenty were defensive priorities – constituencies where McSweeney knew he faced a challenge, usually from smaller parties. There was one big political issue that disrupted Labour's ground campaign more than any other in the months before polling day: the Israel–Hamas war.

When Hamas terrorists killed 1,200 people in Israel on 7 October 2023, triggering an Israeli ground invasion of the Gaza Strip, a conflict erupted that would inflame and distort politics across the West. Amid the horror and international outrage at the killings, left-wing political parties struggled to know how to respond. Initially, many offered Israel their backing. But Israeli Prime Minister Benjamin Netanyahu's retaliation in Gaza provoked rage and anguish at the suffering of Palestinians that was hard to contain.

In Britain, the debate was fraught. Many on the left traditionally sympathise with the Palestinian cause. It had been a central tenet of Jeremy Corbyn's political ideology for decades.

Just days after the 7 October attack, Keir Starmer found himself struggling to calibrate his response without losing traditional Labour voters, especially in Muslim communities. An interview given by Starmer to LBC Radio at the close of the party's 2023 conference explored how Labour thought Israel should respond. Presenter Nick Ferrari asked him if 'cutting off power, cutting off water' to Gaza would be appropriate. Starmer appeared to say Israel 'does have that right'.

Starmer later explained that he had intended his comment to refer back to his previous answer, in which he'd said Israel has the right to self-defence. But Labour failed to correct the error until ten days later. Within hours of the station posting a clip of the interview, it had been widely shared across social media. The damage to Starmer's standing among Muslim voters was widespread. Internally, the episode reignited rows within the party over Palestine that had characterised the Corbyn era. But more importantly, it outraged many Muslims in the UK and a section of left-leaning liberals.

The war in Gaza intensified, and community tensions rose as the Palestinian death toll mounted. Labour MPs representing large Muslim communities feared an electoral threat too. Those concerns grew after a by-election in February 2024 in Rochdale. The seat was snatched from Labour by George Galloway, the divisive firebrand leader of the British Workers Party. When he won, Galloway declared, 'Keir Starmer, this is for Gaza.'

In the general election, a succession of independent candidates stood on hardline, pro-Palestinian tickets in seats in London, the Midlands and the north-west. Labour paid the heaviest price in lost support. The Greens also made the most of taking a tougher stance against Israel in seats where they were competing with Labour.

In some areas Starmer's candidates faced intimidation, which was videoed and shared widely on social media. Naz Shah, who was re-elected in Bradford West, describes how 'death threats [were] routine' during the campaign. Several videos showing her being harassed went viral.

'It was vitriolic. When my team were out campaigning, they were literally threatened with dogs,' she says. On other occasions, 'cars rocked up with men in hoodies' for a rival independent candidate's campaign. 'It was intimidation tactics. They walked into the gardens where we were talking to constituents and just tried to talk over you. It was really in your face – and all men. It was steeped in misogyny.'[24]

Heather Iqbal, Labour's candidate in Dewsbury & Batley, was called a 'genocide agent' and 'child murderer' while out campaigning. Some, including shadow Cabinet minister Shabana Mahmood, were forced to scale back their campaigning amid security concerns.

The re-emergence of Palestine as a political issue also provided Corbyn with a cause to champion. He stood as an independent in Islington North, which he had represented since 1983. The former leader won the seat, in an irritating blow to Starmer on election night.

Thangam Debbonaire, shadow Culture Secretary, lost out to the Greens on election night, in part over Labour's handling of the Gaza war. She said the Israel–Palestine issue in her Bristol Central seat was nuanced:

> The Muslim [community] was always constructive with me. I had a lot of people whose country of origin was Sudan and who felt that I was standing up for the Muslims of Sudan when nobody was giving a damn ... The hate that I got was confined to white liberals, solely, absolutely, and was quite vicious. But it was small.[25]

Debbonaire said Labour's delay in correcting Starmer's LBC interview had damaged her chances. 'What was the point in clarifying ten days later? You might as well not have done it.'

Labour's pollsters found it hard to assess the impact pro-Gaza independent candidates were having in local contests. In Ilford North, Wes Streeting, shadow Health Secretary and one of Starmer's brightest lights, was standing for re-election. Almost no one saw the danger he was in. At one point, an audio file began circulating among pro-Palestine voters. It purported to be a recording of Streeting saying he did not 'fucking' care about innocent Palestinians dying. Streeting denounced it as 'obviously fake' and the social media account that posted it did not provide fact checkers with any evidence to show it was genuine. Labour sources suspect the clip was created using AI of some kind. The file was shared heavily on private messages in the constituency. 'It went through the community WhatsApp groups like wildfire,' said one party source.[26]

On 4 July, six pro-Palestine independents succeeded in ousting candidates from major parties. The biggest shock of election night for Starmer was Jonathan Ashworth, who had a high-profile role in Labour's national campaign. He lost his seat in Leicester South. Again, the issue that cost him was Gaza.

Rishi Sunak called the election hoping to take his rivals by surprise. Labour was more than ready, with what was likely to have been the most efficient, tech-heavy, data-led ground-targeting operation ever seen in British politics. But in a ground campaign featuring more independent candidates and smaller parties than ever, even Morgan McSweeney's dazzlingly successful operation could not see every threat that it faced.

CHAPTER 7

DIGITAL

VANITY METRICS

Jeremy Corbyn left a trail of destruction in his wake.

In the aftermath of Labour's worst election drubbing since the 1930s, the Leader of the Opposition's office was a shattered place. Party structures were a mess and morale was at rock bottom.

In that poisonous atmosphere in the early months of 2020, internal rivals competed for power, trying to build their own empires and looking over their shoulders to dodge the blame for any mistakes – and there was plenty of blame to go around. Colleagues didn't talk to each other. When they did, supposedly privately conversations leaked. In the midst of Covid lockdowns, trying to create a functional team was even harder via video calls.

'It was just a classic organisational meltdown,' said one person who worked in the office at the time. There were teams across the organisation supposedly working on the same project, 'most of which seemed to absolutely hate each other'.[1]

After four years of Corbyn and four election defeats in a row, Labour needed to rethink everything. Nowhere was this more true than in the party's approach to digital operations. Starmer, David Evans and Morgan McSweeney realised that for the party headquarters team to make progress towards winning the next election, its digital campaigning machine would need a complete revamp.

The rise of online publishing and social media since 2010 has transformed the way modern elections are fought and politics is conducted. Social media platforms including Facebook, TikTok, YouTube and X (formerly known as Twitter) demand as much attention as traditional media and can be far more useful for reaching specific target voters. Even newspapers are now heavily weighted towards digital content for smartphone apps and websites.

McSweeney and Evans decided that digital operations would need a seat at the top table in their campaign organisation and they knew who they wanted to take it.

Tom Lillywhite joined the Labour Party in 2016 to vote, unsuccessfully, against Corbyn's leadership. After campaigning for Starmer in his Holborn & St Pancras constituency, Lillywhite returned to help Starmer's leadership bid in 2020. He was instantly hooked and decided to swap life running a small digital agency for the intensity of work at the top of British politics.

• • •

The first UK election campaign to take digital operations seriously was David Cameron's Tory operation in 2015. McSweeney has studied that campaign extensively, to learn from what Ed Miliband's Labour team got wrong as well as what the Tories did to win. His decision to give Lillywhite a director-level role replicates the one Cameron's campaign took in the run-up to 2015.

Cameron's operation presented a blueprint for a highly

professional and focused digital strategy. It sought to exploit all the data available to social media companies about their users – such as who and what they liked, how old they were, what they cared about, where they lived and their shopping habits. Particularly on Facebook, which had the most detailed and accessible data on its users, political campaigners could then target tailored election messages to precisely the tiny batches of swing voters in key seats they most wanted to reach. The Tories also threw more money at digital advertising in that year than anyone in UK politics had done before.[2]

In 2017, Corbyn's Labour had taken a different approach. Their digital budget was not as high as the Tories', but their organic reach – the way videos and ads would spread naturally among thousands of supporters sharing them with friends – was far more powerful.

Under Starmer, however, Labour officials made the case for looking beyond the size of an audience. 'Everyone patted themselves on the back for getting millions of views on videos on Twitter and thought they'd done it,' a party insider recalls. 'But it was just the same people seeing it over and over again. We have tried to move away from those vanity metrics and just talking to ourselves and making ourselves feel good about stuff and take our message to where people were consuming it.'[3]

That meant spending lots of effort making inroads into Facebook groups and cutting out Twitter, which still drives conversations in Westminster but is far less useful for reaching swing voters. 'It was much more important if 500 people saw something in an effective way than if 2 million people saw the same picture,' the same insider says. McSweeney, Lillywhite and others spent time giving presentations to Starmer's shadow Cabinet on why Twitter and 'vanity metrics' no longer mattered in their drive to win power.

At the outset, Lillywhite and his boss took two crucial strategic decisions. The first was that Labour needed to engage in local online discussion forums, politely and respectfully and in ways that showed the party was on the side of voters. The second decision was that it needed the right people in place to make sure that happened.

The most important forums for Labour activists and candidates to join were Facebook groups. These are places where Facebook users can connect and share experiences with other people who have similar interests. Groups exist for sports, parenting, cookery and other hobbies. They also exist for local communities.

The problem for Labour was that many of these local community groups had been hostile to Corbyn's party. Labour HQ believed these Facebook groups were set up by Tory councillors who dominated the discussion and would be aggressive to Labour. There was a lot of resistance among Labour candidates and activists to joining up, but Lillywhite was clear that it was vital. Unless Labour people were in the discussions, making reasonable points politely and offering to help communities with their problems, how would the situation change? A party source explains:

> Facebook groups were really toxic places in 2017 and 2019. Most of them are run by Conservative councillors, they skew right politically. But it is where politics happens in local communities. We have had some people saying we don't want to go in those spaces because they're not very nice, but you've got to be in them, you can't vacate any space, especially those that are promoted so heavily by the Facebook algorithm, especially for our target audience skewing slightly older. That was a prime battleground for us.
>
> We did loads of training with candidates and councillors and said, look, you should be open and honest, it's not about being underhand or sneaky or being activists in them. Just say, 'I'm

standing for your council, what are your local issues and how can I help?' If someone comments about antisocial behaviour, you should comment on that and say, 'I'm really sorry to hear that. Can you send it to me please and I'll do something about it?'[4]

Starmer's team began recruiting a cohort of digital trainees. These were young people who were not necessarily experienced or expert in digital campaigning but were diligent and creative problem-solvers with plenty of energy. They were sent to key marginal seats to run local social media campaigns. By polling day, there were forty-five of these digital recruits embedded in target seats around the country. Their work involved making sure local candidates knew how to produce a good social media video, could run online ads and had a network of volunteers.

The team in HQ kept track obsessively, with checklists and a points system showing how well prepared each target-seat candidate was for a digital campaign and which local teams were struggling. Privately, Lillywhite knew his obsession with these data dashboards was over the top, but it proved to be useful when Sunak called the general election early. It meant McSweeney's officials in London knew exactly which candidates around the country needed extra help to get their local videos and social media ads up and running.

Another significant decision that Labour took was to move away from the 2015 era of micro-targeting of ads on Facebook. The main reason for this was the introduction of restrictions that meant less personal data was available to help tailor adverts to tiny groups of swing voters. It was a decision that the party took at the beginning of 2024, after reviewing the effectiveness of digital ad campaigns during local elections and by-elections. More general ads, carrying key messages across wider groups of voters in swing seats, were seen to deliver a bigger punch per pound. And Labour had plenty of pounds to spend.

'We ended up with 110 people working on digital by the end,' a Labour official said. 'We were running content for Keir, for Rachel, for Angela and the party. And we had this gigantic machine that we had made. We definitely came a long way in that four years – it was blood, sweat and tears to get there.'[5]

DIGITAL BLUES

On the eve of Rishi Sunak's final party conference as Prime Minister, in the autumn of 2023, the Conservatives' digital director resigned. The timing was terrible.

Conference season each autumn is political prime time for every party. Broadcasters and print journalists are guaranteed to pay your people and your policies more attention during the few days of your annual gathering, and the convention is that rival parties do not seek to interfere.

As Tories gathered in the grand Midland Hotel in Manchester, Sunak was preparing to relaunch his candidacy as the agent of 'change'. He would set out three major new policies – scrapping HS2, banning smoking and overhauling A-levels. But the loss of digital leadership the day before the 2023 conference opened would mean they struggled to sell Sunak's new 'change' mission to a social media-saturated electorate.

Cass Horowitz and Dan O'Neill, two special advisers who had been working on Sunak's digital content from No. 10, had to step in as temporary support to see the party through what was always its busiest week of the year. They survived, but Sunak knew he did not have long to get digital operations back on track ahead of an election that was perhaps a year away.

The Conservatives are well versed in effective social media operations. Isaac Levido did not have to argue his case for prioritising digital campaigning inside CCHQ. The Tories' celebrated successes in 2015 and 2019 had been attributed in part to high-quality and innovative digital content that broke new ground in political campaigning. For those who needed convincing, including sceptical Conservative MPs, the figures are compelling: 93 per cent of the voting population is on social media, and Facebook and YouTube reach 91 per cent of British adults over the age of fifteen.

Eventually, Dan O'Neill was persuaded to step in to run Conservative HQ's digital campaign team, but he had two conditions. First, that he would get enough resources and money for spending during the election and in the run-up. And second, that party bosses would back him to deliver not just a good basic operation but the biggest and most intensive digital campaign the country had ever seen. O'Neill was convinced that the party that spent the most on digital would win.

At the time, the Tories had been talking to Frank Hester, a powerful businessman and donor who was interested in backing digital operations. Hester turned into a highly controversial backer for Sunak. The Conservative Party faced pressure to return money he gave when it was alleged that he had said, in 2019, that Diane Abbott made him 'want to hate all Black women' and 'should be shot'. But Hester had pledged around £10 million with potentially another £5 million available if the party could show it was doing a good job on digital, all of which was music to O'Neill's ears.[6]

When he began work inside CCHQ alongside his deputy Tony

Hind, however, they found an organisation in total disarray. There had been little investment or attention paid to digital operations since 2019 and the succession of crises under Truss and Johnson, multiple reshuffles and two changes of leadership had taken their toll. Morale was low. There were only four people in the entire Tory digital team, running everything from social media posts to membership, volunteers and fundraising.

'It was absolutely horrific,' one official recalls. 'The team was completely depleted and demoralised. No one really wanted to come and work for the party.'[7]

There were huge 'black holes' in the digital infrastructure, too. If the Tories ran an online petition on the closure of police stations, for example, people signing it would provide names and contact details. But half of this potentially valuable personal information was going missing because the IT system for handling it was broken.

O'Neill and Hind spent their first three months in CCHQ trying to fix the mess they had inherited. This meant that at the start of 2024 – election year – the Tory operation wasn't even able to focus properly on how it wanted to fight Labour in the critical battlegrounds online.

Typically, digital election campaigns work best if they build on several years of consistent messaging, with an established brand and channels for communicating. The Tories reckoned they needed a year to eighteen months to get the digital team ready for the campaign, but O'Neill did not have that long. By the end of February, three months before Sunak called the election, the Conservatives had hired twenty people into the digital team. Levido and O'Neill had a plan: throw everything at winning the digital contest on Facebook.

Unlike Labour, the Tories have not for many years had large

numbers of activists and volunteers on the ground who can walk streets, knocking on voters' doors. Instead, since 2015, they have relied on clever targeting of swing voters with tailored political ads, in particular via Facebook. 'A huge part of our strategy was gathering data on people so we could understand them and target them on a micro level with our personalised messaging,' one Tory explains. The Conservatives believed this sort of approach can increase the impact of a messaging seven-fold.

O'Neill and Levido agreed to spend as much as £5 million of Hester's donation on ads and other digital operations in the run-up to the election. They would then saturate Facebook and YouTube with the remaining £4–5 million worth of targeted advertising during the six weeks of the campaign.

All the while, they were looking at Labour's plans and thinking that Lillywhite and his team had made a major mistake. It was clear to the Tories that Labour had failed to book significant targeted advertising with Facebook. In truth, Labour strategists didn't need to engage in micro-targeting because they had, in the words of one envious Conservative watching on, 'fuck-you money' – cash to burn. Analysis by Who Targets Me – an organisation tracking digital campaign advertising – published on 1 July found Labour was responsible for 46 per cent of all election ad spending on Meta (which owns Facebook and Instagram) during the campaign. Labour flooded social media in the first week and was responsible for 63 per cent of all parties' spending on digital ads on Meta between 22 and 28 May.[8]

For O'Neill and Levido, the bitter truth was that the Tories, who for years had dominated the party donations league table, were running short of funds. Their plans for throwing up to £10 million on the most intense digital campaign in history kept being delayed and scaled back during the early part of the year. By the spring, reality was starting to dawn. 'When it came to May and we realised we had spent less than £1 million, we thought, "Fuck – there is no money". That had been hidden from us. It was very frustrating,' a Tory official recalls. 'It seemed like donors promised things and didn't deliver. Money that was supposed to be for digital was obviously spent elsewhere.'[9]

Levido was said to have been deeply disappointed. The reality was the Conservatives were fighting an unequal battle online against a Labour Party with superior resources. Labour had more people and more money. Crucially, they also had more freedom to be creative in the kind of eye-catching videos and ads they posted online.

MIDDLE FINGER

Political currency is highly unstable. Credibility and momentum can disappear quickly. When things are going your way, your mistakes are forgiven and every new trick you try is hailed as a stroke of genius. When you're under pressure and seen to be struggling, however, critical voices grow louder and nothing seems to work.

In the digital campaign, Labour were on a roll. 'They had their tails up. Their social media accounts were more fun and controversial,' a Conservative staffer says.[10] By contrast, journalists and even Tory MPs would attack every new video or attention-grabbing post the team in HQ put out, sapping morale.

Sunak instinctively understood the significance of digital and gave O'Neill, Horowitz and Hind plenty of space to get on with their jobs. They and others had served him well, especially during his time as Chancellor, when he built up a formidable personal following and a polished social media profile.

But plenty of Conservative MPs hated what CCHQ officials were putting out – and rang them up to tell them so. In December 2023, BBC presenter Maryam Moshiri was embarrassingly caught out committing a blooper on TV: she showed her middle finger to the camera just as it went live. The resulting image of a BBC newsreader 'flipping the bird' spread around social media and generated plenty of amusement. As any good digital agency would, the Tory team jumped on the mishap and attached their political message to the trend, reposting the image and adding the caption, 'Labour when you ask for their plans to tackle illegal migration'.

The post was a hit and got 20 million impressions. But the tactic sent Tory MPs into a fury. Alicia Kearns wrote, 'Amazed this has not – despite requests – been taken down, it is beneath us.' Tobias Ellwood said, 'Please delete this post.'[11] Depressingly for the CCHQ team of young and under-appreciated staffers, the party's leadership was so worried that MPs could try to topple Sunak that on many similar occasions they caved in.

'MPs were always fucking complaining. They were constantly furious at the memes,' a source involved recalls. Party discipline was broken and the atmosphere at the top was never far from paranoia. Campaign bosses told the digital team that their communications must be acceptable to MPs. The instruction was to 'make the MPs happy'.[12]

Video is king when it comes to creating content that takes off and goes viral on the social media platforms that matter to political campaigners. But many MPs never got the point and would instead demand CCHQ produce a 'graphic' to illustrate a policy point. It all felt very 2010. Nothing could have been more dated.

Tory digital staffers could only watch enviously as their opponents got away with more daring images and videos. 'Labour would do similar things, and their side would remain quiet because they understood the power of unity and of this controversial content cutting through and seizing the agenda,' according to one insider.

CCHQ was a grim place for some. 'There was this culture of genuine fear and anxiety within the building, which impaired creative output as well,' one source says. 'It was like a sad graveyard.'

GAME ON

Candles cast their soft light on the timber-lined, rustic walls. Reclining in a luxurious bubble bath, the movie's famous star, apparently nude, caresses a chilled glass in one hand and gazes intensely into the camera.

The scene is a recreation of Margot Robbie's famous interlude in *The Big Short*, in which she sips champagne in an opulent bathroom while explaining the basics of the subprime mortgage crisis in a cinematic footnote for viewers. Instead of the *Barbie* actress, who regularly features in lists of the world's sexiest women, this particular film stars the stubbly-chinned British comedian Jon Richardson. He swaps an elegant champagne flute for a lager, poured rather sloppily from a can. The bubbles in his bath look like they might not last long enough to cover all his blushes.

Labour's witty digital video 'The Big Short: Rishi Sunak' was released on 3 June, with a month still to go in the campaign. The idea behind it was to remind voters that the Tory leader was wildly rich and made his money working on deals in the financial world that many voters would not like if they knew about them.

The narrator begins: 'Rishi Sunak would love you to forget about how he made his millions before becoming an MP. He wants you to think it's too complicated for you to understand. Or even better, that it isn't notable at all. So, here's Jon Richardson in a bubble bath to explain.'

Richardson takes up the story: 'Basically, before Rishi Sunak got into politics, he was a partner in a hedge fund. Now that was amazingly profitable for him but bad for pretty much everyone else.'

Midway through an election campaign, the video was a risk. It was provocative, featuring a naked male celebrity drinking beer in a bath and swearing freely. (He finishes with a tribute to Robbie's closing line of the original movie scene by saying, 'Now let's fuck him off, shall we?' The bleep is only semi-effective.)

Tom Lillywhite in Labour HQ pushed for this sort of controversial content to be approved. His bosses gave him their backing. Those working in the Labour digital team at the time say it was a focused and productive place where creative ideas were welcomed and staff felt free to experiment without fear of criticism. The contrast with the Tory operation – strapped for cash, risk-allergic and constantly catering to hyper-anxious Conservative MPs – was pointed.

Like Labour, the Conservatives also hired digital campaign managers who could coach MPs and candidates in how to make snappy videos and join community Facebook groups. But they started late and could never match Labour's numbers. By the time of the election, the Tories had twelve digital campaign managers, while Labour had forty-five. In total, only around twenty people worked on the Tory digital operation. Lillywhite's team numbered 110.

Labour outgunned the Conservatives online in every respect: they spent more, employed more people and produced more compelling material with a clearer message. The consequences of such an unequal fight played out in the six weeks of the campaign and on polling day itself.

By the time the King had agreed to Rishi Sunak's request to dissolve Parliament, Labour's army of digital media specialists had been working for months to get ready.

Around 150–200 Labour candidates in key target seats had pre-recorded YouTube videos in which they introduced themselves to voters in their constituencies. Using the miracles of digital targeting, these videos were displayed as adverts only to voters watching YouTube in the relevant electoral district in the first twenty-four hours of the campaign. It was a big advertising outlay, but party election chiefs are proud that they pulled it off and believe it was a huge part of their successful start to the short campaign in May.

Not everything went completely Labour's way. Lillywhite's team cursed when a video that mocked Sunak's national service announcement had to be removed because it infringed the copyright of the movie *Shrek*. The video featured the character Lord Farquaad declaring, 'Some of you may die, but it's a sacrifice I'm willing to make' with the caption 'Rishi Sunak announcing national service'. Gallingly, it seemed as if the Tories had alerted the social media platforms to the infringement. A similar problem occurred when Labour tried a *Harry Potter* meme.

Both main parties only joined the video sharing app TikTok at the start of the campaign. It was Labour, however, that really embraced the platform, which has proven hugely influential among young people. In the first week, the Conservatives posted four items on TikTok, compared with twenty-eight by Labour.

But it was Nigel Farage who became the stand-out winner of the battle for power on TikTok. His videos were spontaneously shared widely millions of times. Often, they were simply short clips of him speaking. Gawain Towler, his longstanding media aide, is dismissive. The TikTok phenomenon was just funny, he says. 'It's not real.'[13]

But for staffers in Conservative HQ, there wasn't much to laugh about.

Some senior Tories look back at Labour's slogan of 'Change' with envy. If only they had been able to come up with something as clear, simple and open to favourable interpretation by willing voters, they say. Instead, they were required to deliver a far too complex message in a highly restrictive sequential way: 'Clear plan. Bold action. Secure future.' Three ideas were two too many, some Tories say, whatever the evidence from focus groups suggested.

Conservative policies fell flat amid public polling that showed Sunak had no hope. Since nobody believed the Tories would win, the party had to focus on convincing voters that Labour would be risky. That primarily meant repeatedly warning of Starmer's alleged secret tax-rise agenda, sometimes in ways that were intended to cause alarm. 'Our whole campaign was designed to make people angry about Labour and to scare them,' a Tory source says. This sort of 'project fear' tactic was uncomfortable for some in the team. It also added yet more messaging to the complicated menu of communications.[14]

Internal analysis suggests the Conservatives' digital effort did yield some successes at the level of individual constituencies, despite multiple challenges centrally. Jeremy Hunt, the Chancellor, held his Surrey seat by just 891 votes, after a particularly energetic digital campaign, including via Facebook groups. Hunt understood the importance of engagement locally and his social media accounts shifted from economic policy to more mundane community issues as the election grew near. His posts reached larger audiences as users shared his messages spontaneously.

Others who benefited significantly from intensive support via digital campaigning included Party Chairman Richard Holden, who only narrowly clung on to his seat, and James Cleverly, the Home Secretary, who saw a huge jump in the audience for his content in the final two weeks.[15]

But the team at Matthew Parker Street didn't have the cash or the time to make a bigger impact nationally. Conservative strategists knew the digital game was over from the start.

In the words of one Labour official asked to sum up the Tory digital operation:

> I thought it was really shockingly bad. It got a bit better, but I thought it was slow, it was Westminster-focused, it was fighting the last election. It wasn't helped by the fact they had no money, which obviously wasn't the digital team's fault there. But annoyingly, I think we could have beaten them on their absolute best day and I think they had a shocker of a campaign. That will always slightly bug me.[16]

CHAPTER 8

CHANGE

Rishi Sunak suddenly understood just how tough this election campaign was going to be.

Oliver Dowden, the Deputy Prime Minister and one of Sunak's closest friends in politics, was doing his best to take down the Tory leader in a ferocious private debating session. Dowden put Sunak through his paces in preparation for his first head-to-head TV clash with Keir Starmer, scheduled for Tuesday 4 June on ITV. Playing the role of Starmer, Dowden did a devastatingly effective job.

Every time Sunak tried to suggest there were positive signs of his plan working, such as falling inflation or progress on immigration or hospital waiting lists, Dowden would hit back: 'You're so complacent; you're out of touch.'

And whenever Sunak attempted to put forward one of his proposals for the next five-year term, such as national service or tax cuts, Dowden would round on him in the rehearsal room. 'You've had fourteen years, why haven't you done that already?'

'It was alarming,' one Tory recalls. 'That was the moment he realised this is how difficult the campaign is going to be. You just saw how effective it was to block off anything and everything.'

Sunak was struggling to come up with what every successful party needs in an election campaign: a way to win what is sometimes called the 'air war'. This is the national campaign, waged mainly on the airwaves of TV and radio, as well as in the digital pages of newspapers via smartphone apps, websites and – in dwindling numbers these days – traditional printed papers.

For most voters in constituencies that are not key battlegrounds, the national campaign in the media will be all they see of the election from the moment it is called until polling day. Headlines touting policies from the major party leaders – such as nationalising the railways, reintroducing national service or reducing taxes – are designed to cut through the noise of daily life and lodge in the minds of otherwise busy voters.

Increasingly, there is an overlap between campaigning in the mainstream media and on social media. What underpins both, however, is a set of key messages that each party tries to promote to voters in an effort to define what the election choice is about.

Party strategists want their core messages to be delivered in compelling ways by leaders and key spokespeople and to resonate with the mood of the public. What Dowden's demolition of his own boss vividly showed was the powerful position Starmer occupied. The Tories' record wasn't good enough to campaign on, and their plans for the future weren't credible either, when polling suggested defeat was inevitable. Britain was demanding a fresh start. The Conservatives knew it.

FALSE START

Seven months before Dowden's debate rehearsal, Sunak stood on the podium in the main hall of Manchester Central's conference complex with dazzling stage lights trained on his diminutive figure. He offered himself up to the nation as the 'change' candidate. For a Tory leader, after thirteen years with the party in power, it was a big claim. To prove his credentials as a radical break from the past, Sunak cancelled the northern leg of the High Speed 2 (HS2) rail project intended to cut travel times between London, the Midlands and the north. Launched under David Cameron and boosted by Boris Johnson, it was the biggest infrastructure programme in Europe. Sunak vowed to spend the multi-billion-pound HS2 budget instead on fixing local and regional rail networks, buses and roads.

He went further. In what turned out to be his boldest attempt to set out a political mission, Sunak tried to distance himself from three decades of government orthodoxy – half of which had been spent under the Conservatives – dismissing the period as 'thirty years of vested interests standing in the way of change'. He went on: 'We've had thirty years of a political system which incentivises the easy decision, not the right one.' Sunak mentioned the word 'change' thirty times in his speech, according to watching reporters who couldn't fail to grasp his point. 'If this country is to change, then it can only be us who will deliver it,' Sunak insisted.

As the 2024 election showed, his instinct, at least, was correct. Voters did want a new start, but with someone other than the Tories. Sunak's short-lived effort in the autumn of 2023 to defy his party's recent history came too late. That simple fact is something his closest allies now believe doomed his campaign for re-election from the outset. One explains:

We had known that the electorate wanted change for a long time. That was the biggest thing that came out of all the research. That was why, with limited success, we tried that change speech at conference, trying to portray Rishi as change, in that he was a different kind of leader, more focused on the long term. But the electorate's desire for change was the single biggest factor in the election.[1]

When it came to the 2024 campaign, Keir Starmer had alighted on the same message. And, for obvious reasons, he was the only person credibly placed to embody the 'change' the electorate wanted. A Tory leader heading a divided and scandal-battered government after fourteen years of turmoil could not plausibly promise to begin something new. It's not as if politics had been a stranger to the concept of 'change' under the Tories anyway. The upheaval of a rolling civil war in the party, with its succession of leadership crises, is a form of change after all. A senior Conservative adviser says: 'The country was exhausted by political drama and they saw the Tories as the cause, or principal actors, in that drama. The appeal of voting for somebody else was to end the drama and that was another thing that hurt us.'[2]

In Isaac Levido's view, it wasn't just the bad behaviour of the government in office that voters wanted to put behind them but politics more broadly. In the last ten years, Levido points out, Britain has seen four general elections, two referendums, two years of Covid, three Prime Ministers in 2022 and the outbreak of war in Europe. 'That sort of backdrop was incredibly disruptive and voters were just sick of it,' Levido says.

In an ideal world, people want to know there's a steady hand on the tiller, that they've got an idea of the direction the government is going in and that the things their government is working on are the right things for them. And they only really want to have to take proper notice and think about a voting choice for a couple of months ... every five years.[3]

• • •

Sunak's ministers and others regard the Tory leader's brief flirtation with being the change candidate and then reverting to offering stability and security (for example, bringing David Cameron back as Foreign Secretary) as further missteps in a long series of errors. Some Tories believe he had a chance to embody change at the very beginning of his premiership. After the sleaze of the Johnson years and the financial fright of the Truss weeks, Sunak was a return to sensible management, a grown-up administrator capable of restoring stability. He could, soon after calming the markets, have shown voters the kind of radical new start they craved by making a concerted effort to distance himself publicly from Johnson and Truss.

Complicating that, however, was his own weak position. He was a man without a mandate, even from his own party. He had to hold his side together, or try to at least, when half of the Conservative Party's MPs would never forgive him for triggering the mass resignations that brought down Johnson. Trashing Johnson's record in public, and to a lesser extent Truss's, would have ignited fresh unrest and risked a leadership challenge. 'His fundamental problem started when he and his team took the decision to undermine Boris,' one Cabinet minister says.

Once you have wielded the knife it is virtually impossible to be seen as anything other than divisive. Some people won't forgive you for that. I don't think he ran a divisive administration in the same way Liz Truss did. In fact, quite the opposite: he knew he needed to keep all sides of the party together and he worked very hard at it. He was actually very engaged in colleague-handling and management. But I don't think there was anything he could have done because he took the crown, in part, by wielding the knife.[4]

Unable to be the change they knew the country wanted, the Conservatives focused their message instead on making the new start Labour promised seem like a gamble that wasn't worth the risk.

CHANGE

Labour strategists had been chewing over a slogan to present to the electorate. It would be emblazoned across leaflets and lecterns and splashed over the battle buses on their road trips around target seats.

There were 'four pillars' of Labour's offer to voters that Pat McFadden, Morgan McSweeney and other campaign chiefs wanted to communicate: Britain needed to change; the Tories had failed; Starmer had changed Labour; and Labour had a long-term plan. These were printed onto posters hung in Labour HQ and formed the basis for most of Starmer's stump speeches.

One senior campaign source says: 'The classic Labour Party way of doing this would be to put a whole Christmas tree of words around it. Like "real change you can believe in" or "change for the UK", "change for the future" or "change for everybody." Instead, McSweeney and his colleagues decided 'let's not bother with the Christmas tree. Let's go for the core word. We'll go for "change".'[5]

Starmer's slogan thus became just one word. The Conservative message was more complex but essentially amounted to the opposite: 'Clear plan, bold action, secure future.' Sunak expanded on the theme in his foreword to the Tory manifesto: 'We must stick to this plan and take bold action to secure the future of our nation and society.'

One of the most important tasks of an election 'air war' is to set the question voters will be asking themselves when they pick up their pencil stub to mark a cross on their ballot paper in the polling booth. This is another of Lynton Crosby's lessons that longer-serving Conservative staffers remember from his successful and highly disciplined 2015 campaign.

'Voters have all got a fixed view of the parties,' one Tory aide explains. Shifting those fundamental views is highly unlikely to be possible in the short, six-week campaign, says the aide. What parties can do is try to define the question voters think this election is about: 'If you lose control of the question, that's when you're fucked.'[6]

It seems odd that the Tories chose to fight the election on Labour's preferred ground – the merits or otherwise of change. As Sunak showed in his conference speech in Manchester, the Conservatives always knew that a fresh start was what the country wanted. The core of their campaign was therefore, from the start, reduced to a negative: to make voters think twice about whether they really wanted to elect Keir Starmer.*

MING VASE

With a massive poll lead, Labour's strategy in 2024 was all about not throwing away its advantage. 'Everyone was terrified of being the

---

* Other elements of the Tories' three-part slogan also featured – 'bold action' in terms of policies like reintroducing national service played into it. But these, some party insiders felt, merely distracted from the core point, which boiled down to urging voters not to take a risk on Starmer.

one that fucked it up and everyone in that campaign will have tasted defeat at least once, if not several times,' one aide explains. Starmer was attempting to tread the same path as Tony Blair in 1997, from opposition to replacing an unpopular Tory government. He was, in Roy Jenkins's famous phrase, like 'a man carrying a priceless Ming vase across a highly polished floor'. Labour's caution-first campaign duly became known as the 'Ming vase strategy'.

But staying on message was a deceptively difficult task. Starmer faced demands from political allies and enemies alike to say more, not less, about what he would do if he won. The apparent secrecy of the Labour leader about his plans for office was one of the Tories' best lines of attack. Sunak continually claimed that Labour was hiding the truth. Sometimes he would assert the contradictory point that Labour didn't have a plan at all. The Tories' private polling showed the electorate was concerned about the lack of clarity from the opposition too.

The risk for Starmer lay in saying too much. If he strayed from his narrow script, he could give the Conservatives a bigger target to tear into and a slip-up could be costly. Theresa May found out in 2017 that being too open about policy – in her case, a confusingly complex proposal on social care funding – can be fatal in the heat of an election campaign. But the 'Ming vase' or 'small-target' strategy was not universally popular internally. Some of the party's own supporters viewed the huge poll lead as an opportunity to be radical and were impatient with Starmer's timidity.

• • •

The critical task for any politician in media interviews is to remain welded to the key messages their party wants to promote. The contest for supremacy in the national campaign is impossible to win unless a party can organise its spokespeople to keep saying the same things until voters get their point, however boring that is. Without the discipline to repeat the core lines, a political party has no message. And without a clear message, a party offers voters nothing but noise.

Not all ministers, or their shadows, are good at sticking to the line and some come across badly on TV. The crucial job of giving interviews on TV, radio and breakfast news programmes needed the parties' best broadcasters. For Labour, the A-team of interviewers included Wes Streeting, the combative shadow Health Secretary, Jonathan Ashworth, a veteran of Gordon Brown's era, and Angela Rayner, the Stockport-born deputy leader who was seen as someone well suited to speaking to working-class voters. Bridget Phillipson, the shadow Education Secretary, Yvette Cooper and Pat McFadden were also competent and clear communicators in the eyes of the party's spin doctors. In an effort to minimise the risks of slip-ups on air, the shadow Cabinet's big hitters were sent for media training at the agency Freuds with Simon Enright, the former communications aide to King Charles and Queen Camilla.

For the Tories, Isaac Levido found himself with a dwindling squad of top ministers to draw on. The problem was that so many of them did not want to do broadcast interviews because they were too busy fighting – unsuccessfully – to hold onto their own seats. Grant Shapps, the Defence Secretary, was a trusted media performer who often dialled in via Zoom from his home office. He lost his seat. Chancellor Jeremy Hunt did almost no broadcast interviews and just managed to save his. Work and Pensions Secretary Mel Stride was among the most frequently used voices on the broadcasts for the Conservatives. One Labour staffer noted, with some admiration for Stride's efforts, that the Tory breakfast show strategy by the end of the campaign amounted to 'the morning Mel'.

FRIENDS AND ENEMIES

As polling day approached, Keir Starmer boarded a private jet on a mammoth tour of England, Wales and Scotland. To the evident delight of this particular football fan, the aircraft was the same one the England football team had used to fly to the Euros. 'One of the flight attendants pointed out that Keir was sitting in Gareth Southgate's seat, which Keir obviously enjoyed,' a Labour source says.[7]

The episode turned out to be a good omen. A few days later, *The Sun* newspaper – still one of the most influential media brands in Britain – came out and endorsed Starmer, with a nod to his passion for football (and a wink to England's quest for glory in the Euros). The paper told its readers Britain needed 'a new manager' and they weren't referring to Southgate. 'Being compared to the nation's football manager was obviously something he appreciated,' the source says.

For Labour, winning an endorsement from *The Sun* was a big deal. Although senior figures try to downplay how much they really wanted the tabloid's backing, *The Sun* has not endorsed a Labour leader since Blair's days. Famously, the Murdoch-owned paper claims it wrecked former Labour leader Neil Kinnock's chances of winning in 1992 with a devastating front page. It certainly did not help Ed Miliband in 2015 when it printed a photo of him looking like a zombie eating a bacon sandwich on polling day and advised readers to keep him out of No. 10.

The endorsement was hard won, it seems, as part of a concerted drive to neutralise potential threats to Starmer's chances. The Labour leader enraged some supporters when he accepted an invitation to Rupert Murdoch's summer party in June 2023. Later that year, Labour backed away from promises to tighten press regulation after the phone-hacking scandal, causing further internal disappointment. But Starmer's communications chief Matthew Doyle knew how powerful the backing from the elderly media mogul's News UK titles could be.*

Part of Labour's strategy to avoid trouble was to erase problematic policies that had been announced already. The risk with U-turns, however, is that they can make party leaders look weak or unreliable. Before becoming leader, Starmer was a pro-European shadow Brexit Secretary in Corbyn's team, offering a potential route to remain in the EU. By 2024, with the UK long since having left the bloc, Starmer had performed a complete reversal, pledging there would be no return to the single market or customs union. It meant Brexit-backing 'hero voters' did not need to fear that Labour was about to lead the UK back into the EU.

In another defensive move, Starmer diluted a pledge to spend £28 billion on action against climate change, which Ed Miliband championed as the shadow minister responsible. The danger was that the Tories would take the huge commitment and convert it into per-household costs in a way that could damage Labour. The question took time to resolve, amid internal tensions over what to do, but ultimately the figure was junked.

Labour's approach was not just about defence. It was also critical to degrade the Tory Party's reputation by attacking their record over the previous fourteen years. Former *Telegraph* journalist Paul Ovenden led Labour's 'attack' team. They amassed an arsenal of 150

---

* Conservative papers such as the *Daily Mail* were never likely to support Starmer. But he won over a host of other editors. By polling day, Labour had the backing of *The Economist*, the *Financial Times* and the *Sunday Times*, in addition to left-leaning papers such as *The Guardian* and the *Mirror*.

potentially damaging news stories ready to fire at the Tories during the campaign. Many were abandoned when other revelations disrupted the plan, but others were timed for maximum impact. 'Everything had been prepared, so it was about executing those stories in different ways,' said one source. 'And there's a skill in doing that. It's like playing a piano and getting the keys in the right order.'[8]

Labour deployed what insiders called 'demoralisation' tactics: stories that would inflame existing divisions among Conservatives, such as rumours of potential defections. In one leaked audio clip unearthed by Labour, the then Conservative MP Lee Anderson was recorded saying he was offered money to join Nigel Farage's Reform UK (which he ultimately did, retaining his seat of Ashfield on 4 July).

THE GRID

Cliques, resentments and rivalries easily incubate in the windowless corridors and cramped offices of Westminster. Genuine friendship in that environment is as valuable as it is unusual. While all leaders have their inner circles, Sunak's is remarkable for how far such personal connections dominate. When Liam Booth-Smith, his young and talented chief of staff, wanted Downing Street to get organised for the campaign, Booth-Smith turned to one of his closest friends, with whom he once shared a home, Jamie Njoku-Goodwin.

During the run-up to the election, Njoku-Goodwin worked with Levido to devise the all-important 'grid'. This is the schedule of ministerial visits, announcements, speeches, policy launches, interviews and press conferences due to take place each day over the six-week election campaign. It is a vital task and one that lies at the heart of delivering message discipline. Without a grid mapping out what to say when, chaos ensues.

Njoku-Goodwin set out several phases to the Tory media campaign. The point was to ensure there was enough variety to capture the fickle attention of broadcasters and national political journalists without having different policies or ministers competing with each other for air time.

For the first three days after the election was called, nothing much was scheduled. The opening clashes were always going to be too noisy for big policies to cut through to voters. The Tory plan was to roll out policy announcements in the days leading up to the manifesto launch on 11 June. This, party strategists hoped, would reinforce the difference between the policy-heavy Tories and the policy-light Labour Party. After the manifesto, the Conservatives planned to step up their attacks on Starmer for the final weeks before polling day, doubling down on warnings that Labour would cost families by putting their taxes up.

On the first Sunday of the short campaign, the Tories launched their biggest new policy idea of the election: mandatory national service. Under the proposal, which Home Secretary James Cleverly took to TV studios to promote, all eighteen-year-olds would be 'compelled' to take some form of national service, which could, if they chose, be in the form of military service. The aim was to 'address the fragmentation in society' through serving as on-call firefighters or special constables, he said. 'The important bit is about that society coming together.'

It was radical. The intention was to shake the country awake and make sure anyone not aware there was an election happening would pay attention. It was meant to demonstrate the first part of Sunak's three-part slogan: bold action. The policy was genuinely close to Sunak's heart and his team expected it to dominate the entire campaign. They had been working on it, on and off, for much of the previous year.

'Rishi was always very worried about the breakdown in national values, national identity and the decline of that sense of national community, particularly among younger generations,' one of those involved recalls.[9] General Patrick Sanders, head of the army, had been warning that the UK needed greater defence resilience, while Will Tanner, one of Sunak's most senior policy aides, and Liam Booth-Smith were among those inside Downing Street backing the idea of some form of national service.

Similar policy ideas had also won support in the past from some Labour figures, including former Home Secretary David Blunkett and David Lammy, Starmer's shadow Foreign Secretary.[10] And, crucially at this election, the concept of national service polled well among voters tempted to support Nigel Farage's Reform UK party.

But when the policy landed at the start of the 2024 campaign, not everyone on the Conservative side was delighted. For some on the libertarian wing of the party, the worst element of it was the fact it was compulsory, especially following Sunak's plan to make smoking illegal, one generation at a time.

A day after the policy was announced, Steve Baker, a Northern Ireland Office minister, told the media it was 'developed by a political adviser or advisers and sprung on candidates, some of whom are relevant ministers'. He suggested that he would have had strongly negative views on it if he'd been consulted.

'I'm afraid by going in with the smoking ban and then national service, you couldn't say the party stood for freedom,' Baker says. 'And once you say that, my view is that the Conservative Party loses its reason to be.'[11]

Adding insult to injury was a glaring error in one of the announcements on the national service policy, which wrongly suggested participants would have been 'commissioned' into the armed forces (the word refers to officers appointed officially with a document signed by the King, not to all service personnel).

'I'm afraid I troubled [Sunak's political secretary] James Forsyth quite a lot,' Baker says.

> James was very good and very tolerant. And I messaged him quite often trying to be absolutely as constructive as possible because I would like to win … But at one point, I remember messaging, 'If it goes on like this, it'll be everyone for themselves. If the national campaign is this incoherent, everyone will just do their own thing.'

That's when message discipline falls apart.

SMALL TARGETS

On 13 June, Keir Starmer strode into the airy atrium of the Co-operative Group's Manchester headquarters to launch his party's manifesto for government. Wearing a big smile, he was jacket-less, with his shirtsleeves rolled up and deputy leader Angela Rayner alongside him, soaking up the applause from party supporters packed into the venue.

He hadn't got far into his remarks when a heckler, apparently from the party's Corbynite left, started shouting, condemning the manifesto document for containing 'the same old Tory policies'.

'Thank you very much,' a stern-faced Starmer responded. 'We gave up on being a party of protest five years ago. We want to be a party of power.'

Although the interruption was uninvited, it served perfectly to remind viewers of McSweeney's key message from his 2021 memo 'Labour for the Country'. The party needed a clear public demonstration that it had changed from the Corbyn days, with the leadership winning a 'conflict' to prove the point. Starmer said as much himself in his ad-lib response: 'That's not in the script but that is part of the change.'

The truth is, the protester had a point. Labour's manifesto ambitions had been scaled back to a small-c 'conservative' offer, broadly in the same ballpark as the tax and spending outlook the government had been working within. It wasn't Corbyn's radical socialism. And even compared to the tax-cutting Tory election offer, it wasn't particularly revolutionary. Labour promised not to raise income tax, VAT or National Insurance. Their openly declared tax increases were easily packaged as moves designed to show the party was on the side of ordinary working people against the elites – adding VAT to independent school fees, abolishing the 'non-dom' tax status, banning the use of offshore trusts to avoid inheritance tax and closing an income tax loophole for private equity fund managers.[12]

And there would be no moves to reverse the Tory government's two-child cap on benefits, which prevents people claiming universal credit or child tax credit for more than two children per family. That battle had been fought a year previously at the National Policy Forum, the consultation designed to engage members, the public and business in developing plans for the manifesto. 'That's where the arguments were thrashed out around the size of the offer that we would be able to make at the election,' a party source says.

> People actually knew for quite some time internally, even if it wasn't clear externally, the tram lines we were operating in. Keir and Rachel had intellectually won the argument with the rest of the shadow Cabinet that we were only going to be able to do this if we were trusted on the fiscal discipline.[13]

The manifesto included Labour's six 'first steps for change', which were deliberately modest, with concrete promises including cutting NHS waiting times and delivering 'economic security'.* Wes Streeting, the shadow Health Secretary, explained the idea was to 'under promise and over deliver' in order to rebuild trust.

To those running Labour's campaign, this wasn't timid – it was a bold departure from the way the party had campaigned (and failed) at previous elections. One senior party figure says:

> I don't think it's caution. I think it's duty, because what you're doing in taking the approach that we took is saying we're not going to run a campaign through stakeholder management to keep various bits of the Labour Party happy and assemble a compendium of policies which is clipped together in a manifesto, which then loses, none of which come into force, and you get another five years of the Tories.
>
> People use terms like 'caution' and 'safety first' and 'small target' and things like that. There's another way to put this, which is, we decided not to be the kind of Labour Party that the Tories find easy to beat.[14]

BIG IDEAS

As they drew up their manifesto, the Tories were in the opposite position. Unlike Labour, they had to attract attention to try to break through to a sceptical public that had stopped listening. That's why

---

* The six first steps were: deliver economic stability, cut NHS waiting times, launch Border Security Command, set up Great British Energy, crack down on antisocial behaviour, and pay for 6,500 more teachers by ending tax breaks for private schools. Starmer also made a bigger pitch, pledging 'mission-driven government', with longer-term goals of cutting violent crime and achieving economic growth and clean energy, among other things.

the party launched the big national service policy at the start of the campaign. Initially, they had hoped it could run through as a key dividing line for debate until polling day, but events got in the way.

Sunak, who always wanted to get to grips with details, was particularly keen to retain close oversight of the manifesto as it developed. There were around eight 'tier-one' policies which Sunak's officials submitted to him that he demanded further work on. These included the national service plan, various tax cuts, National Insurance cuts, a migration cap and the decision on whether potentially to pull the UK out of the European Convention on Human Rights (ECHR), in order to give the government more leeway to tackle illegal migration. Sunak ultimately decided not to make a big deal out of the ECHR policy in the manifesto, but he wanted to stay on top of it.[15]

Another key policy that Sunak heavily influenced was on welfare savings. In an early draft of the manifesto, the Conservatives proposed cutting welfare by £18 billion over the course of the next five years. This was a high figure and a big claim to make for potential savings from the benefits bill. But it was based on an estimate from the respected think tank the Institute for Fiscal Studies, so officials believed they could credibly include it in their manifesto.[16] In the end, the PM chose a lower figure of £12 billion in welfare savings to include in the plan. Like Starmer, Sunak didn't want to over promise. The difference was, Starmer didn't need to.

'The thing that motivated him most was fiscal credibility,' one former aide recalls. The reputation Sunak had built up at the Treasury mattered to him.[17] It must have been a painful irony for him to take over as Prime Minister immediately after the Truss–Kwarteng experiment had trashed the Tories' reputation for managing the economy.

For a Prime Minister who was still attached to the methods and mindset he had as Chancellor, fighting an election campaign on a promise of tax cuts would be playing on home turf. Frustratingly for his colleagues, Sunak did not succeed in articulating a clear reason why he believed cutting people's taxes was a good thing. Even in the weeks after the election defeat, his own senior team could not with confidence set out what his overarching vision for tax cuts really was – or for government more broadly.*

One option would have been to say the Conservatives are the natural party of hard-working people, just as David Cameron and George Osborne had done in 2015, and that cutting taxes would reinforce the party's commitment to 'working Britain'. Some in the Cabinet hoped the Prime Minister would embrace a message like this. He never did.

Instead, the Tory strategy appeared to have been that cutting taxes would be welcomed automatically as self-evidently a good thing. Who doesn't like keeping more of the money they earn, after all? The best attack on Labour would therefore be to warn that Starmer had a secret plan to put taxes up. To make that claim stick, what the Tories needed was a number.

---

* In interviews for this book, senior Tories were not able to set out with any clarity or confidence what Sunak's vision had been.

CHAPTER 9

TRUST

'You can't win unless you are trusted on the economy, and you can't win unless your leader is trusted,' says Deborah Mattinson, Labour's strategy director.[1]

Elections in the UK are generally won by the party that voters see as having the best candidate to be Prime Minister and the best credentials for handling the economy. What underpins both is the question of trust. Does this leader have the strength of character to take the right decisions and keep the country safe? Can their party steer the economy towards more prosperous times?

In 2022, the shambolic disintegration of Boris Johnson's government ruined the Tories' reputation for leadership. Liz Truss and Kwasi Kwarteng's mini-Budget disaster then crashed the Conservatives' credentials on the economy a few months later.

The repeated implosions of the government in 2022 gave Labour an opening. But the party still had to persuade voters it could be trusted with power. 'Disillusionment with the Tories wouldn't be enough,' Pat McFadden, Labour's national campaign chair, says. '[Voters] had to see a Labour Party that they could trust, particularly on the issues of economic competence and national security.'[2]

Jeremy Corbyn, the leader for the past two general elections, had given voters plenty of reasons to be suspicious. He had made the party seem unpatriotic and economically irresponsible. But Starmer had turned that around, embracing the union flag and presenting a sensible image of lawyerly professionalism, in contrast with the disarray in the government's ranks. Rishi Sunak's main hope was to use the opportunities of an election campaign to chip away at Starmer and make voters think twice about whether they really could trust him. As so often in the past, Sunak's weapon of choice was tax.

TAXING LABOUR

Keir Starmer was kicking himself. The campaign was not yet two weeks old, and Labour's leader felt he had let his own side down badly in his first key test.

It was Tuesday 4 June and Starmer had just finished the ITV leaders' debate with Rishi Sunak. It was a typically shouty affair, in which moderator Julie Etchingham had to warn both men not to talk over each other. But Sunak landed one punch that sent Starmer reeling and rocked Labour's campaign. Independent Treasury officials had costed Starmer's plans and the Prime Minister told the live TV audience that 'he would put up everyone's taxes by £2,000'.

It was a figure that the Conservatives had pulled together based on a variety of sources, with some input from civil servants under their control at the Treasury. Labour believed it was essentially made up. They long expected the Tories would put a spurious number on their tax-raising plans at some point in the campaign. Yet when it happened, they did not seem prepared.

For the first half of the live TV debate, Starmer did little to counter Sunak's repeated claims about Labour's tax plans. One Labour official watching on TV felt he perhaps didn't know quite how to expose such a blatant untruth while live on air. When he tried to reply, Etchingham said they would be coming to a section on taxes later in the debate.

The impression of Starmer, however, was of a politician who was leaden-footed and stuck for a good answer. One Labour source explains Starmer's slowness: 'There's part of him that thinks, "Well, are you seriously going to be saying these things that you know aren't true?"'[3]

During the commercial break, Labour's communications director Matthew Doyle went to speak to Starmer inside the ITV studio in Salford. He encouraged his boss to hit back hard at Sunak's claims in the second half of the programme. By that point, however, it was too late. Most of the newspapers had already started writing up their coverage based on the first few minutes of the debate. And TV news editors also take material from early exchanges for their evening bulletins, which often follow as soon as debates conclude. That is why landing key points early is vital for politicians taking part. 'It's an odd format,' a Labour aide says. 'In the House of Commons, you're not allowed to say someone's a liar and someone's lying. You are [allowed] on TV.'[4]

Labour's strategy director Deborah Mattinson was running a live focus group of viewers watching the debate. She fed her findings into the Labour team in the ITV studio, including politicians who were talking to the press in the 'spin room' and offering their entirely partisan verdicts on the debate to the media after it had finished.

The initial snap poll of viewers watching gave Sunak a narrow victory but other surveys called it a dead heat. In truth, aside from landing his tax attack effectively, it wasn't a great night for Sunak either. The audience laughed when the Prime Minister said NHS waiting lists were coming down, groaned when he blamed strikes for the waiting lists and laughed again at his national service plan.

For Starmer, though, the occasion had been a failure. The Tories had been better prepared, more aggressive and more ruthless. This was what an election was like. 'He was annoyed with himself,' one Labour source says. 'It was the only point in the campaign that he was pissed off, but he was pissed off with himself.'[5]

• • •

The Tories began laying their trap for Starmer in early spring. Jeremy Hunt's chief of staff, Adam Smith, teamed up with Sunak's political aides, including economic adviser Tim Pitt and Liam Booth-Smith, to think of ways to embarrass Labour during the election campaign. One obvious and well-trodden route was to ask civil servants to come up with 'costings' for opposition policy options – in this case, highlighting the implications for Labour's proposed tax changes.

Ministers from both main parties have done the same thing for decades, using the same official Whitehall form to request the work. In Labour's last year in office in 2010, for example, Gordon Brown's government commissioned the Treasury to produce scores of different costings. The aim is to come up with a credible answer, using civil service brains and leveraging their political independence for added credibility, to make opposition policies look as bad as possible.

'We were really quite strict and we thought the figure is actually higher than £2,000,' one aide involved this time recalls. 'But we arrived at that figure.' The process is not without risks for politicians hoping to unearth ammunition with which to hurt the opposition. The civil service is bound to publish the results of its analysis, even if they are not helpful to the governing party that commissioned them.[6]

Yet even though it's clear that the civil service was involved, back in Labour HQ, Starmer's chief of staff, Sue Gray, and economic adviser Spencer Thompson moved to challenge the Tory figures. Thompson drafted a letter to the permanent secretary to the Treasury in the name of Darren Jones, Rachel Reeves's deputy, setting out Labour's concerns.

Permanent secretary James Bowler duly confirmed that the Tories had added up his officials' numbers with figures from elsewhere to come up with a giant total of £38 billion. 'I agree that any costings derived from other sources or produced by other organisations should not be presented as having been produced by the civil service,' Bowler wrote. 'I have reminded ministers and advisers that this should be the case.' Civil servants were 'not involved' in calculating 'the total figure used', he said.

The official government statistics watchdog also warned the Tories that saying Labour would hit households with a £2,000 tax rise was potentially misleading and confusing. The Tories weren't making it clear enough that this number was spread over four years and most people wouldn't understand, the watchdog said. Other seasoned Whitehall figures, including former Cabinet Secretary Gus O'Donnell, hated the practice of getting civil servants to come up with opposition costings and called for it to be abandoned.

Labour aides found it reassuring that Sue Gray knew from her civil service days that the Conservatives were pushing the rules of how to use independent officials for political ends. That gave Rachel Reeves's shadow Treasury team the confidence to hit back. But there was a risk in doing so.

Before they decided to attack Sunak, Starmer's team debated

whether they were all simply falling into the Tory trap. By challenging what they knew to be a Conservative falsehood, they would inevitably bring further attention to the story, amplifying the original damage. Everyone would be discussing how much Labour was going to put up taxes by – which was exactly Isaac Levido's campaign plan – when Labour wanted to focus on the Tories' disastrous record.

In the end, Starmer felt so strongly that Sunak's dishonest claims should be called out for what they were that he personally authorised his team to accuse the Prime Minister of telling a 'lie' in public. Amid such highly charged arguments, the story ran and ran, and for a couple of days the Conservatives were in control. The election campaign, in its first few days, was being fought on Tory turf. Something was finally going Sunak's way.

THE IRON LADY

Morgan McSweeney knew that the Tory tax attack was damaging and felt it had been one of the two weakest moments of Labour's campaign. The other was how the party had responded to the Diane Abbott selection furore, which took too long to resolve.

What was so difficult for Labour about the tax bombshell claims was that the party had spent so much energy trying to reassure businesses and the public that Labour could be trusted with the economy and would not jeopardise household finances. As far back as the spring of 2021, after the Hartlepool by-election disaster, Starmer and his top aides knew that turning Rachel Reeves into a credible custodian of the economy was going to be vital to delivering victory. But auditioning to be the country's first female Chancellor of the Exchequer – a job Reeves has craved her whole political career – was hard work.

In the early days, voters in one focus group were shown images of Starmer and Reeves together visiting a manufacturer. They were wearing the typical fluorescent safety vests that MPs are forced to put on.

'It's such a cliché, politicians in high-vis jackets,' snorted one voter. 'I know,' replied another, 'but why's he brought his wife with him?'

The team at Labour HQ was alarmed that Reeves was so anonymous that people could mistake her for Starmer's wife. If Labour was going to overcome its bad reputation for fiscal risk-taking, Reeves would need to boost her profile dramatically.

Earlier in her parliamentary career, Reeves, a former national chess champion and Bank of England economist, was dismissed as too 'boring' to have a top role, an impression not helped by what was characterised as a monotonous public speaking style. Labour insiders knew a different Reeves. She is 'a force of nature' with a laugh 'that could shake walls', one colleague says. Her powerful personality and strength of character, alongside her economic credentials, were what party strategists wanted to show off to the electorate. 'If you are a naturally strong woman in politics, it makes no sense to downplay that,' one party insider explains.[7] Reeves was told to make sure she included in every interview or speech the fact that she had been an economist at the Bank of England to hammer home her qualifications for running the Treasury.

Over her three years as shadow Chancellor, she developed a guiding principle that she called 'securonomics', an unsubtle neologism designed to convey the point that Labour, unlike Liz Truss's Tories, prized economic security for families as well as the public finances. She did her utmost to show voters she was serious and would take on anyone, including in her own team, to deliver economic stability and growth.

In a barnstorming Labour conference speech in 2023, she outlined her 'iron-clad fiscal rules', including debt reduction and a promise not to borrow to fund day-to-day public spending. She vowed to enhance the authority of independent bodies such as the Bank of England and the Office for Budget Responsibility, both of which Truss had trashed. Her choice of imagery – cladding her pledges in 'iron' – was also deliberate and revealing. The speech, and the booming style in which it was delivered, owed much to Gordon Brown, who was known as the 'Iron Chancellor' in his time in Blair's New Labour governments. It was also, Reeves's allies say, a nod to the original Iron Lady, Margaret Thatcher.[8]

• • •

'With Rachel, you get somebody who is personally affronted by waste,' said one source. 'This is not just something which is developed as a political strategy … it just happens to be something that she absolutely abhors.'[9]

Reeves practised what she preached when it came to frugality. She would regularly return from a business breakfast with a stash of pastries for the team in her office as she could not bear to see them thrown away. She would also bring in a packed lunch in a Tupperware box rather than buy a sandwich from a shop. Before he developed a Pret baguette habit during the election campaign, Pat McFadden did the same.

Importantly for Labour veterans who endured the 'TB–GB' wars between Blair and Brown, Reeves and Starmer are genuine friends as well as political partners. Throughout the campaign they were regularly in touch, speaking or texting daily.

In 2015, Ed Miliband floundered when the Tories released a letter signed by 100 big business leaders backing David Cameron. In 2024, Labour was first out of the traps, with a similar letter from business figures backing Reeves.

When the Tories quibbled over whether some of the firms were legit, Reeves challenged them to release their own list. Chancellor Jeremy Hunt was unable to do so. Instead, the Tories told the *Financial Times* that they would be focusing on small firms. One Labour source remembers:

> We were just punching the air. Not only have we got our list out first, they haven't even got a list. It was shorthand for a lot of the work we have done and what we've achieved and how bad they were and what they'd done to the economy. It was [with] that *FT* piece that they had conceded defeat on the economy.[10]

THE OTHER CHANCELLOR

While Rachel Reeves was desperate to become Chancellor, Rishi Sunak, in many ways, was reluctant to stop.

On Friday 10 March 2023, the interconnected world of global finance suffered another dangerous spasm. In London, government staffers' phones began lighting up with messages of alarm from their contacts in the tech world: Silicon Valley Bank (SVB) had collapsed and hundreds of the UK's most promising tech firms, which were its customers, faced disaster. The Treasury institutionally was 'caught asleep at the wheel' and didn't know the bank was in such trouble until very late in the process.[11] Tech execs called Downing Street in desperation. Without an urgent government intervention by Monday morning, UK tech firms were facing insolvency. Start-ups employing up to 50,000 people were potentially affected.

Sunak was always a passionate advocate for the British tech sector. The crisis hitting the UK arm of SVB was a huge threat to his ambition to make the country the 'next Silicon Valley'. It was a perfect storm for Sunak to navigate – the former California dweller and start-up founder, as well as ex-Goldman Sachs banker, had served as Chancellor in the pandemic and knew how to get the Treasury to take mould-breaking decisions in a hurry.

Sunak worked with what observers described as a fierce intensity all weekend, from 7 a.m. on the Friday through until Sunday evening, immersing himself in the details of the crisis-hit companies. With Treasury and Bank of England officials, he pulled together a plan to sell the failing bank on to HSBC and stop the tech firms running out of cash.

'He was in Zoom calls saying, "Get me the cap table for SVB. Show me their investments." It was Rishi the investment banker coming out,' says one of those involved. 'He fought the Treasury machine to save [the situation]. I am completely convinced that if he had not been driving the process, a load of UK tech businesses would really have suffered.'[12]

Dealing with high-pressure financial decisions and orchestrating Treasury interventions was Sunak's sweet spot. He felt comfortable and knew he was the most competent leader for that work. The last Chancellor who moved next door from No. 11 to 10 Downing Street was Gordon Brown. Both men shared a reluctance to give up control over the finance ministry once they had taken over the premiership, and the economic gods were unwilling to release their hold on them either. Just as Brown battled the 2008 financial crash, so Sunak was responsible for righting the ship that Liz Truss had capsized.

When it came to selling his achievements and his plans for the future to voters in 2024, Sunak remained most passionately interested in the government's economic and fiscal policies. After raising taxes to their highest level in seventy years during the pandemic, he had championed an agenda to cut them again. His flagship move was slashing National Insurance contributions, a tax on working people.

That appetite for detail and technical intervention suited Sunak at the Treasury. It also delivered some of his successes as Prime Minister, such as the Windsor Framework, according to Grant Shapps, who served as Defence Secretary in Sunak's government. 'The Windsor Framework was an absolute triumph – technical, technocratic, difficult. His level of application got that over the line very nicely,' says Shapps.

He was in the right place being Chancellor. But being Prime Minister isn't as easy as it looks. That instinctive decision-making is not always about the polls, it's not always about reading the brief until you can recite it inside out. It's about a much more light touch than that. And because he was the extreme opposite of Boris, we went from one extreme to the other in this regard.[13]

CLASS WARRIORS

In order to win, Labour needed a leader who would look more prime ministerial than Sunak and at the same time appear to be more in touch with voters' lives.

There was a risk that some voters would assume 'Sir Keir', with his knighthood, was a wealthy member of the aristocracy. Labour spin doctors and speech writers made a concerted effort to cast Starmer as an ordinary working-class boy, who simply studied hard for his success as a lawyer. 'Keir had one advantage,' recalls Mattinson, who had analysed the way voters felt about party leaders in her focus groups. 'People could imagine him in Downing Street. Unlike Corbyn, he looked the part. But voters didn't know much about him and it was very important to get his beliefs and his compelling backstory out there.'[14]

The other side of Labour's campaign to win on leadership involved pointing out how rich Rishi Sunak really was, repeatedly and without much mercy. The party's social media team amplified Sunak's cringe-worthy mishaps to portray him as grotesquely out of touch with ordinary people's lives. Two months after becoming Prime Minister, he volunteered at a soup kitchen and memorably asked one visitor, 'Do you work in business?' The man replied, 'No, I'm homeless.' As Chancellor, he appeared at a photocall at a petrol station and seemed unsure how to make a contactless card payment. Both incidents became online 'memes' that Labour exploited.

This perception of Sunak, widely held by the time the general election was called, had roots in a scandal that emerged six months before he was elevated to the role of PM. Sunak's wife Akshata Murty had 'non-domicile' tax status. It allowed her to avoid paying UK tax on income earned abroad, which included the shares she held in her father's company. She would later repay the amount saved out of what she called a 'British sense of fairness', admitting it had become a 'distraction' for her husband.

This prepared the stage for Starmer to prosecute a controversial argument at PMQs in January 2024. 'He doesn't get what a cost-of-living crisis feels like,' said the Labour leader, glowering over the dispatch box in the Commons. 'He doesn't know any schools where kids no longer turn up, and he doesn't understand what it's like to wait for a hospital appointment. Doesn't the country deserve so much better than a Prime Minister who simply doesn't get Britain?'

Claiming the UK's first British Asian PM didn't 'get Britain' was risky. Some saw it as an attempt to play race politics, but Starmer's team insist it was intended to cement Sunak's image as a disconnected member of the 'super-rich' elite. 'Sunak's wealth was so embedded in the country's psyche, it was coming up all the time in focus groups,' said one Labour source.

Then there were what Starmer's media critics derided as his 'class war' policies. Tory-supporting newspapers slammed Labour's plan to apply VAT to private school fees. Conservative candidates began branding shadow Education Secretary Bridget Phillipson's proposal a 'tax on aspiration'. One *Daily Mail* front page claimed some private institutions could close as a result, with the headline 'Keir's Class War Threat To 200 Private Schools'. Others warned that moves to end non-domicile tax status would force successful and wealthy businesspeople to flee the UK.

Labour saw many of these attacks as 'hilariously bad'. Far from being a drawback, implementing VAT on school fees was one of Labour's most effective policies, insiders believe. 'Precisely because there was an element of tension and conflict, [voters] knew it wasn't just "motherhood and apple pie",' said one source. 'They knew there were going to be some people who were going to potentially lose out, and some vested interests who were going to be really unhappy about it. They found it more credible because of that.'[15]

THE BIG MATCH

'It's real people, so I'll just go and give them answers.'

Keir Starmer should have been a bag of nerves. In a few hours' time, the would-be Prime Minister was due to face a televised grilling. The probing would not come from Rishi Sunak or a seasoned political journalist, but the potential risks were just as great.

It was 20 June and he was due in front of a BBC *Question Time* live television audience. They could ask him anything they pleased. As Gordon Brown discovered when he met Gillian Duffy on the campaign trail in 2010, encountering a member of the public in full view of the cameras can be more dangerous than half an hour with a BBC political editor. Brown was infamously caught on a microphone referring to Duffy as 'some sort of bigoted woman' after she asked him about immigration.

Starmer's team is well used to drilling him for public debate and had prepared him intensively for his first TV clash with Sunak, on 4 June. This time there was a major obstacle in the way of their usual preparation routine: the football was on.

The Euros had been in full flow during the campaign and always threatened to distract public attention away from the politics. Sunak got in trouble by asking a group of voters in Wales if they were looking forward to watching the competition – after Wales had failed to qualify. Instead of preparing for his TV grilling, Starmer was much keener to watch Gareth Southgate's England take on Denmark.

'We were all wondering, how is this going to go?' says one person involved. 'He did zero rehearsal.'

They should not have worried. By this point, Starmer, like all of Labour's top team, knew the script and his job was simply to not deviate. It became monotonous, but Starmer did what he was told and stuck to his lines. One of his defining characteristics is his hands-off approach. Unlike Sunak, Starmer is ready to delegate and willing to take advice. One Labour source explains how he operates as a boss:

> He's a perfect candidate because he's a candidate. He doesn't try to be campaign manager, or speechwriter or logistics manager. He's good at properly backing his people and making everyone

understand that they have his support to do the job. That doesn't mean that he doesn't understand that people can make mistakes, but I've never known him to overreact to that.[16]

Starmer's deputy, Angela Rayner, also took part in TV debates against senior Tories and representatives from the Lib Dems, Greens, Reform UK, Plaid Cymru and the SNP. In preparation, she would watch a team of Labour officials rehearse a mock-debate, with her chief of staff Nick Parrott playing her. Former Gordon Brown aide Damian McBride played Farage, 'at which he was excellent', one source recalls.

• • •

On his tour of the country, from one media clip to the next, Starmer rarely boarded the official Labour battle bus. He preferred the train, in order to be able to speed back to London as quickly as possible to be with his family, if he could.

Living on the move during a frenetic six-week national campaign is exhausting. Starmer wanted to keep life as normal as possible. When he and his team were staying in a town, they would often go out for dinner to an Indian restaurant, in his case for a vegetarian curry and a beer. Those who joined Starmer for the ride and the rice dishes included communications director Matthew Doyle, his deputy Steph Driver and private secretary Jill Cuthbertson.

Starmer tried to stay healthy. Where possible, he would be based in a hotel with a pool or a gym. A habitual early riser, he would take a dip around 6 a.m. while he was away. 'He was like Michael Phelps,' one aide jokes. During the day, Starmer would not snack but would often order salads and fish with a side of chips when stopping for a meal. His mood often brightened when he was approached by a member of the public for a chat or to pose for a photo. But the campaign was an endurance test, even so. 'You knew every day you ticked off was one day closer to polling day and getting to the decision of the British public,' says one source close to the Labour leader. 'It's a combination of adrenaline and sheer willpower that keeps you going.'[17]

· · ·

'There were moments where you could tell he had the hump or he was a bit grumpy,' says one of Starmer's aides. 'But it would always be centred around himself. He wouldn't take it out on others.'

Starmer was not relishing the prospect of his second head-to-head debate with Sunak. Being slow to correct Sunak's claims that Labour would hike taxes by £2,000 in the first debate on 4 June had put the campaign under pressure. A snap YouGov poll after the clash had given Sunak the edge, with 51 per cent to 49 per cent for Starmer.

He resolved to put in a punchier performance at the rematch on BBC One on 26 June. 'He's very competitive,' says one Labour official who knows him well. 'If Keir thinks he's not good at something, he will work very hard to get better at it.'[18]

An aide recalls how Starmer told a fellow frontbencher before facing Sunak again that since he couldn't beat the shouting Tory leader, he'd have to join him. 'Look, I've just had to accept that the British people are going to have to watch two grown men shouting at each other, because if I don't shout at him, everyone's going to say that he beat me and I didn't debate him very well,' Starmer said. 'And if I try to answer properly, I'll get cut off after twenty seconds.

So I've just had to accept that it's not going to be fun for anyone, no one's going to be at all enlightened by it, but that's my job.'[19]

Starmer and Sunak clashed over immigration, trans rights and integrity in politics. It was a scrappier encounter than the first. When Sunak repeated the £2,000 tax claim, Starmer could be heard bellowing, 'That is a lie'. Despite his dislike of 'yah-boo' politics, the more aggressive approach paid off. While YouGov called it a score draw, Starmer had denied Sunak the clear win he needed to turn the Tories' fortunes around.

The Conservatives believed, with some justification, that Starmer was a wooden debater and would not do well in the format. Isaac Levido wanted at least two more head-to-head TV contests between the two leaders. Labour, leading in the polls and with more to lose, declined. In their position, Levido would have done the same.

PART III

THE CAMPAIGN

CHAPTER 10

D-DAY

REMEMBRANCE

The British Normandy Memorial at Ver-sur-Mer stands at the top of a hill overlooking the sand dunes of Gold Beach, where tens of thousands of troops waded ashore on D-Day.

Broken concrete pill boxes and other defences jut out from the grassy landscape, where cows now graze. At nearby Arromanches, the bulky 'Mulberry' harbour – a feat of engineering towed across the Channel to support Allied supply ships – looms out of the bay. Museums, memorial plaques and stone monuments record the vast collective effort that made the D-Day landings a success.

More than 130,000 Allied soldiers crossed the English Channel to confront German gunfire on the Normandy beaches in June 1944, in what is still the largest seaborne invasion in history. Within a year, western Europe was free. Streets, hotels and landmarks now carry the names of the region's long-dead liberators: Montgomery, Eisenhower and the troops they commanded.

In these towns and villages, the history of D-Day is permanently present. For the veterans of the battle, the hellish scenes they encountered in the sand and saltwater have also left their mark.

• • •

The number of former soldiers well enough to travel back to the French coast to observe the anniversary has dwindled in the eight decades since the war ended. In 2004, for the sixtieth anniversary, hundreds sailed from Britain to France, put on their medals and marched through the streets of Arromanches in a parade in front of the Queen and assembled Presidents and Prime Ministers. Local French women, too young to have known the war, reached their arms out to the ageing veterans and kissed them as they passed, with tears in their eyes.

By 2024, only twenty-five former servicemen were able to make the ferry crossing from Portsmouth for the events in Normandy on Thursday 6 June. The eightieth was likely to be the last big anniversary veterans would be able to attend.

There was never any doubt that Rishi Sunak had always planned and wanted to be there. He told his team the D-Day commemorations were a priority, regardless of the election, and care should be taken to ensure they did not become politicised. The Tory leader is a committed supporter of the armed forces and has championed government donations to veterans' charities. For the first time, he elevated the post of veterans' minister to the Cabinet.

One Tory aide recalls Sunak's instructions: 'He said, "This is incredibly important. It's important we spend this time recognising the sacrifices people have made." He really cares.'[1]

Despite Sunak's good intentions, his mishandling of the D-Day anniversary commemorations amounted to one of the most damaging blunders in recent British electoral history. Instead of pausing politics out of respect for the fallen, his decision to leave the official events in Normandy a few hours early – and return to the UK for a TV interview – gave the impression that he didn't care at all. When David Cameron, the ex-PM serving as Foreign Secretary, posed for a picture with the leaders of France, Germany and the United States, Sunak's glaring absence became the bad news story that derailed the entire Conservative campaign. If there was one moment that terminated the Tories' already slim chances of avoiding a wipeout, this was it.

How did a Tory Prime Minister who took so much pride in his support for veterans – and had just proposed reintroducing national service – end up doing only half a job of commemorating the eightieth anniversary of the defining battle of the Second World War? In the words of one of Sunak's closest aides, 'It was just a complete cock-up.'[2]

• • •

In the middle of May, before the election was called, officials working for Sir Tim Barrow, the PM's national security adviser and a highly experienced diplomat, drew up a plan for Sunak's attendance at the D-Day commemorations in Britain and France. Their memo, which was sent to the Prime Minister, left no room for doubt about what was expected. The note summarising the latest schedule explicitly stated that the PM was due to attend three 'core events' – the UK commemorations in Portsmouth on 5 June, the British event in Normandy the following day, and the international event later on 6 June. This memo then listed the world leaders who would be present at the international event: US President Joe Biden, German

Chancellor Olaf Scholz and the host, French President Emmanuel Macron. 'That is the first paragraph of the note,' one official said, recalling the advice to the PM. 'It said, "You are there."'[3]

The memo from the foreign policy team spelled out what would happen at these events, including at the international leaders' gathering, which Sunak would go on to miss. He would arrive at the VVIP reception point in Saint-Laurent-sur-Mer and would be taken to his seat, the memo said. There might be a chance for short, informal conversations with other world leaders on arrival, it added. The Prime Minister did not have a speaking role, with only Macron scheduled to make an address. Afterwards, there would be a forty-minute car journey to a leaders' reception, which would provide another opportunity for informal discussions between the Prime Minister and Macron, Scholz and Biden.[4]

Most damningly of all, the document makes clear that no decisions are needed from the Prime Minister. The schedule was set. But at some point between mid-May and 6 June, Sunak decided otherwise.

DIPLOMATIC INCIDENTS

On 5 June, Sunak, Starmer and others had gathered in Portsmouth for the first part of the anniversary commemorations, which included 500 troops, a 79-piece orchestra and a Red Arrows flypast. It must have been a surreal moment, coming just hours after the two men had clashed angrily in the ITV leaders' debate. At the time, the Tories were ramping up their attacks on Labour's tax plans while Starmer was authorising his team to accuse the Prime Minister of telling a lie. Politics hadn't paused at all.

After the military displays and speeches were done, Starmer travelled to France with his core team of media and logistics advisers.

After spending the night on French soil, Starmer woke, put on his smartest suit and went to Ver-sur-Mer, where the British Normandy Memorial is located, to meet UK veterans with King Charles and the PM. Other senior figures at the event included French President Emmanuel Macron, Defence Secretary Grant Shapps and Foreign Secretary David Cameron.

Back in London, POLITICO's morning newsletter 'London Playbook', which has become essential daily reading for insiders at Westminster, dropped into the inboxes of party staffers working on the election campaign. Starmer's team in France got wind of the news contained in the email that Sunak would not be staying in Normandy for the international event, at which Ukrainian President Volodymyr Zelenskyy was also expected. As 'London Playbook' put it:

> The even bigger event… is Macron's 2.30 p.m. ceremony on Omaha Beach with 12,000 participants and 25 heads of state and government. Ukrainian President Volodymyr Zelenskyy, U.S. President Joe Biden, German Chancellor Olaf Scholz, Canadian PM Justin Trudeau and Dutch PM Mark Rutte are all expected. So is Prince William.
>
> But but but… While Starmer and his Shadow Foreign Secretary David Lammy are due at Omaha Beach, Sunak is not expected to be there. Defence Secretary Grant Shapps and Foreign Secretary David Cameron are standing in, with Playbook hearing the PM will be back in Britain early afternoon. One U.K. official downplayed any suggestion he'll be missing a big day of diplomacy. Sunak has next week's G7 for that… and he does have an election to turn around, after all.
>
> A Tory spokesperson said… Sunak is 'honoured to play a part

in D-Day commemorations over the two days.' He'll be back on the election trail proper on Friday.[5]

Starmer's team couldn't understand. Was the Prime Minister really going to leave the D-Day events early? Labour aides checked with British diplomats who were in France at the event and they confirmed the PM's plans meant he would not be at Omaha Beach. Initially, Starmer's team worried a member of Sunak's family might have had a medical emergency that meant he needed to dash home.[6]

King Charles, who had been receiving treatment for cancer, also left Normandy before the international event. One senior Tory suggested this may have been relevant to Sunak's decision, as the Prime Minister did not want to upstage the King. David Cameron was reportedly 'apoplectic' at Sunak's decision but couldn't stop him going home.[7]

After lunch, the international event began at Omaha Beach. Starmer was there, along with Cameron and Shapps, who as Defence Secretary had taken on the role of leader of the UK delegation in the PM's absence. Prince William was forced to listen as Macron made a highly political speech about the European election, which the British side regarded as inappropriate. Macron then beckoned Cameron over for a chat. 'Mr Macron said he wanted to have a word with me,' the Foreign Secretary later explained to the BBC.

> We had an exchange and then he said 'let's have a photo of the quad' – which is Britain, France, America and Germany. And so there we were, having a photograph. It wasn't an event or a meeting or anything as substantial as that.[8]

For Sunak, the image was a disaster. As he made his way back to Britain, he was telling his team how moved he had been speaking to veterans and hearing their stories during the morning. It was a great event, he said, genuinely pleased with how well his trip to Normandy had gone.

'Then in the evening, out of nowhere, this picture showed up of Cameron, Biden, Macron and Scholz. And we were just like "What?!" It was the first I knew that Biden was actually there,' recalls one person involved. 'If we had known Starmer, Zelenskyy and Biden were going to be there we'd have been like, one we're trying to make this non-political, but OK, if he wants to politicise this, we should probably stay around.'[9]

This claim of ignorance about the guest list is an astonishing one from a senior member of the Conservative operation. All Sunak's team needed to do was read the original memo from civil servants, which made clear that Biden, Scholz and Macron would be attending the event and that Sunak was expected to be there too. And if they needed a reminder, it was all laid out – along with Zelenskyy's arrival – in POLITICO's Playbook email first thing on the morning of the anniversary. His plans could easily have been changed, even at that late stage.

Multiple members of Sunak's senior team blame a communications breakdown between the political unit running his election campaign and the permanent civil service who were responsible for organising events like the D-Day commemorations. Protocol dictates that when an election is called, political advisers leave government buildings and move into their party headquarters. That makes it harder for the political side in CCHQ and the impartial civil service, still working inside No. 10, to stay in touch. This, Sunak's allies insist, is the root of the 'cock-up' over D-Day. One explains:

Essentially what happened was No. 10 thought this was what the campaign wanted. The campaign thought this was what No. 10 wanted. And so no one really questioned what the plan was and that's how you ended up with a cock-up. The campaign thought they were handing the Prime Minister back to the official government machine for a day. The government machine thought their instructions were to get him back by X time, and it was just a complete cock-up born of both sides thinking that the other side had taken the strategic call.[10]

The backlash was relatively muted, at first.

At 11.22 p.m. on 6 June, Labour put out a quote from the party's media attack dog Jonathan Ashworth, accusing the PM of a 'total dereliction of duty'. Plenty of Tories privately agreed but stopped short of commenting in public. One warned that the only reason Sunak wasn't facing a leadership challenge as a result of his skipping the ceremony was because it happened in the middle of an election campaign.

The following morning, on Friday 7 June, only the Labour-supporting *Daily Mirror* splashed Sunak's early trip home on its front page. While most papers carried front-cover pictures of the D-Day events, there was no page-one coverage of Sunak's absence in the *Daily Telegraph*, the *Daily Mail*, the *Daily Express*, *The Sun* (which later backed Labour) or *The Times*, which quoted remarks by Macron, Biden and the King.

But while Grant Shapps was preparing for the morning round of broadcast interviews on radio and TV stations, Sunak's team inside Matthew Parker Street headquarters believed they were in crisis. The BBC were covering the criticism of the Prime Minister and it felt like it was going to blow up into a big story.

The question of what to do came up at 5.40 a.m. when Isaac

Levido chaired the campaign's regular first call of the day. Sunak's team discussed whether he should apologise. 'There was a debate,' one said. 'We were trying to work out basically what he was meant to apologise for. There were some people saying he shouldn't apologise – if he apologises you're basically saying he's done what everyone says he's done.'¹¹

Levido felt strongly that Sunak had to bite the bullet and say sorry. The media story was building and the fear was that any Tory who went on broadcasts would be asked repeatedly why the Prime Minister had skipped his D-Day responsibilities. The problem was 'that picture of Cameron with the other world leaders' made it look like Sunak should have been there longer. 'If it wasn't for that picture – there were pictures of him at D-Day with British veterans. He'd been there,' a senior adviser says.¹²

On a second call at 6.30 a.m., Conservative campaign chiefs decided the Prime Minister should issue a full apology. Levido called Sunak, waking him up, and told him that an apology was not optional but essential. The bleary-eyed Prime Minister at first didn't understand. 'Hang on,' Sunak said. 'We were following official advice. I thought it was right.' Despite misgivings and a debate about the phrasing, the group agreed that an apology was the best way to try to bring the controversy to a quick end. One Tory strategist explains:

> It felt like what would end up happening was you'd spend days refusing to apologise and finally have to apologise. We were in the space of, he doesn't want D-Day to be politicised, so apologise, try to shut it down and move on. Obviously, that didn't work. It stuck for days and days.¹³

At 7.45 a.m., Sunak said sorry in a post on X:

The 80th anniversary of D-Day has been a profound moment to honour the brave men and women who put their lives on the line to protect our values, our freedom and our democracy. This anniversary should be about those who made the ultimate sacrifice for our country. The last thing I want is for the commemorations to be overshadowed by politics. I care deeply about veterans and have been honoured to represent the UK at a number of events in Portsmouth and France over the past two days and to meet those who fought so bravely. After the conclusion of the British event in Normandy, I returned back to the UK. On reflection, it was a mistake not to stay in France longer – and I apologise.

SACRIFICE

The apology achieved the opposite of what Levido and his team had intended. Instead of drawing a line under the affair, it turbocharged the story. In a television interview later, Sunak faced a brutal interrogation from Sky News's Sam Coates. 'These men made the ultimate sacrifice and you couldn't even sacrifice a whole afternoon,' Coates told a chastened Prime Minister, before quoting a 98-year-old veteran who said Sunak had 'let the country down'.

The PM apologised, again. Asked why he hadn't stayed, Sunak said, 'The itinerary for these events was set weeks ago, before the general election campaign.'[14] He had apparently forgotten what civil servants had told him in their original memo in mid-May, when the schedule was fixed.

It was open season for Sunak's critics, including within his own party.

First, Veterans Minister Johnny Mercer told *The Sun*'s Harry Cole that Sunak's decision to leave Normandy early was 'disappointing' and 'a significant mistake'.[15] Later that evening, Cabinet minister

Penny Mordaunt, taking part in a BBC election debate with six other senior politicians from rival parties, said the Prime Minister had been 'completely wrong'. Mordaunt, herself a navy reservist who had been Defence Secretary and MP for a Portsmouth constituency, said, 'What happened was completely wrong, and the Prime Minister has rightly apologised for that, apologised to veterans but also to all of us, because he was representing all of us.'

The BBC 6 p.m. TV news bulletin is among the most important media moments of the day for politicians of all stripes, attracting an average audience of 4 million viewers. That night, the first half of the entire programme was devoted to Sunak's D-Day disaster. The coverage lasted twelve minutes and thirty seconds. In television terms, it was an eternity.

'We lost the election in a much bigger way because of this issue,' one still furious senior minister says. 'Voters across the country saw the apology and thought, "If he's saying he's bad then he must be bad."' The minister says a better approach would have been to reject the criticism, stressing how much Sunak had done for veterans and how long he had spent with them during the anniversary events in Portsmouth and Normandy. No. 10 should have robustly pointed out that the international event was for heads of state, which is why the UK was represented by Prince William. 'My voters, Conservatives, just needed a reason to know he's been fantastic for veterans, no one has done more. There would have been a fraction of the argument, it would have been a one-day thing. Instead, he owned it, wrongly.'[16]

• • •

When Keir Starmer got back to London, he called staffers in the party's war room together for a 'stand-up meeting'. The Labour leader wanted to share his reflections on two days of commemorations.

'There was no political gloating,' one of those present recalls. Instead, he focused on how much Labour had changed, thanks to everyone in the room. The party was now a party of public service, decency and patriotism, in tune with the values of those veterans he had spoken to in Portsmouth and Normandy.

'He talked about the people he'd met quite vividly – people who were very frail, veterans who were in wheelchairs.' Somehow, Starmer said, these men in their nineties managed to lift themselves out of their seats to stand for the King.

'You could hear his voice waver, especially talking about the people trying to stand from their wheelchairs,' one staffer says. 'I think he's acutely aware of people with physical frailty and disability, due to his mum and her situation. He knows what it's like to feel maybe impaired, and somehow, despite that, achieve something, even just for a moment.'[17]

Only four years after Corbyn, Labour had completed its transformation from a party of populism and pacifism to an offering far more closely aligned with the values of the public. It was 'a fundamental reckoning about who we are', the Labour official says. 'There was a stillness in the room as it dawned that this was a culmination of how the party has genuinely changed.'[18]

Rishi Sunak was deeply frustrated. He felt the criticism was unfair, especially given that the event he missed was the 'glad-handing' with world leaders, while he made sure he had attended those events where British veterans were present. But the damage had been done. Polling by YouGov found two-thirds of voters believed Sunak's decision to leave Normandy before the international events had concluded was either 'somewhat unacceptable' or 'completely unacceptable'.

Reform UK leader Nigel Farage claimed the incident showed Sunak did not understand 'our culture' and was not 'patriotic'. Senior Tory and Labour politicians condemned Farage for his remarks. Cabinet minister Mel Stride said Farage's comments were 'deeply regrettable' and made him feel 'very uncomfortable'. He added, 'I'm very proud of the fact that we have a British Asian who is right at the top of the government.'

Labour's shadow Justice Secretary Shabana Mahmood called the comment a 'dog whistle' and a 'classic' Farage move. 'We can all see exactly what Nigel Farage is doing, he's got form, it is completely unacceptable. This is a man that has a track record of seeking to divide communities who just wants to do it with a veneer of respectability whilst he's at it.'

• • •

Senior Conservatives disagree about the extent to which the D-Day fiasco was damaging, with some arguing that voters forgave the Prime Minister for making a mistake but didn't forget it entirely. Others say it blew up their campaign, especially for support from so-called 'red wall' voters, who had historically identified with Labour but backed Brexit and voted for Johnson in 2019.[19]

Labour's strategy director, Deborah Mattinson, agreed. She had made a priority of trying to change Labour's image to make the party seem more patriotic to these voters in particular. That had been hard work after the anti-war campaigner Jeremy Corbyn's years in charge, when Labour was caricatured as a party that wanted to leave NATO, scrap nuclear weapons and disband the army.[20]

Key steps along the way included getting the whole Labour conference to sing the national anthem after the Queen died and displaying the union flag in political videos and on leaflets. D-Day was the big Tory blunder people referred to in focus groups during the election. 'It confirmed a bunch of things about Rishi Sunak that they already suspected were true – that he didn't care about the things they cared about,' Mattinson says.[21]

After losing their reputation for honesty under Boris Johnson and their credibility on the economy under Liz Truss, Rishi Sunak's D-Day debacle saw the Conservatives surrender their claim to be the patriotic champions of the armed forces. In the middle of an election campaign when they wanted to focus on security, the party of Winston Churchill gave up the right to tell the nation's wartime story too.

CHAPTER 11

BAD BETS

If you had to pick a man who looked like he would never take a reckless, potentially career-ending bet, it would be Tony Lee.

The Conservative Party's campaign director and a loyal Tory for decades, Lee is mild-mannered, conscientious and deeply thoughtful, according to people who know him well. He speaks slowly, quietly and deliberately, with a soft West Country burr, and was widely trusted as a 'rock-solid' colleague at the heart of party HQ.

'He is easy to get on with,' said one colleague who's known Lee for more than twenty years. 'He's the sort of person that I would sit here and chat with. You'd regard him as totally confidential. You could talk to him about people and feel that he wasn't going to go dashing back to reveal what you'd discussed. Very trustworthy.'[1]

As director of campaigning, Lee would have been inside the very tight circle of top Conservatives who were required to prepare for the general election. He had to know the date that the Prime Minister planned to hold the vote before it was made public knowledge, in order to prepare the party machinery as much as possible for the ground war. Leaflets would need to be printed, candidates selected and given guidance, electoral paperwork completed, and volunteers brought in to bolster the team in Westminster and around the country. Only a handful of trusted senior Conservatives – excluding almost all of the Cabinet – knew that Sunak planned to announce 4 July as election day. Lee, multiple sources say, had to be one of them.

On 20 June, the BBC reported that Lee and his wife Laura Saunders, the Conservative candidate for the seat of Bristol North West, were being investigated by the Gambling Commission over an alleged bet relating to the timing of the election. The implications were potentially very serious. Using confidential information to gain an unfair advantage when placing a bet could be a criminal offence under gambling laws. Lee took a leave of absence when the news emerged, party officials announced at the time.

It was a devastating blow to the Conservatives, only a week after Rishi Sunak's parliamentary aide Craig Williams admitted putting 'a flutter' on the election 'some weeks ago'. *The Guardian* reported that Williams, who was standing for election in Montgomeryshire & Glyndwr, bet £100 on a July election only three days before the Prime Minister announced it. The episode hit Sunak hard. Williams apologised for his 'huge error of judgement'.

One foolish decision could, perhaps, be explained away. But when it was reported that Lee and Saunders were also being investigated for allegedly betting on the election, the damage was infinitely worse – to both the party's election campaign machinery and its already tarnished image among voters. Neither Lee nor Saunders publicly commented at the time, no doubt for legal reasons amid an ongoing investigation.

Sunak declared he was 'incredibly angry'.[2] For Tory staffers who were trying against the odds to cling on to as many MPs as possible, the loss of their campaigning boss in these circumstances punched a hole deep into team morale. People felt betrayed. 'Tony and I used to communicate multiple times a day,' says one Tory. 'It was unbelievable.'[3]

One of those in the inner circle of advance knowledge about the date explains how protective they all were of the secrecy surrounding the election date: 'I had literally not told a single soul. Not my partner, not my parents, not my dog. You couldn't tell anybody. It was fucking sacrosanct.'[4]

At the same time, the very nature of the political calculations that Sunak and his most trusted aides made when it came to calling the election mean no date was ever certain until the words came out of his mouth on 22 May. Officials point out that if two Tory MPs had defected to Reform UK on 21 May, for example, he probably wouldn't have gone to speak to the King.

The investigations by the Gambling Commission and the Metropolitan Police had practical implications too. Senior campaign figures, including Liam Booth-Smith, the PM's chief of staff, and many other top officials in No. 10 and CCHQ were questioned by investigators, taking up their time and distracting them from their work trying to fight the election. Booth-Smith was interviewed as a witness and spent twelve hours answering questions in the middle of an election – a deeply frustrating interruption that naturally affected his capacity to work on the campaign.

For party communications director Alex Wild, the gambling scandal made it impossible to push the core Tory message in the media about the risk of a Labour government putting up voters' taxes. That impact lasted for a crucial week in late June, close to the end of the campaign. It was hard to fight back when party officials did not know how many more names would emerge as having had an ill-advised 'flutter'. A Met Police officer working in Sunak's close protection unit was arrested. The number of police officers under investigation then rose to seven.[5]

As the story spiralled, Isaac Levido, who was deeply frustrated and angry, had to try to keep his core team of thirty or forty staffers inside the Matthew Parker Street headquarters focused on their work. He called a team meeting and said: 'What happened with Tony and Laura is very upsetting and disappointing. A lot of us know him very closely and have got feelings, but we need to focus on our jobs.'[6]

The real damage, of course, was to the party's standing with voters. 'I felt sick,' one senior party official said. 'I thought, this is going to kill us.' Members of the public made their disgust clear to candidates on the doorstep and in the party's internal focus groups.

'It was about money and it spoke to just more Tory fucking around, fiddling while Rome burns, selfishness,' another senior Tory strategist said. Voters saw it as just more 'insider Westminster politics – these people not focusing on you. People were just like, "How do I make this stop?" In an election they only have one lever: to vote against us. It was incredibly damaging.'[7]

The problem of candidates allegedly putting bets on the election wasn't completely restricted to the Tories. Labour suspended Kevin Craig as candidate in Central Suffolk & North Ipswich, after he admitted putting a bet on himself to lose. But the major damage was done to the Tories. Some in Sunak's Cabinet think the furore merely confirmed voters' worst impressions and made little difference to the overall result. 'It was all over by then,' one said. But after reflecting on the defeat, which included many seats only narrowly lost, Tory campaign chiefs estimate that the betting scandal may have cost the party as many as sixty seats. It's impossible to know for certain.

Anger has hardened in the weeks since polling day. At the time of writing, nobody involved in the inquiries has been charged, let alone convicted of any crimes. Regardless of whether any allegations are ultimately proven, one question dogs the thoughts of party staffers: how did the names of the Tories under suspicion leak to the press in the middle of an election campaign?

When the Gambling Commission contacted CCHQ to inform the party about its investigation, it demanded cooperation and complete secrecy. Yet the names of those caught up in the inquiries – including some interviewed merely as witnesses – emerged rapidly in the media.

One senior party source suspects some form of conspiracy:

> The Gambling Commission told us this was a highly confidential, highly sensitive investigation that they needed us to cooperate with – which we faithfully did. But the fact that names were getting put to us by the media almost immediately after names were being put to us by the Gambling Commission, or names even being put to us by the media before the Gambling Commission put them to us, is a scandal. Either it was being leaked out by the Gambling Commission or the Met was leaking it.[8]

The leaks, the senior Tory says, 'influenced the outcome of the election': 'It's an outrage, which should not be forgotten when their investigation concludes.'[9]

The Metropolitan Police and the Gambling Commission both say they have no evidence of leaks from within their investigations. 'We are not aware of any evidence to substantiate these claims,' a Met Police spokesperson says. 'If anyone has such evidence, they can of course come forward with it formally, but as yet no reports have been received.' A spokesperson for the Gambling Commission adds, 'We are not aware of, or have any suspicions of, any leaks from our staff.'

Regardless of who did or didn't do the wrong thing at the bookies, the gambling scandal rebounded badly on the Tories because the headlines at the time reminded voters of the morally dubious behaviour prevalent under Johnson: ministers and their aides acting hypocritically in their own self-interest, having parties during lockdown and lying to try to get away with it. The drip-drip of leaked names that made the news also robbed the Tories of the chance to get their election campaign messages out.

Levido's analysis of his final round of internal polling before voting began on 4 July confirmed the problem that his party just could not shake. Voters said they wouldn't back the Tories for two main reasons: they'd 'had their time' and they had 'behaved badly' in office.

CHAPTER 12

ENTER FARAGE

THE END OF THE PIER

'That moment was probably the moment that I thought, we've won this,' a senior Labour official recalls.

At 4.15 p.m. on 3 June, at a hastily arranged press conference and after initially ruling out standing in the election, Nigel Farage announced that he had changed his mind. And that changed everything.

Inside Labour's headquarters, Morgan McSweeney and his team running the campaign couldn't believe their good fortune. 'It was one of those rare moments when everyone stops what they're doing, gets out of their seats and huddles around the TV,' the party official recalls. McSweeney's team knew that Farage's entry into the election – taking over from Richard Tice as the Reform UK Party leader and standing in the seaside town of Clacton in Essex – was Rishi Sunak's worst nightmare.[1]

For over a decade, Farage has posed an existential threat to the Conservatives, splitting the right-wing vote and allowing Labour to win seats that would otherwise go to the Tories. Only when Farage's

Brexit Party decided not to stand candidates against Boris Johnson's pro-Brexit Tories in 2019 did the Conservative Party win a big majority. His re-entry into the contest one month from polling day would doom Sunak's hopes in many seats. And Labour knew it.

McSweeney wore a broad grin as senior staff gave each other fist-bumps after Farage's announcement. 'Morgan's face was just a picture,' said one who was there. 'He had a very content smile and went back to work.' However unpalatable Farage might be, McSweeney knew Labour had just been handed a huge slice of luck.

• • •

Senior Tories heard that Farage had been 'sniffing around' in Clacton-on-Sea for months in his quest for a potential seat. Part of Sunak's calculation in calling an early election in July was to catch Farage 'a bit off guard' and make it much harder for him to get a campaign up and running, one Tory said. Initially, it worked. After Sunak announced the poll, Farage said that he wasn't ready to run and would instead join in only to campaign for other candidates.

He was still bearing the scars from his unsuccessful run for Parliament in South Thanet, Kent, in 2015. Back then, a determined Tory campaign threw everything it legally could at stopping Farage. Then, it broke the law to throw in some more. The seat was flooded with Conservative activists bussed into the area to deliver thousands of leaflets for the Tory candidate. Then the party failed to declare its election expenses correctly, and a senior figure involved in the Thanet campaign, Marion Little, was convicted of breaking electoral law and given a suspended jail sentence in 2019.

'Thanet taught him a lesson,' says Gawain Towler, who has been by Farage's side as a press adviser for years.[2]

But supporters kept telling Farage they wanted him to lead them. This had an impact and one day, after the Reform team had been on the promenade at Skegness campaigning, it dawned on Towler that Farage's resistance to joining the battle was melting. 'It was people coming up to him saying, "Nigel, I'm really pleased you're campaigning. Why aren't you leading us?"'

Then on a Zoom call later that day, Towler saw a look on his boss's face that he recognised. 'I've seen that before, the cogs were whirring,' he says. 'It was an "Oh fuck, I'm going to have to do this, aren't I?" face. He felt duty-bound.'

Announcing his decision at the press conference, Farage said:

> I have decided, I've changed my mind. It's allowed, you know. It's not always a sign of weakness. It could potentially be a sign of strength. So, I am going to stand in this election. I'll be launching my candidacy at midday tomorrow in the Essex seaside town of Clacton. So, midday tomorrow, Clacton, at the end of the pier.

Watching on from Tory headquarters in Westminster, Conservative chairman Richard Holden gave an impromptu speech to staffers. 'This isn't about the future of the country, it's all about Farage,' he said. Then he went to Clacton-on-Sea in the afternoon to show his support for the Tory candidate whose job it would be to try to fend off the Farage onslaught, Giles Watling. 'It was all just a nightmare,' one Tory recalls. 'Awful.'[3]

TORY TORTURE

Farage has been tormenting Tory leaders for years, a pantomime menace always lurking behind them ready to steal their thunder, their voters and even their MPs. As leader of the UK Independence Party (UKIP), he drove David Cameron's Eurosceptic colleagues into a frenzy and a revolt that forced the then Prime Minister to promise an 'in/out' referendum on Britain's EU membership.

In the campaign that followed in 2016, Farage played a leading role pushing the anti-immigration message that helped deliver the vote in favour of Brexit. When Theresa May was failing to get her EU exit deal approved by Parliament, Farage's Brexit Party stormed to victory in the 2019 European Parliament elections, winning more votes than any other party. Amid the carnage, May stepped down as Prime Minister.

For his part, Rishi Sunak suffered the defections of three MPs to Labour in the weeks before the election. The threat of Tories jumping ship to join Farage was longstanding and still present: before the 2015 election, two MPs left Cameron's Tories for UKIP. In March 2024, Lee Anderson, the former deputy chairman of the Conservative Party, whom Sunak had suspended over Islamophobic remarks about Mayor of London Sadiq Khan, joined Farage's Reform UK – and then held his seat of Ashfield at the election. Lucy Allan, a Tory MP who stood down at the election, endorsed the Reform candidate standing in her seat to replace her, much to her colleagues' dismay.

There were other Tories thinking about joining Farage, too, according to Towler. They might have kept their seats if they had. Andrea Jenkyns, a Conservative MP standing for Leeds South West & Morley, boldly put a photo of herself next to Farage on one of her election leaflets. Sunak's image did not appear.

'Nigel always got on well with her in the past,' Towler says of Jenkyns. 'People behave badly in elections. If you really wanted to have a photograph with Nigel, you should have defected and been our candidate. And Nigel would have come and campaigned for you.

And you'd have saved your seat. But you didn't, and now you're no longer an MP.'[4]

MILKSHAKES AND BEER

It was a typical Nigel Farage campaign: unscripted, inflammatory and full of unpredictable public encounters.

Farage loves to mix with the crowds. He delights in the way his plain-speaking grabs media and public attention, even when it's negative, and feeds off the energy of being recognised wherever he goes.

In Blackpool on 20 June, he unveiled a poster warning that migrants crossing the English Channel in small boats constituted a 'national security emergency' before dropping into Blackpool's football supporters' club. Fans were busy sinking pints of beer and watching Gareth Southgate's team scrape a draw with Denmark in the Euros. Despite the distraction of the sport, Farage was mobbed.

Towler, who was with him, recalls:

> It was mad. It was great. There was cheering and singing, 'There's only one Nigel Farage.' The point is, can you imagine any other senior British politician walking into a football supporters' club during an England match? Farage loves it. He adores that contact. We spent a couple of hours there. Of course it wasn't all just cheering, there's lots of chats. Don't get me wrong. Not everybody in that room is a supporter. They're pleased to see him. But he's able to reach beyond his own supporters by just making himself available. And very few [politicians] do [that].[5]

On another occasion in Skegness, Farage was followed around by four young men dressed in bright pink for forty minutes, waiting for autographs. He preferred large-scale rallies, in a similar vein to Jeremy Corbyn's crowd-pleasing events from the 2017 election, and he held rallies in Devon, Birmingham and Sunderland.

But there was a downside to Farage's old-school, shoe-leather campaigning style too. On his first day of campaigning in Clacton-on-Sea, he was confronted by a woman who threw a milkshake in his face, soaking his suit and hair. A 25-year-old was later arrested. The experience is not unusual for Farage but no less alarming for it.

'I don't know what was thrown at me, but it hit me in the face, fair and square. Quite frightening,' he told a TV crew soon afterwards. Asked why it keeps happening to Farage, he replied: 'Because I go out and meet the public, nobody else does ... No one goes out and does the old-style street campaigning the way that I do. And this is the risk that goes with it and I'll be honest, it is quite scary.'[6]

Intimidation while campaigning was a worryingly common feature for many candidates in 2024. After the election, Commons Speaker Lindsay Hoyle warned that the level of threats against MPs was the worst he has seen. Many Labour MPs and candidates reported abuse during the course of campaigning, especially from pro-Palestine activists who hated Keir Starmer's position on the Israel–Gaza war. This trend is clearly not trivial. Two MPs have been murdered in their constituencies in the last eight years – Labour's Jo Cox in 2016 and Conservative David Amess in 2021.

Towler thinks Farage doesn't get much sympathy for having liquids thrown in his face because attitudes are biased against Reform in the left-leaning media:

> Don't tell me it's not scary because you don't know what it is as it flies. People laugh at it. Fine, crack on, but you don't know what it

is. That is quite worrying. But it's interesting how we have people going on about the threats to politicians. Funnily enough they never mention Farage. Because he's 'a dodgy right-wing bastard who therefore deserves to get everything that comes at him'. It's basically the approach from the Beeb and everyone down.[7]

• • •

Farage launched the party's manifesto on 17 June in Wales. Except he called it a 'contract', disliking the mainstream political term 'manifesto' because it signified broken mainstream political promises, he said. Holding the event at a community centre in Merthyr Tydfil was Towler's idea. 'It said everything we wanted it to say just by being in the cheapest council estate in south Wales. "Nobody cares about this place. We do." Where did the Tories hold their events? At Silverstone.'[8]

Farage argued that the fate of Wales showed what a failure Labour would be in power, and how useless the Conservatives would be in opposition. 'Since devolution, the Welsh have been ignored by the London political establishment and let down by the Labour administration they elected,' he said. 'Meanwhile, the Tories have been the official opposition almost solidly since 2016 and have achieved zilch, which probably explains why we are neck-and-neck with them in the polls in Wales.'

The Reform 'contract' promised controls to migration, scrapping net-zero climate targets and sweeping tax cuts. The 'establishment' in London didn't like it much, with economists at the Institute for Fiscal Studies saying the Reform spending calculations were out by 'tens of billions' of pounds a year. That was never really the point.

Wales had been a happy hunting ground for Farage's 'tribe' before.

In 2016, UKIP won seven seats in the devolved Welsh Senedd. In the 2024 general election, the party finished almost level with the Conservatives, on 17 per cent to the Tories' 18 per cent. Party insiders are targeting the next Senedd elections in 2026.

• • •

With a small budget and very limited resources for a ground war, Reform UK had to focus on getting attention via the national media and social media channels. It was a classic case of all publicity being good publicity. Until it wasn't.

On 11 June, Farage sat down for a set-piece BBC *Panorama* interview with presenter Nick Robinson. His argument was that 'there isn't a right in British politics' because the Conservatives had vacated that space by promoting high-tax, big-state policies. Only Reform UK could provide a robust opposition to Starmer with a big majority, he said. Then he turned to 'the big one', immigration: 'Since the Conservatives came to power, our population has risen by 6 million. And you wonder why you can't get a GP appointment, you wonder why the roads are clogged, you wonder why you can't get a house.' So far, so on-brand.

Then Robinson pulled up a picture of Vladimir Putin, describing him to Farage as 'the man you said was the statesman you most admire'.

'Hang on a second,' Farage intervened. 'I said I disliked him as a person but admired him as a political operator because he's managed to take control of running Russia.'

Robinson replied that when Putin sent his troops across the border, Farage blamed the West. 'We have provoked this war,' the Reform leader responded. Senior Conservatives say this moment was Farage's only major mistake in the campaign and allowed the Tories to push that point with voters tempted to back Reform.

Yet there were other difficulties for Reform UK. An undercover investigation by *Channel 4 News* found activists spouting racist and homophobic comments as they worked on Farage's campaign in Clacton. One of them, Andrew Parker, was recorded suggesting migrants arriving on British shores on small boats should be shot as 'target practice' by the army. The same individual referred to Prime Minister Rishi Sunak as a 'fucking P***'. Another Reform activist referred to the Pride flag as 'degenerate'.

In a statement given to the programme, Farage said he was 'dismayed by the reported comments of a handful of people associated with my local campaign'. He said the individuals concerned would be thrown off the campaign, adding, 'The appalling sentiments expressed by some in these exchanges bear no relation to my own views, those of the vast majority of our supporters or Reform UK policy.' Farage later suggested Parker, a part-time actor, may have been part of a set-up by the broadcaster, a claim *Channel 4 News* denied.

For Sunak, the target of the racism shown in the report, the episode was upsetting. 'My two daughters have to see and hear Reform people who campaign for Nigel Farage calling me an effing P***,' he said. 'It hurts and it makes me angry, and I think he has some questions to answer. And I don't repeat those words lightly. I do so deliberately, because this is too important not to call out clearly for what it is.' Speaking at a campaign stop in Teesside, Sunak added, 'As Prime Minister, but more importantly as a father of two young girls, it's my duty to call out this corrosive and divisive behaviour.'[9]

Back in London, Tory officials watched with admiration as the Prime Minister made his stand against racism. Isaac Levido says:

What was somewhat lost or brushed over was an incredibly significant moment in British politics, when the Prime Minister actually said what he was called on television. Whilst it didn't necessarily have an impact on the race, it was a big moment. It was a big moment for him – and importantly, many other people in the country who could very personally relate to it – and I was very proud of him that he did it.[10]

There were other failures too. Farage threatened legal action against the vetting firm that had been hired to look into the backgrounds of 400 Reform candidates. The work was not completed in time for the election campaign, which meant the party unwittingly fielded prospective MPs who had praised Hitler or previously supported the extreme-right British National Party.

In the aftermath of the election, Farage has promised to 'professionalise' his party and root out the few 'bad apples' who'd crept in through inadequate vetting processes. Towler, who had to deal with some of the crisis around candidates, admits that a small percentage were 'egregious'. He said he had to deal with about sixty problem cases, 'of which twenty were egregious and sackable'. 'We're talking about 3 per cent of our candidates were dicey. Racist or homophobic or whatever.'[11]

MY ENEMY'S ENEMY

When the results came in on the night of 4 July, Reform UK won 4.1 million votes – 14.3 per cent of the total share – and five seats in Parliament, including Farage's own in Clacton. The biggest impact of the pro-Farage surge was to wreck the Conservative Party's chances of a revival.

As a senior Tory says, Farage's talents put Reform in an ideal position to exploit Conservative mistakes: 'He is an incredibly able campaigner and an incredibly effective communicator and then events worked in his favour. The D-Day and the gambling stories just served attack lines up to him on a platter. And he's very effective.'[12]

The polling that predicted a Labour landslide also helped Farage's cause:

> Farage had caught fire and there was an emotional connection to him among voters we were targeting. Then we had the media saying Labour are ahead by a million miles. Trying to convince people that their vote counts, they can affect the outcome by stopping a Labour supermajority, was incredibly difficult in that situation.
>
> When Nigel Farage got into the race, it catalysed a group of voters. Half of the people who were voting for Reform were disaffected Tories who were just upset and eminently persuadable. We did get some of them back at the end. But then there was another half that basically had the attitude, 'You can all get lost, I love this guy, maybe Reform can win 100 seats and be the official opposition and also I don't believe the news so don't put any stats to me.' It was very Trumpian, although Farage is a far more able communicator than Trump, in a way. He really catalysed those voters and it just became almost impossible for us to reach them.[13]

• • •

Keir Starmer made tackling racism in the form of antisemitism inside the Labour Party one of the central pillars of his leadership. As Prime Minister, he found out in the first days of his new government that the racist far-right is a threat to civil order, with rioting stoked by online disinformation spreading through cities across England. The trigger was a mass stabbing targeting children in Southport, Merseyside, on 29 July.

Nigel Farage insists he has zero tolerance for racists in his party and has vowed to grip the organisation and root out bigots. Even so, he and his allies sounded sympathetic to the 'protesters' in the summer of 2024, whom they say were angry about uncontrolled migration. They condemned 'two-tier' policing that they say treats white British demonstrators more harshly than protesters from racial minorities and for progressive causes. 'It's awful. But what's awful? Is it the riot or the person stabbing people? It's probably the person stabbing people,' Reform UK's Towler says.

Many of Starmer's senior strategists, including Morgan McSweeney, regard Farage's presence in the national debate as poisonous. They would far rather he had no platform at all. Yet during the 2024 election campaign, McSweeney was pleased when Farage joined the contest and happy to allow him a free hit at the Tories to gain a calculated, tactical advantage.

Labour's central campaign directors told candidates – including the party's contender against Farage in Clacton – not to fight Reform too hard. They knew that almost every vote for Reform was one taken from the Tories, and every minute Sunak's team spent fighting a strengthening Farage was time they could not devote to taking on Labour. All that could only help Starmer. 'We knew in Ashfield and we knew in Great Yarmouth in particular, two weeks out, that Reform were going to win and we needed to do something about it,' one veteran activist says. 'The party told us: do not attack Reform and do not attack their candidates. Because they are facing the Prime Minister and if you take down Reform that will impact nationally.'[14]

One party source says McSweeney decided that in the 'short-term' battle of an election campaign, Labour should treat Reform as 'your enemy's enemy' – and therefore a helpful tactical alliance against the Conservatives. In the longer term, Farage toxifies the debate and is bad for political discourse, McSweeney believes, according to colleagues. Another senior Labour official says the party's decision not to fight Reform in 2024 should not apply in future: 'Moving forward, that won't be sustainable and we will have to review that. But for this particular campaign we wanted to make it a fight between Labour and Tory, and that let us ignore them.'[15]

A third Labour strategist says:

> We knew that the voters we needed to get were 2019 Tory voters and we were comfortable enough that the Tory voters who wanted to vote for Reform were probably not accessible to us. They were probably more right-wing than the Tory Party ... You can't run a perfect campaign for every single seat. You have to run a campaign that is going to win.[16]

• • •

Analysis after the election suggests Labour's majority would have been far smaller if Farage had not fought the Tories. One report indicated that Reform cost the Conservatives eighty seats.[17]

Reform now has five MPs in the Commons, and with 14 per cent of the vote they can claim a bigger share of broadcasters' airtime at the next election. Farage has set his sights on overtaking the Tories and even appears to believe he can oust Labour and form a government in the years ahead.

Labour might need to re-examine its own mission in politics if it is to find an answer to Farage's challenge. Reform is doing well in parts of the country that have been failed by successive Labour and Tory governments.

According to the think tank Onward, Farage's new home town of Clacton ranks among the 1 per cent most deprived districts in the country. Nearby Jaywick Sands – which also falls within Farage's constituency – is the most deprived of all neighbourhoods in England. Economic activity in the area is low at 51 per cent, compared to an England average of 80 per cent.[18] In 2015, when Farage toured deprived estates in Ramsgate as UKIP leader, residents were astonished to find a real-life politician on the doorstep paying them any attention at all.

Labour found it politically expedient to get out of the way as Reform sank its teeth into the Tories. As the right split, Starmer's candidates, in many cases, were the ones who benefited and found themselves elected to Parliament. But some in the Labour team believe the calculated tactical alliance with Reform was not comfortable for Starmer's party, with its history of fighting against the politics of division and seeking to cast itself as on the side of the poorest in society.

RACE

This election was fought in a political climate that many participants say was vicious and deeply unhealthy. Candidates and their teams – on the left and the right – suffered threats and intimidation, and in Nigel Farage's case, physical attack. In some areas, the Israel–Hamas war, which has fuelled a rise in antisemitic and Islamophobic hate crime, dominated the contest and triggered menacing behaviour, directed mainly at Labour candidates.

Against this troubled backdrop, Rishi Sunak – the country's first British Asian Prime Minister – found himself targeted because of his background. There was the Reform activist caught on camera calling him a 'fucking P***'. Then there was Farage himself saying Sunak's early D-Day exit showed he didn't understand 'our culture', which provoked allegations of 'dog-whistle' prejudice from Labour and Conservative politicians. And – some Tories privately argue – there were the campaign ads, stunts and soundbites that came from Keir Starmer's Labour Party.

While none of the Conservatives who agreed to be interviewed for this book believe Starmer himself holds racist views or that there was overt racism in his campaign, a number – including several senior figures close to the leadership – feel Labour crossed a line more than once.

They point to an attack advert that Labour launched against Sunak, suggesting that he did not believe paedophiles should be locked up. There was already a narrative in the media around Asian men and child abuse, especially following the Rotherham child sexual exploitation scandal. These adverts caused concern within Labour too.

A Labour source says in response, 'We won't apologise for making the Tories wear their record of failure over 14 years. The Conservatives hollowed out the criminal justice system leading to record low charging of sex offenders. They never addressed this fundamental point.'[19]

The Conservatives interviewed also note that while Sunak, as a wealthy former banker, might be a target for seeming 'out of touch' with working-class voters, saying that he 'doesn't get Britain', as Starmer did, is a different point and a step too far. Even accidentally, it resonates with prejudice that has often been directed at people of colour from immigrant backgrounds, these Conservatives say.*

The same Conservatives also cite specific election stunts targeting Sunak that they say played into racial stereotypes. In one, Labour mocked up a corner shop front, with garish yellow-on-blue lettering and a picture of Sunak's face. It resembled a local discount store or off-licence.

The mocked-up shop's name was 'RISHI'S MEGA MORTGAGES' and it promised: 'Every deal will leave you worse off!' In the windows were plastered the words 'RISHI'S RAW DEALS'. The detail that made Tories stop and think was the addition of Sunak's smiling face, crudely cut out and added to the shop sign, complete with a twinkly white star shining from his tooth. Labour did a similar stunt in January, mocking up a different shop front (these shop fronts were actually former offices, Labour sources say) in blue and yellow. The signage also featured the twinkly toothed PM. 'Who runs off-licences in this country?' one Tory asked, pointing to the stereotype. 'I think there was some pretty nasty subtle stuff going on.' Another said the Labour message amounted to saying Sunak was like a 'slick Asian shopkeeper – don't buy from him'.[20]

Eagle-eyed Tory researchers also spotted that Labour had played around with filters on images of Sunak that they used in social media content. The effect, they said, was to make his skin seem darker. These Conservatives have shared their evidence with the authors (who make no claim to being experts in photography). It is clear at least one picture looks like it has been darkened when it is compared with the original photo of Sunak. Using filters is clearly

---

* The Labour source points out that 'the full exchange' in Parliament shows the context for Starmer's comment, which makes it clear that he was talking about 'Rishi Sunak not resonating with the struggles of ordinary people'. For more on this, see Chapter 9.

not unusual in advertising. There may be a question over whether, in this case, it was wise. A Labour source says, 'We totally reject that images were ever doctored to depict this.'

For many Labour supporters and politicians, providing the Conservatives with any shred of a reason to complain, however quietly, that Starmer's team engaged in 'dog-whistle' campaign tactics would be sickening. Many might also note the irony of the Tories complaining about something they have been criticised for doing themselves in the past.

The Labour source responded to these complaints, saying:

> We totally reject these claims. As we found throughout our time in opposition and during election campaigns, the Tories would desperately throw mud at the wall and hope something sticks. They repeatedly used rogue tactics such as reporting politicians to the police and confecting scandals to smear their opponents without foundation.

Sunak himself rarely speaks of the racism he has suffered personally. In the election campaign, he made one notable exception, after a Reform UK activist was secretly recorded referring to him with racist slurs. Sunak's reticence, his allies say, comes from not wanting to be defined by the colour of his skin, for positive or negative reasons. Immigration was also such an electrified subject for his government that it may have seemed too difficult to raise his background without inviting an unpredictable debate.

In his farewell speech, Sunak acknowledged, in a typically understated way, his pioneering achievement as the first British Asian to lead the country. As usual, though, he referred to his religion, not his skin colour:

One of the most remarkable things about Britain is just how unremarkable it is that two generations after my grandparents came here with little, I could become Prime Minister and that I could watch my two young daughters light Diwali candles on the steps in Downing Street. We must hold true to that idea of who we are. That vision of kindness, decency and tolerance that has always been the British way.

In one sense, it was only unremarkable because Sunak never wanted to talk about it.

Starmer did. A couple of hours later on 5 July, standing in the same spot, the new PM said, 'I want to thank the outgoing Prime Minister, Rishi Sunak. His achievement as the first British Asian Prime Minister of our country – the extra effort that will have required – should not be underestimated by anyone. We pay tribute to that today.'

It was, no doubt, a sincere appreciation of his predecessor's achievement from someone who fought and beat antisemitism in his own party. McSweeney, too, cut his teeth as a campaigner defeating the BNP in east London, as did Hollie Ridley, field operations leader and now Labour's general secretary.

Starmer, his team says, always had red lines: among the things he would 'never' authorise in pursuit of victory was any suggestion of using Sunak's Asian background against him. Nobody in the Labour campaign, as far as is known, would ever have suggested it anyway. At the very least, however, there may be questions over whether Starmer and his key lieutenants, despite their personal records of fighting prejudice, took enough care to make sure their campaign was completely beyond suspicion.

CHAPTER 13

FALL GUY

THE JUMP

Ed Davey was having second thoughts.
 The Liberal Democrat leader had spent much of the campaign squeezing into tight swimming outfits and wet suits, falling off paddle boards and generally making a fool of himself for the cameras. On 1 July, the slog of the election was nearly over. With three days left before the polling stations opened, Davey was attached to a bungee cord and invited to throw himself off the top of a crane, high above Eastbourne. This stunt was the only one of the contest that had made Davey nervous. His team were a little worried too.

The Liberal Democrat leader did not always know far in advance what eye-catching campaign gimmicks he'd be required to indulge in. But PR-conscious party officials worried that their most senior politician, literally in free-fall, might actually throw up in front of the TV cameras. Despite focusing their campaign on sewage, not even Lib Dems wanted to see that. So, party press officers told Davey it was bungee day in the morning and he should skip breakfast to minimise the risks.

Even so, the team were nervous and so was he. They had one rule – if Ed was ever unsure about a stunt, they wouldn't do it. No questions. This time, everyone was unsure, but nobody said let's not do it. So, the bungee plan went ahead.

• • •

Wearing navy chinos and a dark green jumper, Davey stepped gingerly to the edge of the blue metal caged platform, suspended in the air. After a couple of deep breaths, he stepped off the edge and plummeted with his arms outstretched towards the ground, shouting, 'Vote Liberal Democrat!' The bungee cord did its job and yanked Sir Ed back up again. He bounced and dangled, spinning upside down for a while, arms still held out in a wide V, exhorting viewers to 'do something you've never done before' and back his team.

Davey says the best advice he received was 'don't look down, look at the horizon and dive for the horizon'. The Lib Dem Eastbourne candidate, Josh Babarinde, made the mistake of glancing at the ground. 'What did he see? He saw a cemetery!' says Davey. 'He needed a little bit more persuasion.'[1]

During the campaign, Davey had gone on daytime TV to get a makeover, fallen repeatedly into Lake Windermere, whizzed down a slip-and-slide water-shoot on an inflatable yellow ring, ridden the rollercoasters at Thorpe Park and taken an aqua aerobics class.[2]

Party chiefs explain there were three points to Davey's stuntman craze: first, it got media attention for a small party that had won only eleven seats at the previous election; second, it gave voters something to know about the Lib Dems' relatively low-profile leader; and third, it guaranteed an opportunity for Davey to give interviews in which he could promote his key policies.

In the early days of the campaign, Davey was 'inevitably a little bit worried' that the risk of looking like 'a fool' who was 'not serious' was going to backfire badly. He 'pushed back' at stunt ideas a couple of times but was reassured by his team that the strategy was working.[3]

'He never said "No" to anything,' one Lib Dem source recalls. 'He got it. Every time we did it he got loads of interviews and the first question was about the stunt but the next ten questions were on policy. The bungee was the only one when he got a little bit nervous, but he never said no.'[4]

Back in Lib Dem headquarters on Vincent Square in Westminster, aides would gather around the TV, watch their 'centrist dad' leader making a spectacle of himself and laugh. 'It was like a party. He absolutely loved the campaign.'

The record-breaking results when they came were a vindication of everything that Davey and his campaign team did. It was a remarkable and dramatic revival for a party that four years earlier had been down and very nearly counted out.

A BLEAK HOUSE

After the 2019 election, the Lib Dems looked like they were over.

For a third election in a row, voters had comprehensively rejected the party, leaving it with only eleven MPs. Just as the Lib Dems had done in 2017, they positioned themselves as the party to stop Brexit. And they got the same result: a humiliating rebuff. Leader Jo Swinson even lost her own seat in East Dunbartonshire.

In the months that followed, as Boris Johnson pushed his bare-bones Brexit deal through Parliament with his eighty-seat majority and took the UK out of the EU, the Liberal Democrats struggled to regroup. Staff turnover at headquarters in London was high. The office was a miserable and dysfunctional place to work, according to those who were there at the time. 'It was quite a tough environment,' one said. 'The party lacked confidence. It's almost like there had been a bereavement,' another said.[5]

Swinson had declared she believed she could be the next Prime Minister and ran a campaign that was heavy on the air war of national messaging but too light on meaningful ground operations. Voters, apparently, just wanted to get Brexit out of the way, and couldn't stomach the idea of Jeremy Corbyn in No. 10, so gave Johnson his victory. There was no room for a third force in English politics. 'The party had really high expectations of 2019. We had ended up going down one. It was a demoralised place,' one person who worked there says.

The Covid lockdown that followed did not help alleviate the 'bleak' atmosphere, another party worker recalls. 'We were on five per cent in the polls. Most of the staff had left. It was a bit of a state. It felt like a party very much on its knees – it felt awful to be blunt.'[6]

With Swinson out, Ed Davey took over, first on an interim basis and then permanently. From the outset, he had one key mission: to rebuild from the ground up in order to win. 'We needed to really listen to people. The party had got out of touch with listening,' Davey says.

Dave McCobb had been working for the Lib Dems on and off for decades. He was elected as a councillor for the party aged twenty-two in Hull and had plenty of experience helping to work on national campaigns. During Swinson's ill-fated bid to win power in 2019, McCobb was one of the officials in the room who felt the campaign was making fatal mistakes. He viewed with dismay the attempt to win via an air war message of opposing Brexit with only scarce resources for grassroots campaigning.

'Between 2015 and 2019 we had five people trying to support target seats across the UK at regional campaigns officer level. It was tiny,' McCobb recalls. 'Nowhere near enough to support a proper campaign across the UK. It meant if there was one by-election, the entire team had to go do that, there was no capacity.'[7]

When the party's new chief executive Mike Dixon offered him the role of campaigns director, McCobb agreed on one key condition: that the party rebuild a proper grassroots network that would be able to assemble a campaigning army on the ground in enough target seats and councils to make a difference.

For his part, Davey was already fully signed up to the need for a rethink. 'Ed won his seat the way I think it works, so we had a very clear shared view,' McCobb says. 'It is about building a ground organisation, identifying the issues voters care about, campaigning on them and promoting candidates as really effective advocates for a local area. That's what Ed did to win his seat in the first place.'

Between them, Dixon, Davey, Davey's chief of staff Rhiannon Leaman and McCobb agreed on their plan to bring the party back to life and claw back some long-lost territory on the electoral map. Gradually they began rebuilding the party's infrastructure, increasing the size of the campaign team from five to almost twenty by the time Sunak called the election in May 2024.

On video calls during the pandemic lockdowns of 2020, they resolved to focus ruthlessly on the target seats that they believed were winnable and rejected the idea of fighting a thinly spread national campaign. McCobb set out a twin-track approach to targeting, with a core group of around thirty-five target seats. The party would aim to saturate these constituencies with volunteers and campaign leaflets in a concerted attempt to win attention and support from voters in the years that lay ahead before the election. These were to be the seats that the party would aim to win from the Tories if, as was expected, the Conservatives remained reasonably popular with Johnson as their leader. If Tory fortunes deteriorated, the group of target seats could be expanded.

There was a second wave of a further sixty to seventy constituencies where the party would work hard with its local candidates over the course of the five-year parliament. If these local campaigns generated enough momentum, they would be elevated to the top tier of target seats and receive more intensive support and resources from the central party.

McCobb ran a tight ship. He measured the performance of every local team in each of the key target seats. They were set goals for how many volunteers they recruited, how many leaflets their teams delivered and how many voters they made contact with during door-to-door canvassing. The target seats list was revised every six months. If local teams weren't putting in the work, they would be dropped, while those working harder and showing progress would be added in to the top-tier list.

'We set some really clear campaign metrics,' McCobb says.

> All those things we were tracking constantly from April 2020 right through until polling day. In 2019, there were many seats where people were very open to the idea of voting Lib Dem, they just didn't think we could win there. So, the thing we needed to do was not just have an electorate that was open to voting for us, we

needed a ground organisation capable of running a big enough campaign that people understood we were the choice there.[8]

By the time of the 2024 general election, the Lib Dems had thousands of volunteers in their key seats, numbers that the Conservatives could hardly imagine. Hundreds of activists were already running regular leaflet rounds in all of their target constituencies. The best-performing of all – former leader Tim Farron's Westmorland & Lonsdale seat – boasted 680 volunteers delivering a round of leaflets every week. In many of the Conservatives' priority seats, the Tory volunteers just didn't materialise, leaving candidates reliant on a handful of friends to help.

BLUE WALL BURRITOS

In the spring of 2021, Dame Cheryl Gillan, who had served as the Conservative MP for Chesham & Amersham in Buckinghamshire since 1992, died, triggering a by-election in a seat that had been Tory since its formation in the 1970s.

It was as chance for Dave McCobb and his cohorts to put their new ground-up, localist approach to the test.

A group of party officials, including McCobb, went to the constituency, visiting towns and villages and knocking on as many doors as they could. Their mission was simply to listen. They asked residents what they liked about the area, what their views on politics were and what they cared and worried about. Even though they had voted in a Tory MP in 2019, many locals did not like the direction Johnson was taking in government. McCobb decided to throw everything he could at the seat.

But it was still the longest of long shots: Gillan had held the seat for the Tories in 2019 with 55 per cent of the vote, while the Lib Dem candidate trailed on 26 per cent. Boris Johnson remained widely liked. Nationally, the Lib Dems were on just 7 per cent, with the Tories on 43 per cent. In Chesham, however, Johnson was not such a popular figure.

'They hated him there,' says one party official. 'They were One Nation Conservatives that liked law and order, and they liked integrity in the way politics is done. They couldn't vote for these Tories and they needed a viable option – and that's what we were.'[9]

During the by-election campaign leading up to the special vote on 17 June 2021, Lib Dem candidate Sarah Green and her volunteers told voters they shared their local concerns around damage being done to the natural environment, including through sewage pollution.

McCobb told journalists he believed the Lib Dems could win the contest. None believed him. And then the result came, shocking political pundits and commentators who had forecast a Tory win. Green took 57 per cent of the vote, easily beating her Tory rival, who had 36 per cent. Davey confesses he was 'a little bit surprised' himself. 'It was quite a tough ask but we managed to pull it off and that cemented our view that the strategy we had been developing was the right one,' he says.[10]

The party had focused on the issues voters wanted to talk about – which included the NHS and sewage. The party official quoted earlier says, 'Ed made a strategic decision that Brexit had happened and people didn't want to talk about Brexit any more. But they did want to get rid of the Tories.' The victory was a much-needed boost for the party, giving weary activists confidence and vindicating Davey's leadership. It also changed views of Johnson, in the public and in Westminster. 'That by-election was the first time that Boris Johnson looked beatable,' says McCobb.

Leaman, Davey's chief of staff, had been convinced that they needed a visually arresting image to celebrate their triumph and capture public attention. There had been some talk in the media of the Tories losing support in the so-called 'blue wall' – traditional Conservative voting districts in affluent parts of southern England. The idea was that Johnson had reoriented his hard-Brexit Tories too far towards those Leave-voting former industrial heartlands in what used to be Labour's 'red wall', at the expense of blue wall Conservative strongholds like Chesham.

Leaman proposed that Davey should be filmed knocking down a wall of blue bricks with a big orange hammer. The stunt would be a visual demonstration of intent, she believed. Some were deeply sceptical about the idea. 'We were in the village hall in Chesham and we said, "Are we definitely going to do this blue wall thing?" and we said, "Yes. We're doing it. We are doing it,"' one of those present recalls.

Party activists lined up holding Lib Dem diamonds in the background and – due to the persistence of the pandemic – still wearing their Covid face masks. Davey gave a short speech in which he promised to show what happened when 'a really powerful, strong orange force goes against a blue wall,' before swinging his orange hammer and making a mess of a neat row of plastic blocks.[11]

It was here that the party first learned the power of the stunt. While some viewers found it naff, they still saw it on the news and remembered it. 'It was visually interesting and it was on TV bulletins for days afterwards,' a party source says. 'So, every time we won a by-election, we did it. The more we did these stunts, the more airtime we got to talk about the things we wanted to do.'

More by-election successes followed as McCobb's ground war strategy paid off. In December 2021 the party won the North Shropshire by-election. By this time, Johnson was deep in trouble over Partygate, among other scandals. The following June, the Lib Dems took Tiverton & Honiton with a campaign that urged voters to 'show Boris the door', and a few days later he resigned.

In the summer of 2023, the Lib Dems had another opportunity to road-test their election machine with a by-election in Somerton & Frome. The Somerset constituency had been Lib Dem for eighteen years until the Tories took it in their devastating raid on the party's strongholds in the West Country in the post-coalition election of 2015.

The reality of political ground campaigns is rarely glamorous. It involves bundles of leaflets stuffed into car boots, hour after hour of pounding the pavements delivering election literature, trying to engage complete strangers in moderately polite conversation and making do with some improvised working space wherever you can find it.

McCobb and his team set up their campaign office in a former warehouse near Frome station, which was being refitted as small unit office space at the time. The party got a good deal on renting a room on the site, on the condition that builders and electricians could continue with their renovation and rewiring work at the same time.

The key difference in this contest was that the Lib Dems did not feel they were coming from behind. When the campaign began, they knew they were already on course to win it. McCobb decided it was time to reformulate his general election strategy.

He called his team together for a Mexican lunch at the Burrito Boi restaurant opposite the station, which had become a regular haunt for the campaign team. McCobb and his heads of campaigns in England, Wales and Scotland decided it was time to raise their ambitions. McCobb explains, 'That was the week I realised there was a much higher probability that ... the Tory vote wasn't just going to spring back when a general election was called.' McCobb's team then decided to double their target-seat list. He says:

> We looked at the second tier and identified another middling thirties' worth of them and said we're going to start putting serious effort and focus into these as well. So, from about a year out, we were going from mid-thirties to mid-sixties in terms of seats we were seriously putting effort in, with always an understanding that if we hit the general election and the Tory vote goes up, we focus on the core seats. But if the Tory vote doesn't go up, we are in a position to capitalise on that opportunity. They were really good burritos.[12]

OBSESSION

For most of his career in Parliament, Ed Davey was not usually picked out as the fun guy in the room.

When the Liberal Democrats were in opposition before 2010, he was one of the party's most effective media attack dogs, a broadcast bruiser taking on Gordon Brown's Labour government as foreign affairs spokesman. That serious demeanour saw him through three difficult years in Cabinet as part of the power-sharing 2010–15 government with the Tories. The decision to enter into coalition with David Cameron ultimately doomed the Lib Dems for a decade. Davey himself lost his seat as the party was all but wiped out in 2015.

When he became leader in 2020, after yet another miserable

election failure the previous December, Davey said his party must 'wake up and smell the coffee'. Voters do not think that Lib Dems 'share their values' or are on their side, he said. 'I am listening now.'

Davey made winning back voters' trust the hard way, through the painstaking work of thousands of conversations with voters, the centre of his plan to rebuild the party. The end goal was always clear to anyone working inside headquarters in the years that followed, according to a Lib Dem official:

> They were obsessed with winning. I can't say how obsessed HQ was. We were obsessed with the blue wall target seats. That came from Ed, from the top down. Ed was obsessed and that filtered through every Member of Parliament, and every press or policy person too.[13]

Like their party leader, the issues voters wanted to discuss weren't glitzy. In fact, they were the opposite: a creaking health service, inadequate support for carers and sewage polluting waterways were frequently raised concerns. They became the core of the Lib Dem campaign.

While the groundwork was vital, Davey's media team, including his press secretary Timothy Wild, were always clear that the character and image of the leader himself would be critical when it came to the election campaign. Davey's reputation as the combative, serious technocrat from the coalition years never did him justice, his team felt. Luckily, he remained relatively unknown, which made it possible to give him a makeover as leader.

'The first thing we wanted to deal with was the bruiser vibe,' says one party source. 'He's a friendly guy, he loves chatting to people, he jokes around and although he takes politics seriously, he never really takes himself too seriously.' Showing the fun side of Davey's character became an important part of the party's election planning.[14]

In many ways, Davey is the antithesis of the slick, high-production-value TV politician. Another aide says, 'He has the centrist dad vibe. It's very much him. Ed is an embarrassing dad. I have seen him dance. He's a dad on the dance floor. In a lot of ways, it's quite refreshing how he's normal.'

The second strand to the strategy was to encourage him to talk more about his own life – what's known in political circles as the 'backstory'. Davey's backstory is a powerfully emotive one. His father died when he was four and his mother was diagnosed with a terminal illness when he was just twelve years old. He nursed her until he was fifteen, when she passed away, after which he lived with his grandmother and brothers. What few beyond his circle of trusted friends and colleagues knew about Davey was that his caring duties had continued as an adult. His son John has an undiagnosed brain condition that means he can't walk by himself or talk.

'He never really talked about his own backstory and he was literally advised in the past not to talk about it at all,' one colleague says. 'Ed has got one of the most powerful backstories of any political leader in the world.'[15]

• • •

Bringing your family into the front line of an election campaign is a risk for a politician. The Blairs and the Camerons happily posed with all their children on the doorstep of No. 10. As a result, they found intimate moments in their children's lives were treated as fair game for a hungry media. Tony Blair's son Euan was arrested aged sixteen for being 'drunk and incapable', a fact that made its way into all the main press and broadcasters, not least because the then Labour PM had only days before proposed spot fines for drunken behaviour. When David Cameron left his eight-year-old daughter Nancy behind at a pub where they'd been having lunch, it was similarly covered by every major news outlet including the BBC. Keir Starmer has taken a radically different approach. He refuses even to permit the media to know the names of his children, let alone offer them up for press photos.

The election campaign was Ed Davey's big moment to introduce himself to voters and he decided to take a leap – metaphorically, for once – and open his own family's story for public consumption.

In a remarkably personal and emotional campaign video, Davey not only discussed his childhood, marked by the tragically early deaths of his parents, but also life as a father caring for his son, John. It even featured John on film too. Davey says it was 'by far' the biggest and most difficult decision to discuss John in this way. With his wife, Emily, Davey tried to 'carve a line' between showing John on film and protecting him. That meant not including much of his face or voice in the broadcast. 'John will never be able to say yes or no to whether he wants to be talked about,' Davey says. 'So, it was us as parents having to work out what we did.'

> Having crossed the line and agreed to talk about my son, which was not an easy line to get over, the response from people was so enormous – people saying thank you for talking about it – we then almost felt an obligation to talk about it. It was a process, not an event or a strategy. It was who I am.*[16]

---

* Putting the care agenda at the heart of the Lib Dem campaign in a way that led to electoral success rather than disaster, is an achievement. It has long been an unfashionable topic in British politics with the potential to derail election campaigns. In 2017, Theresa May's social care funding plans were branded a 'dementia tax' (by critics including the Lib Dems), contributing to her government losing its majority at the election. In 2010, the Tories called Labour's proposals a 'death tax', sinking the chances of a cross-party deal on reform and damaging Gordon Brown's campaign for re-election.

Davey's wife Emily has multiple sclerosis, which the couple have also talked about in public. Asked in the election film if his mother would be proud of him, Davey became upset and had to pause, before saying he hoped she would.[17] This is a question he always finds tough, his aides say.

Davey's campaign activated two powerful emotional responses in ways his team recognised he was unusually well suited to deliver. Daisy Cooper, the party's deputy leader, summed up the approach: the Lib Dems, she said, have shown they can make people 'laugh' and make people 'cry'.*

Reducing voters to tears might seem like an unusual election pitch. But it reveals a deep truth that politicians forget at their own peril. As the Conservative election strategist Lynton Crosby put it in 2015, while celebrating the Tory campaign he ran which destroyed the Lib Dems across swathes of southern England: 'In politics, when reason and emotion collide, emotion invariably wins.'

It is another irony in this election of reversals that the Lib Dems took Lynton Crosby's maxim on the supremacy of 'emotion' and turned it back on the Tories with devastating effect, retaking many of the seats his campaign won from them nine years earlier.†

Davey finished the 2024 election as the highest rated of all the UK party leaders. The Liberal Democrats won seventy-two seats, a record increase on their previous tally of eleven. It was the party's best result for more than a century.

---

* The combination of humorous and emotive content is something Davey says was part of the strategy: 'Although some people said I'd been a bit of a fool falling off a paddle board, even though we had this serious message, the [election broadcast] video I think showed people that actually I was quite a serious guy, who could talk about difficult issues in a way which grabbed attention in a very different way. So, humour – falling off the paddle board – and now there was raw emotion. And bringing the humour and the emotion together worked.'

† Lib Dem president Mark Pack calculates that of the twenty-seven seats the Tories took from the Lib Dems in 2015, the party now holds twenty-three after the 2024 election. It won back some – including Davey's – earlier.

CHAPTER 14

SCOTLAND

For almost a decade, Scotland was a one-party state. The Scottish National Party (SNP), under Alex Salmond and then Nicola Sturgeon, ruled with undisputed power across the land. It had gained total dominance on the strength of separatists' swollen grievances, after the referendum of September 2014 rejected their campaign for independence. The shift in Scottish politics appeared to be permanent: in 2019, the SNP won forty-eight out of Scotland's fifty-nine Westminster seats. Labour held just one.

On 4 July 2024, Keir Starmer's party surged back, taking thirty-seven Scottish seats and consigning Sturgeon and Salmond's former colleagues to a historic wipeout. The SNP was reduced to just nine MPs.

Labour's successes in Scotland were its first major inroads into territory the party was once able to bank on for support. In many ways, the story north of the border mirrored the political transformation in England – Labour gained at the expense of a tired government beset by scandals and leadership crises, after many years in power. But like in the south, Starmer's team still needed to seal the deal with voters in order to benefit from the SNP's travails. And Labour nearly didn't bother with Scotland at all.

In the early days of the party's preparatory planning for the general election, there was 'tension' within Starmer's top team over whether Scotland was worth the effort. 'There were a lot of people arguing to Keir that this would distract from the strategy we needed to win the general election,' one party source explains.[1] The concern was that the campaign that would be needed to win over swing voters in England and Wales was radically different from the one that would be required to secure victory in Scotland. English voters who could be tempted to back Labour and Scottish voters were 'two different audiences', the source says.

Most of the 'hero voters' Labour's research expert Deborah Mattinson had identified were found in the English and Welsh seats that Johnson had won in 2019 (the Tories secured their majority entirely in England and Wales, losing seven Scottish MPs). They generally backed Brexit, were socially conservative and economically on the left. 'Obviously, the hero voter thing works in Wales, but it doesn't work quite in Scotland, so we had a slightly different definition of voters there. You've got a different profile of voter and voting patterns,' one campaign source says.[2]

Starmer, however, was adamant that Scotland must not be abandoned as a lost cause, even though Labour had a huge task to regain support from its starting point of just one MP. 'Keir was always very clear that he wanted to be Prime Minister of the UK, and being Prime Minister of the UK with one seat in Scotland was going to be a problem for him,' the Labour source says. 'He was always very invested in what was a politically high-risk strategy of trying to win seats back in Scotland.'[3]

It also mattered to Morgan McSweeney. He lives in Scotland with his wife, Imogen Walker, who was one of the candidates elected for Labour on 4 July. McSweeney realised that it was not possible to run the Scottish campaign from Westminster and in the end a separate strategy was devised. For it to succeed, however, the party needed the right people and a hefty slice of luck.

Richard Leonard had been Scottish Labour leader since 2017 and had overseen the failed campaign in 2019. A grey-haired former trade union official, Leonard was not even Scottish – he retained some of the Yorkshire accent of his county of birth. After Jeremy Corbyn resigned, Leonard had a good claim to being the most senior Corbynite in the UK. His brand of politics, which tended to emphasise the socialist successes of the past, was out of tune with Starmer's new, more centrist agenda. In January 2021, Leonard stood down. Anas Sarwar, a charismatic, Glasgow-born Muslim former MP, twenty-one years younger than Leonard, took over the following month.

• • •

'We were lucky.' The verdict of one of Starmer's most senior aides candidly tells the story.[4] Labour's revival in Scotland owed much to the disastrous and sudden collapse of the SNP, which had been ruling from the devolved Scottish Parliament in Edinburgh since 2007. After the country voted No to independence in 2014, the SNP stormed to an astonishing result in the UK general election in 2015 under Sturgeon's leadership, winning fifty-six out of the country's fifty-nine Westminster seats. It continued in the same vein until Sturgeon's star came crashing down to earth.

Sturgeon resigned in February 2023, insisting she just felt 'almost instinctively' that 'the time is right' to let someone else take over, even if many would think it was too soon. 'In my head and in my heart, I know that time is now,' she said. In the weeks and months that followed, first Sturgeon's husband Peter Murrell, the party's chief executive, and then the former leader herself became embroiled in a scandal the likes of which Scottish politics had rarely seen. Murrell was charged with embezzlement. Sturgeon was arrested and released pending further investigation. It was all part of Operation Branchform, the police inquiry into alleged possible fundraising fraud in the SNP. Sturgeon, Murrell and the SNP have denied wrongdoing.

'We were gifted what happened with the SNP and Nicola,' says the same Starmer aide.

While in England the scandals and crises that swung political fortune in Starmer's direction date back to 2022, the transformation in Scottish politics is much more recent. The first sign that the SNP's woes would convert into success for Labour came at a by-election in October 2023 in Rutherglen & Hamilton West. The special vote followed a different sort of wrongdoing by the SNP.

Rutherglen's MP Margaret Ferrier incurred the wrath of the public and her SNP colleagues after she broke lockdown rules and travelled hundreds of miles by train despite testing positive for coronavirus in 2020. The parallels with Dominic Cummings's trip to Barnard Castle were obvious. Outraged voters in the seat eventually got the chance to oust her by signing a petition and deploying a little-used power to 'recall' their MP. That triggered a by-election to find someone else to represent the area.

On 5 October 2023, Michael Shanks won the seat with a massive 24 per cent swing to Labour. Sarwar, Labour's leader in Scotland, declared, 'The clock is ticking on two failing governments.' Labour was able to win over Tory voters, many of whom would be strongly pro-union, as well as soft Scottish independence supporters in

Rutherglen. That meant Labour stood a fighting chance of coming out on top under the first past the post general election voting system in swathes of seats that were previously out of reach.

Gordon McKee, a close ally of Sarwar's who won the Glasgow South seat in 2024, recalls that the victory celebrations after that by-election win were a landmark in giving the party confidence. The revelry continued into the early hours at the campaign's base next to the Burnside Hotel in Rutherglen. Jackie Baillie, deputy leader and Scottish Labour stalwart, was joined by Sarwar, the victorious candidate Shanks and a host of buoyant campaigners. 'It was completely packed and it was incredibly joyful,' McKee recalls.

> It was about 4 a.m. Everybody started popping champagne and drinking. It felt like a moment. Almost everyone in that room had been through the really difficult times and we'd had ten years of real misery. It was the first proper celebration that I'd ever had in the Scottish Labour Party.[5]

Starmer boarded a train to Rutherglen for a rally alongside the newly elected Shanks and Sarwar, all visibly thrilled. 'You blew the doors off,' he said.

• • •

Meanwhile, the SNP continued on its apparent mission to emulate the disasters that had hit the Tories in London. After one leader quit and was engulfed in scandal, the next one set himself on course for the scrap heap too.

In April 2024, Sturgeon's replacement as SNP leader and First Minister of Scotland, Humza Yousaf, decided the power-sharing deal with the Greens wasn't working any more. Tensions had been building over a succession of issues, but the final straw was an interview by the co-leader of the Greens, Patrick Harvie, in which he refused to accept a landmark report raising concerns about treating trans children with puberty-blocking drugs. Yousaf was incensed. He sent a letter to the Green Party leaders terminating the governing agreement and firing them as ministers. It was a completely self-defeating move. Almost instantly it became clear that Yousaf would face his own no-confidence vote in Parliament, which he would likely lose. He cut his losses and resigned after barely a year in post, leaving the once-mighty SNP in the mire.

John Swinney took over. While he was seen as a competent figure who had served as a party deputy for many years, he had been expected to retire before long and lacked the charisma of Sturgeon or Salmond. In the end, he also lacked the time to make much of a difference: two weeks after Swinney became Scotland's First Minister, Rishi Sunak called the general election.

• • •

With polls showing Keir Starmer was set for No. 10, Labour had a compelling argument to make to voters in Scotland: 'The SNP want to send a message to Westminster. We want to send a government.'[6] The party raised its ambitions from hoping to win six seats to targeting twenty in the election campaign. Sarwar and his team realised they had a chance of a breakthrough in Scotland's 'central belt' – the stretch of the country with the highest population density, including the major cities and towns of Glasgow, Edinburgh, Paisley and East Kilbride. Many constituencies in these areas had swung to the SNP after 2014.

One campaign source says:

There's a lot of evidence now to suggest that Scotland's central belt tends to work as one bloc. Whether it's Rutherglen, Motherwell or Falkirk, you have the same profile of voter – working-class or middle-class, tends to identify strongly as 'Scottish'. Once you win that group, you can win everything. Unlike in England, where you have lots of different voter groups geographically close to each other, you don't have that in the same way in Scotland.

Kirsty McNeill, who was elected Labour's MP for Midlothian on 4 July and then made a junior minister in the Scotland Office by Starmer, says the SNP's failure to improve crumbling public services was crucial to her party's success. Voters were 'desperate to see the Tories out' and regarded Starmer as a viable new PM and the best way to dump Sunak.

One of the analogies that I used was: do you want someone sitting at the back of the bus shouting, or do you want someone up at the front of the bus who knows the bus driver? What do you think is more likely to get the bus going in the direction you want?[7]

The SNP scandal did not feature heavily on the doorstep during the short campaign but gave voters an excuse to ditch the party Sturgeon used to lead, according to McKee. 'People didn't care so much about the scandal,' he says. 'I think it gave a lot of SNP voters permission to move on. They didn't have to admit they were wrong about independence, it was more "the SNP has changed, so I can change as well".'[8]

While Starmer and McSweeney were keen to let Sarwar's Scottish

Labour team run their own campaign, there was one English figure who was seen as a good fit north of the border: deputy party leader Angela Rayner. Known for her big personality and working-class roots, Rayner was dispatched to Scotland on the Labour battle bus, meeting Sarwar in Livingston where they posed together on a giant swing. She particularly enjoyed her trip to a whisky distillery, according to one party source: 'Angela did manage to polish off a series of shots and went to the shop and took some away with her, which perhaps isn't the style they would have got from any other visiting UK-level politician.'[9]

Sarwar and Starmer ended the campaign with thirty-seven MPs, taking back chunks of their former heartlands from the SNP, while the Tories held on in some parts of the border. The results in Scotland took Starmer's majority from a big win to a monumental one. The Lib Dems won six seats.

In a final bitter pill for the SNP, Blair McDougall, who led the successful No campaign in the independence referendum a decade earlier, took the symbolic constituency of East Renfrewshire for Labour. In 2015, the SNP were crowing after winning the seat from Jim Murphy, who was Scottish Labour leader at the time.

Stephen Flynn, the SNP's Westminster leader, who clung on in Aberdeen South, said on election night, as thirty-nine of his colleagues lost their jobs, that his party had been 'swept away by the Starmer tsunami'. McSweeney, who was never wholly satisfied, privately rued the fact that Labour hadn't done better. If he'd been able to get another 100 activists into Scotland, he thought, Labour could have won even more.[10]

CHAPTER 15

POLL AXED

GIVING UP

It was early June, the frenetic election campaign was nearly two weeks old, and the PM's chief of staff, Liam Booth-Smith, found himself with a spare half-hour. So he started drafting Rishi Sunak's concession speech. Work never began on what the Prime Minister would say if the Tories unexpectedly won.[1]

In truth, Sunak's team always thought they were likely to lose. By week two, they knew they would. Inside CCHQ, internal seat projections ranged from the dire to the apocalyptic. One person involved said internal estimates around this time suggested the Conservatives could end up with as few as thirty seats, a total wipeout that would kill the party as a political force.[2]

Isaac Levido needed to change course dramatically. He and his team of research specialists, led by pollster Zach Ward-Elms, had been testing a plan they long suspected they might need. It was hugely controversial. Effectively, the Tories would admit to voters that they were not likely to win.

Labour, they would say, was on course for a huge victory that would give the unknown, untested Keir Starmer unlimited power to do whatever he wanted. And nobody knew what that was because Starmer wasn't saying much about his plans for office. The new campaign message would be to vote Tory so someone can keep Starmer honest.

Levido set out his thinking in a strategic note to party bosses on 10 June. In it, he cited evidence from Ward-Elms's polling, focus groups and analysis that voters liked the party's policies, such as on national service, tax and pensions. They just didn't believe the Tories could win and so dismissed the policy plans as irrelevant. Levido's strategic note continued:

> The polls have not moved in our favour. In fact, the opposite has happened. This is being driven by voter expectations. Voters have seen frequent polling and media commentary that Labour are expected to win, and win big. Our own polling shows that only 20% of voters think that the Conservatives will win, to 70% who think Labour will win. 34% think that Labour will win 'a big majority'. This means that while voters support our policies, these announcements are not driving a change in voting behaviour because voters do not believe they will ever be introduced.[3]

The persistently negative polling had shaped public expectations to such a degree that the prospect of a Conservative government was 'not credible', the note said. That meant voters felt liberated to support smaller parties that aligned more closely with their views, like Reform UK or the Liberal Democrats. It also meant many saw no point in voting Tory – a disastrous situation for Levido and Sunak.

Therefore, we must reframe the choice at this election to harness expectations that Labour will win to our advantage. We must prove to voters that their vote does have worth, not by preventing a Labour Government altogether, but by preventing an overwhelming Labour majority that will leave Labour unaccountable and free to do things that are unpopular with voters.[4]

Levido and Ward-Elms had analysed the attitudes of key groups who had backed the Tories in the past but were 'defecting' to other parties this time. Their target audiences were those who were switching to the Liberal Democrats and those who would be switching to Reform. These voters were convinced Labour would win but had doubts about what that would mean.

Tory polling and focus groups highlighted three key concerns that these target voters had about Labour. First, they worried that Starmer would do things in power that he was keeping secret. Second, these voters thought Labour would change election laws to rig the system and keep themselves in power for longer by, for example, lowering the voting age to sixteen. And third, they believed Starmer was 'weak' and would not be able to stop left-wing factions and his strident and outspoken deputy Angela Rayner from taking over.

These ideas resonated powerfully, particularly among voters minded to ditch the Tories in favour of Reform. Some 87 per cent of Tory switchers to Reform felt Starmer would do things in power that he was not telling the public about because he has no convictions, the party's research found. The same proportion – 86 per cent – thought tax rises were among Starmer's secret plans. And 82 per cent thought Starmer was too weak to stand up to Rayner and Labour's left wing. Among Lib Dem switchers, scepticism about Starmer was lower but still significant enough to give the

Conservatives an opening: around two-thirds of Tory to Lib Dem switchers (60–65 per cent) held the same concerns on these issues.[5]

Levido had a plan. His memo described how these same voters, 'when pushed', recognised that only the Tories could provide the sort of robust opposition needed to hold Labour to account. The two beliefs – that Starmer could not be trusted with a big majority and that only the Conservatives could hold him to account – gave the Tories a final chance to win back voters from Reform and the Lib Dems.

Levido needed a punchy message to land the point.

> The campaign must motivate voters by asking them to reject a large Labour majority. To do so, the campaign must vocalise that Labour are on course to win a large majority, or 'supermajority'. That such a supermajority presents a grave and lasting risk to issues that voters' care about. And that the Conservatives are the only party able to prevent that undesirable outcome.[6]

The strategists chose the word 'supermajority' because they knew it was a striking and unusual term to British ears. It was drawn from American politics and would be likely to excite the media.

There were other options available to the Tories. They could have redoubled their attacks on Starmer for his record running the Crown Prosecution Service. They had tried to blame him in the past for failing to prosecute the paedophile TV presenter Jimmy Savile. But Levido knew there was one message that counted above all in the closing weeks of the campaign. When voters were making their decision, the Tories needed to do whatever they could to make sure the defining question of the election was, 'What is the consequence of a Labour supermajority?' And the answer should be that people's taxes were going to go up. Levido was determined to make sure that at this late stage, this message must be delivered with a discipline that had been lacking from the party for so much of Sunak's time in office.[7]

There was no guarantee that this switch in tactics to warnings of a supermajority would work. Another even more radical step might be needed. The strategic note said:

> It may be the case that this move does not instil sufficient consequence to voters' choice such that they will consider the impact of their vote. In that circumstance, and subject to the time left before election day, the campaign may wish to switch to advocating for the Conservatives to be a strong opposition. However, this would be a significant decision for the Prime Minister at that point, and should be taken with due consideration to the risks involved.[8]

One big risk was internal: that Conservative activists and candidates would hate the 'supermajority' message so much and be so demoralised by party bosses effectively giving up that they would ignore CCHQ and do their own thing or not bother to help campaign on the doorstep at all.

Sunak and his team accepted Levido's proposal. In fact, the 'supermajority' warning was already being deployed in targeted digital communications because postal voting had begun. Grant Shapps picked up the theme and ran with it before CCHQ had intended to roll it out, telling Times Radio on 12 June, two days after Levido's note, 'You don't want to have somebody receive a supermajority.'

> If you ended up with a party with a massive majority, unchecked power, able to do anything that they wanted, and with the

instincts, we would argue, of Keir Starmer's party on all sorts of things – from raising people's tax to their lack of support for increased defence spending – we think that would be a dangerous place to put this country.[9]

Back at party headquarters, officials were surprised to see Shapps roll out the new message so soon. The campaign team had been planning to launch the 'supermajority' warning in the national media a few days later. But since it was already public on the airwaves, they decided to 'go with it', in the words of one strategist. The reaction was instant.[10]

'It had an awful impact on the ground,' one Tory aide recalls.

There were lots of complaints from activists. If you're going out knocking on doors, it's dispiriting. But we were very careful with our language. We weren't conceding the election, we were saying, 'If the polls are right, Labour is heading for a supermajority.' But there were lots of activists that got quite dispirited and turned off by that, understandably.[11]

Shapps was not the only Cabinet minister to see the impending disaster and choose to go his own way in the campaign. Levido gave Jeremy Hunt a pass to stop doing broadcast media. That meant that instead of travelling to studios in London, the Chancellor could remain in Surrey fighting – successfully – to keep his Godalming & Ash seat.[12] Some regarded Hunt's absence from the airwaves as a major loss in a campaign the Tories wanted to make about tax. But Hunt was one of very few to survive the Lib Dem surge that swept so many Tories away. James Cleverly, the Home Secretary, and Claire Coutinho, the Energy Secretary, were too busy fighting for their own seats to film social media videos for the national campaign after the first two weeks.[13]

The news kept getting worse for the Tories. On 19 June, two big seat-projection polls predicted in public what Levido and others had warned was a risk in private. The YouGov for Sky News seat-projection research put the Tories on just 108 seats and Labour on 425.[14] Meanwhile, Savanta's survey for the Tory-loyalist *Telegraph* newspaper was truly apocalyptic for Sunak, giving the Conservatives just fifty-three seats to Labour's 516.[15]

• • •

In the second half of the short campaign, another problem hit the Tories. The money was drying up. A few months before the election, the government raised the maximum spending limits during a campaign, expecting to rake in the cash from the party's traditional business backers. But when it came to the crunch, those donors, who were seeing the same dire polls, never showed up. Promises had been made, and as soon as the campaign kicked off, donors would be expected to 'get off the bench', in the words of one senior Tory. This time, loyal party backers politely looked the other way. Some did still give money, because they wanted to be encouraging, but it was a fraction of what they would usually provide and nothing like what the party required.[16]

The result was that Levido did not have the resources he needed to fight Labour's better-funded operation. While the Tories could muster about twenty full-time digital campaign specialists, Labour had 110. One senior Conservative said:

It's not rocket science. These people are businessmen. They didn't make their money by throwing it away, and they like to back winners. When it becomes increasingly clear you're not likely to win, they still give you money, they just don't give you as much. The idea that we ran out of money was not true. We would just have liked more. It would have gone into seats, digital advertising, more mail.[17]

Sunak tried to stay focused on his task, keeping up a packed schedule of campaign visits. He took a tour of a sheep farm in the hope of providing some engaging video showing him out in the open air, feeding animals. Unfortunately for the luckless Prime Minister, the sheep ran away.[18]

TACTICAL VOTERS

In an art deco building above a Tube station in the middle of London, there is a small warren of offices packed with data screens, white boards and campaign posters. There are TVs, a kettle and some snacks. This is the headquarters of Best for Britain, the biggest and highest-profile anti-Tory tactical voting organisation in the country.

There was no formal pact between Labour and the Liberal Democrats in 2024 to coordinate their campaigns in order to wreck the Tories' chances and kick them out of power. But Best for Britain did step in to join the dots.

Best for Britain was founded by campaigner Gina Miller, who became famous for challenging Boris Johnson's plan to shut down Parliament during Brexit negotiations. In previous years, the group had pushed for Parliament to have a final chance to reverse Brexit via democratic means. After the country left the EU, it shifted focus to backing pro-European parties and campaigning primarily against the Conservatives.

In 2024, their twin tasks were perfectly clear: 'Lock the Conservatives and other populists out of power for a generation' and get as many pro-European MPs elected to Parliament as possible.[19]

The group made tactical voting a core part of its mission to get rid of the Tory government. Midway through the campaign, they published recommendations to help anti-Tory voters choose who to back in 451 of the 650 parliamentary constituencies via a dedicated website. They ran billboard adverts stating, 'A change of government is Best for Britain.'

According to the group's own analysis, it was a roaring success. Best for Britain defined 2024 as 'the tactical-voting election' and said some 17 per cent of voters, equating to about 5 million people, had voted tactically. Cary Mitchell, director of operations and strategy at Best for Britain, said:

> Our analysis of the results ... estimates that 91 Labour and Liberal Democrat MPs in England and Wales have tactical voting to thank for their elections. Without tactical voting, Liz Truss and former Conservative ministers Grant Shapps, Penny Mordaunt and Thérèse Coffey would all still be MPs. We changed minds, and changed politics as a result.[20]

During the campaign, Best for Britain was in regular contact with the election teams working for the Lib Dems and for Labour. As well as commissioning their own MRP research, which provided seat-level projections designed to show who was winning and who was the best challenger against the Tories, the group scoured Labour and Lib Dem lists of target seats. Best for Britain came up with its recommendations by analysing the data from the polls, the target-seat information from the parties – which was generally available publicly if you knew where to look – and other factors.

On 17 June, the group published its recommendations in those 451 seats. Analysis later suggested the recommendations had proved 'correct' in 445 of them, meaning that in all but six of these constituencies, Best for Britain's preferred candidate won or came second.

• • •

Tactical voting has always happened. Sometimes it is easier than others. In 2019, the defining question of the election was Brexit. If you wanted to 'Get Brexit Done', you could vote for Johnson's Tories. But the choice for voters who didn't was not simple: the Lib Dems were proposing to cancel Brexit without another vote, while Jeremy Corbyn's Labour offered a tortured compromise of a second referendum in which his government would remain neutral. For Remainers, it was a messy and confusing choice.

In 2024, the question facing the electorate was simpler and there was much more agreement on the answer. Was it time to kick the Tories out and give Labour a chance? Strategists in all the main parties agree that tactical voting played a significant part in the outcome. On the Labour side, McSweeney's team noted how voters clustered to the Lib Dems in seats where the Lib Dems were second to the Tories and the swing from Tory to Labour was much smaller.

In Dave McCobb's view, the Lib Dems also benefited from Best for Britain and other groups validating their argument that his party was the real challenger to the Tories in key seats. That endorsement was something Ed Davey's team could put on election leaflets to prove to voters that backing the Lib Dems locally would really matter for the country. 'Most of the different tactical voting sites were all aligned about who's best placed to beat the Tories, and most of them were aligned on most seats most of the time, which created a much clearer landscape,' McCobb says.[21]

Labour officials, understandably proud of their stellar campaign result, are less willing to concede that any outside organisation beyond their own dazzling campaign played much of a role in their victory. One senior strategist says voters themselves are 'very astute' and could work out what to do themselves just by looking online. 'All this stuff about voting pacts or deals or putting money into tactical voting sites was just a complete waste of time because voters could use the Google machine,' the strategist says. 'They just worked it out and it's not hard for them to do so.'[22]

Deborah Mattinson, Keir Starmer's polling guru, is more ready to accept that the tactical voting campaigns made a difference, even if they didn't shift Labour's own campaign. 'Did they change anything we did? I don't think so, really, but they were certainly helpful,' Mattinson says.

> In the end, change was the overwhelming mood of the country, and people, including people who'd only ever voted Tory, were wanting to get rid of them. It was that straightforward. Lots of people would do anything that they could, and it was very helpful for them to be told.[23]

The day before Best for Britain announced its tactical vote recommendations in those 451 seats, the group contacted both the Labour and the Lib Dem campaigns to check that its proposed advice to voters was right. Both parties gave the green light.[24] There wasn't a pact and the outreach came from Best for Britain, rather than from the politicians. But both the Lib Dems and Labour encouraged and welcomed the work that this pro-European, anti-Tory campaign group had done.

TAXING POLLS

Martin Boon runs one of the UK's most reputable polling firms and has been a leading name in the industry for decades. He's just about had enough of political polling, and he's not alone. Even though the polls in 2024 correctly predicted a big Labour win, they were wildly out when it came to estimating the support the major parties would receive.

For months, national polls in the media gave Labour a lead over the Tories of 20 points or more. That pattern continued deep into the short campaign, the gap narrowing only slightly in the final few days. But when the results came in on the night of 4 July, the Labour lead had halved to 10 points, Starmer's side winning 34 per cent and the Tories 24 per cent of the final vote. When it came to the size of the gap between the two main parties, the pollsters got it 100 per cent wrong.

'This is either the very worst or the second-worst polling performance since 1979, depending on what you look at,' says Boon, who led research at ICM before co-founding Deltapoll with Joe Twyman, formerly of YouGov. 'It was a terrible polling performance.'[25]

The tendency for pollsters to give Labour a higher vote share than they eventually receive and to understate support for the Tories is not new. 'This has been a feature of opinion polls since before I started,' says Boon. In media shorthand, the trend has been described as 'shy Tories' in the past – the suggestion being that

Conservative supporters are more reluctant to reveal their preferences during surveys than Labour backers. But it is far from certain whether this is the real problem. The truth is that nobody knows what went wrong.

What is clear is that the flaws in the system are huge and getting worse rather than better – at least when it comes to the most common type of polls that seek to paint a picture of the headline vote shares. 'There is something fundamentally wrong with the data we collect,' says Boon. 'Many pollsters have already come out giving themselves pats on the back,' he adds, referring to the bragging rights some in the industry claim when their polls more closely (or less inaccurately) reflect the final election result. 'I find that risible.'

There were some individual decisions in 2024 that suggested pollsters were unsure themselves. At YouGov, which produced powerfully influential research for *The Times* and Sky News, pollsters totally changed their methodology at the start of June, in the middle of the election campaign.

YouGov found their MRP model, which estimated parliamentary seat results, gave different vote-share results from their standard 'voting intention' poll, creating a confused picture. YouGov resolved this by putting the voting intention survey through the MRP model.*

The most significant change from YouGov putting its headline voting intention poll (with a smaller sample) through its MRP model was that the new system would mean asking people how

---

* MRP – standing for multilevel regression and post-stratification – is a statistical model pollsters use to estimate constituency-level election results, which uses a very large national survey sample. The MRP model estimates results for different parliamentary seats based on the characteristics of voters who live there – such as age, educational background, employment income, past voting behaviour – in light of how people with the same characteristics said they would vote in the large national poll.

they would vote 'in their specific constituency', to take account of tactical voting. The result was a narrowing of Labour's lead over the Tories and a 2 per cent jump in the Lib Dem share.[26]

The polling failure in 2024 has escaped scrutiny in the media. That's likely to be because the overall picture painted by the pollsters in the voting intention surveys they conducted – which pointed to a big Labour win – was exactly what voters delivered when it came to the tally of parliamentary seats. But those polls were a long way off the final vote share that Labour won in particular.

Does it really matter? Boon clearly thinks so and is worried that the structural failure to account for right-leaning voters is embedded in polling around the world. The errors almost never overstate the Tory vote in the UK or the Republican vote in the US, he says.

During the campaign, Conservative candidates in many areas were convinced the race was much closer than the national polls were suggesting, according to anecdotal evidence. Robert Hayward, a Tory peer and election analyst, says candidates would frequently ring him for advice on the polling, which he believes distorted the contest. 'The constant theme that I heard from candidates, whether they won or lost, was that the polls were wrong,' Hayward says. 'If you are an inexperienced candidate and you've got televisions telling you one thing and you've got party workers coming in on a day-by-day basis utterly demoralised, then ultimately you begin to believe what's being put in front of you by the media.'[27]

Top advisers to Sunak are also deeply frustrated at the polls and the way they were allowed to completely dominate media coverage in the weeks and months before the vote. Some of Sunak's closest allies and friends, as well as members of his Cabinet, have privately expressed cold fury at the way the polls exaggerated how far behind

Labour the Tories truly were. If Conservative MPs had known they were only 10 points adrift, it's possible fewer would have quit Parliament ahead of the election. The party would probably not have been so demoralised and unruly, they say, if MPs had not been fed a daily diet of doom by the media reporting the latest wipeout prediction.

Most importantly the entire media's discussion of politics and the public perception of the state of the race would have been different. Voters' expectations would have changed. Turnout may have been higher if a Labour landslide had not seemed a foregone conclusion. The Tories may not have needed to resort to their 'supermajority' line. Though, of course, the impact of such a hypothetical scenario is impossible to determine with any certainty. Some on the Labour side say the poll lead didn't help them – as it made the Conservative message warning of a 'supermajority' plausible and probably led some potential Labour voters to stay home or back other parties. 'There probably was a swing away from Labour caused by the polls,' one Labour source says. 'People were worried about it but not nearly as worried as they should have been.'

Politicians and election strategists on both sides see the case for changes. Some are making their views clear. For Isaac Levido, it's time that the media dialled back its coverage of polls in the campaign. The polling industry should also get its house in order and face tougher regulation, he believes.

'If the British Polling Council is going to hold themselves up as a proper regulator, they need some teeth to enforce proper rules on their members, with sensible sanctions if those rules are broken,' Levido says. 'If you try to ban these polls outright, the media will just find a way to publish anyway. But if some of these polling organisations are sanctioned by a governing body, that would help.'

In Spain, for example, polls are banned in the final few days before the vote under electoral law. Levido thinks a moratorium is also needed in the UK.

> I'm not arguing that we would not have lost. But the inaccuracy of the polls and the reporting of them by the media increasingly play an outsized role in election campaigns. The polls are, frankly, given far too much attention relative to a proper policy debate and it significantly influences how voters behave. I'm not sure it's realistic to ban polls for the whole campaign period, but I certainly think some sort of blackout in the final couple of weeks, as some other countries have, would be healthy. Other countries have blackouts on TV advertising in the final two or three days of the campaign, too.[28]

Another senior Tory adviser is in favour of banning all polls for the entirety of the six-week campaign. Even Morgan McSweeney, Starmer's campaign chief and new chief of staff, is said to see the case for a ban, according to a Labour source. It's not likely that the new government will pass any legislation to bring a moratorium into law, but McSweeney was aware how polling disproportionately dominated media coverage of the campaign.[29]

Certainly, if the pollsters were less prominent, or silent for a period, the public would have a chance to hear more about parties' policies and the debate would focus more on questions about the relative qualities of rival candidates for Prime Minister.

On the over-reporting of polls by the media, McSweeney and Levido, apparently, agree. 'There should be far more media scrutiny of the pollsters and their results,' Levido says.

Commercially, there's an unhealthy incentive with pollsters and the media where newspapers want a shock poll because it's a good headline. They don't want a boring poll that says the same thing as all the others. Of course, media organisations want good stories and that's understandable. But if there are questions over the validity of these polling results, that's unhealthy.[30]

Boon has virtually no sympathy with the complaints of party strategists. But he, too, sees the argument for banning polls in the short campaign. This move would also likely make him quite a lot of money, as the only people who would commission polls would be hedge funds and other investors that have the means to pay for political insights.

BOTS AND GRIFTERS

Boon has made a study of polling failures. 'Pollsters are market researchers trying to do their best. Every single one of us wants to produce the most accurate prediction.'[31]

The problem, he says, is not that the polling companies cannot process the data properly. All polls have to take account of variations in the sample of, say, 2,000 adults who answer the questions on their voting intentions. Pollsters also need to find ways to handle voters who say they 'don't know' who they will support. Often, pollsters will decide to weight some factors more than others – such as which party a respondent voted for in the past – in an attempt to make the overall result more accurate. But nothing ever seems to work when it comes to correcting the pro-left bias.

For Boon, the real scandal, however, is in the raw data itself. The business of conducting market research has changed radically in the past twenty years. Polling has moved away from telephone surveys to online questioning. With that, the polling companies have generally lost sight of the evidence-gathering process itself. Instead, completely separate 'panel' companies have sprung up to recruit thousands of respondents online. These firms, which Boon says are not regulated, advertise for survey respondents on websites and offer to pay them to answer questions in an online form. There are major problems with this model, according to Boon.

First, there is no visibility for pollsters as to who is in their panel of, say, 2,000 anonymised respondents. It is possible for one panel company to sell the same panellists to multiple polling firms, who would not know that this was happening. Second, pollsters also have no idea which websites the panel companies advertise on. If the websites are politically skewed, the sample of respondents they recruit is likely to be skewed too.

Since panel companies pay respondents for their time, a third problem emerges – what Boon refers to as the issue with 'bots and grifters'. People who just want to make money will click through a survey as fast as they can without even reading the questions, never mind providing honest and considered answers. Some even set up artificial intelligence 'bots' to complete multiple surveys on an industrial scale, in order to make a healthy income.

Boon's firm, Deltapoll, inserts test questions into its surveys to try to catch these fake respondents who are either not honest or not human. One test question asked people to select which vehicles they had a licence to drive from a list. The list was somewhat unusual and included a US navy aircraft carrier, a highly specialised and unique piece of construction equipment only found in Germany, and the Millennium Falcon from the *Star Wars* films. Only 89 per cent correctly answered 'None of the above', meaning one response in ten was from a 'bot' or a 'grifter'.*

More in Common, a research organisation, was among the pollsters with the better records this time, correctly placing the Tories on 24 per cent and giving accurate results for Reform and the Lib Dems in its final survey of the campaign. Even so, the poll overstated the Labour vote by 4 points. In its post-election analysis, More in Common suggested a number of theories as to why its Labour result was too high:

> Since every pollster overstated Labour's performance, it appears there is a wider problem with established polling methodologies that needs to be addressed, even if public opinion polling in general remains accurate. We find it plausible that around one percentage point of this error on Labour's vote could come from people changing their minds in the last week of the election campaign, and another percentage point could have come from unrepresentative Muslim subsamples. The rest may be explained by selection bias on online panels, random sampling error, or another unidentified cause.[32]

At the time of writing, the British Polling Council (BPC), the industry body, had no plans to formally investigate the errors in the voting intention polls that occurred in the run-up to the 2024 election. In the interests of 'transparency and accountability', the body has started to collate and publish research findings from individual pollsters who have looked into the 'over-statement of the Labour

---

* It is also possible that people found the question amusing and treated it as a joke. That is still not in the spirit of a survey for which the expectation is that respondents will give truthful answers in exchange for payment.

vote intention share'.[33] The BPC also promises a 'public event to synthesise insights' from this work when more data is available, 'early in 2025'.

Meanwhile, pollsters keep polling, and the media keep reporting what they say as if it were true.

HINDSIGHT

At one of the darkest hours in Tory headquarters, Isaac Levido's team considered a nuclear option: to concede defeat before a single voter had picked up a pencil in a polling booth.

The idea would have been to shock the electorate in to paying attention to what they were about to do. Rishi Sunak would have given a speech. He would have said the state of the polls, public and private, clearly showed Labour was going to win. He would have cancelled the rest of the Conservative campaign. There would be no more policies. There would not even be a manifesto. The whole Conservative campaign message, from that point on, would have been to ask voters how big Labour's victory should be. The Tories would in effect have focused on competing for second place and the right to form the official opposition.

'Rishi Sunak would come out and we would not even have done a manifesto,' one Conservative aide explained. 'He would have given a speech saying, "I am not going to be Prime Minister again. We have lost. The country now must think very carefully. Do we want a Labour Party with completely unfettered power?"'[34]

It didn't happen. Senior Tories were hesitant even about embracing the 'supermajority' term. But some Conservatives now think the 'shock tactic' of conceding weeks early would have stopped voters 'sleepwalking into something they hadn't thought about'. In part, that's because the 'supermajority' warning, which Conservatives pushed hard in the final three weeks of the campaign, really worked.[35]

Levido's internal research on the eve of polling day showed that the two biggest reasons why voters were backing the Tories again were that the Conservatives would 'hold Labour to account' and that voting for Sunak would mean they 'can prevent a Labour supermajority'. The two biggest negatives dragging down support for Labour were the flip side of the same 'supermajority' coin: the 'expected Labour majority' and Labour's 'refusal to say what they would do if they win'.[36]

In the months after the election, Liam Booth-Smith privately wondered whether the big mistake the Conservatives made was ever trying to win in the first place. If Sunak and his inner circle had been willing to accept that they were doomed from the moment he walked into No. 10, perhaps calling the election even earlier – in May 2023 – would have limited the losses. It's a harsh judgement on a devastating defeat, made in the merciless glare of perfect hindsight.

And perfect hindsight is a high bar for political strategists to meet, when none of the country's most experienced media pollsters can reliably say what voters truly want.

PART IV

THE ELECTION

CHAPTER 16

ELECTION NIGHT

Rishi Sunak woke to a chilly morning in North Yorkshire on 4 July, polling day. Though the air was cool, the sun shone. Wrapped in a pale blue, half-zip sweater, he left home early with his wife Akshata and arrived at the polling station to vote just after it opened at 7 a.m. He managed a grin and a wave for the cameras, but he must have known his time as Prime Minister was nearly up.

Back in London, Sunak's team were busily putting out a stream of social media videos, including one featuring the PM telling voters not to give Labour a 'blank cheque'. It's a quirk of the country's outdated election laws that campaigning videos are permitted on social media but banned on mainstream broadcasters once the polls are open. A string of ads during the day on Sunak's social media accounts told voters that Starmer could not be trusted with a 'supermajority'.

The final, eve-of-vote polls were in. All predicted thumping wins for Starmer. *The Sun* newspaper, a tabloid bellwether of the national mood, declared in a slightly guarded way that it was backing Labour. The front-page headline on 4 July referenced England's football team, who were competing in the Euros: 'AS BRITAIN GOES TO

THE POLLS, IT'S... TIME FOR A NEW MANAGER (AND WE DON'T MEAN SACK SOUTHGATE.)' *The Times*, the other crucial Murdoch-owned daily, declined to endorse any party. The *FT* reported that internal Tory projections showed the Conservatives were only confident of holding eighty seats. An optimistic result would see Sunak finish with 140.

In the Tories' Matthew Parker Street HQ in Westminster, Isaac Levido kept in touch with teams on the ground around the country. These days, with a vastly depleted army of Conservatives to deploy, there is not much information coming back from polling stations. In parties that are well resourced, volunteer 'tellers', working on behalf of candidates, stand outside polling stations and tick off the 'elector numbers' of people who have been to vote. The aim is to identify who has not yet voted and pass this information back to a candidate's team, so they can go and knock on doors to encourage their supporters to go to the polling station.

The information is useful for campaign bosses too, because it tells them how the contest is going in real time and what their teams on the ground need to do in the hours that remain before polls close. But for the Tories, telling operations are a distant memory. 'The party doesn't have tellers any more,' one senior Tory says. 'You've got so few people, you're not going to have someone outside a polling booth telling. They should be out knocking on doors, getting people to vote.'

• • •

The sun was out in north London too, as Keir Starmer and his wife Victoria turned up at their local polling station in a community hall inside a Camden housing estate. Reporters had spotted the actor

ELECTION NIGHT

Charles Dance arriving to vote at the same polling station earlier in the day.

Two months previously, the Starmers had voted in the same place for the local elections, although the Labour leader was dressed down then in a T-shirt and a casual navy jacket. This time, he had put on a smart dark suit, white shirt and pink tie. Starmer also wore a stiff smile as his burly security detail made a hole in the crowd for him to pass through. There were plenty of police and press shouting questions. The scene told a story: power had already begun to shift Starmer's way.

Labour HQ in south London was deserted. Apart from Tom Lillywhite's digital team, almost everyone else was out pounding the pavements to encourage Labour supporters to exercise their democratic rights and eject the Tories from office. Campaign bosses had sent a memo out a few days earlier saying they didn't want anyone in HQ on polling day. 'It was like a ghost town,' one source recalls.

Morgan McSweeney and Hollie Ridley, the field operations chief, were also at headquarters, keeping in touch with teams of local activists around the country. After voting, Starmer arrived at HQ and locked himself away with Sue Gray to plan who would be in his first Cabinet. McSweeney dipped in and out of the appointments meeting, though preparing for government was Gray's domain. Starmer wanted to keep his Cabinet team in the same jobs in government that they had shadowed in opposition.

McSweeney's team, meanwhile, needed to decide where to redeploy activists in the ground operation to get the vote out. It became clear during the day that shadow Culture Secretary Thangam Debbonaire was doomed by a surge in support for the Greens in Bristol Central. Nobody knew the powerful shadow minister Jonathan Ashworth was also in trouble.

Using all the digital tools they had built up, Ridley and Lillywhite were able to monitor, in real time, how voter turnout was going. Ridley would tell Lillywhite which seats looked like close calls and needed an extra burst of digital messages to be sent to voters to encourage them to turn out and vote. They could also text party members to mobilise them. In the afternoon, buses of party volunteers drove out of safe London constituencies to target seats in places such as Bexley. While candidates in safe seats were all allowed access to some voter data on polling day, many were told after 12 p.m. to leave their home territory and reinforce the party's efforts in key marginals such as Portsmouth North, Penny Mordaunt's seat.

Starmer went through the speeches that had been prepared for him with Matthew Doyle, his communications director. There were drafts for the remarks he would make on election night – at his constituency count in Holborn & St Pancras and at the victory party at Tate Modern – and then there was the first statement he would make to the country as Prime Minister before entering No. 10. Everyone hoped these would be the speeches he would get to deliver.[1]

Labour's digital team had been preparing for polling day for months. One critical concern was the risk of a mass spread of disinformation on the day. They needed to be ready to rebut lies about Labour candidates or election processes, which could cascade out of control within minutes on social media. 'We had quite an active group who were sitting in HQ monitoring, and they would get lots of stuff taken down about polling stations being closed and things like that,' one person involved recalls.

McSweeney realised that in less than twenty-four hours, he was likely to be going to work in No. 10, arriving on his first day in government in front of the world's media. And he didn't own a suit.

ELECTION NIGHT

The campaign chief, who had orchestrated Keir Starmer's rise from the rubble of Labour's 2019 defeat, navigated bitter internal battles with his party and was on the point of taking Labour into Downing Street, went out shopping for clothes.

• • •

In the Liberal Democrats' Vincent Square offices, Dave McCobb had spent days trying to calm his colleagues down. He flatly refused to make any prediction of the final number of seats the party would win. His reluctance to give numbers, as with Labour's campaign chief Pat McFadden, was partly down to superstition.

'I spent a lot of the last week telling everyone anything over thirty-four would be the best result ever for the party in over 100 years,' McCobb says.[2]

The office was quiet, with most people out knocking on doors in constituencies. Staff who were due to work on the overnight operation took a break during the day. After eating an early dinner, they arrived back at HQ in the evening for a briefing from McCobb. Senior party officials, including Ed Davey's chief of staff Rhiannon Leaman, his press secretary Tim Wild and communications chief Olly Grender, all gathered around to hear McCobb's thoughts. At last, he was ready to give some numbers.

'Seventy-two wasn't there,' recalls one person present. 'We were looking between fifty and sixty seats. I didn't believe it. I still thought we would get thirty to forty.' There was no alcohol in the office, the person says. 'We had all eaten earlier. We were drinking lots of Diet Cokes. We live off that.'

• • •

In what has become a Tory election night tradition, the party's top team of campaign directors took a five-minute walk from their headquarters in Westminster to St Ermin's Hotel, a grand, red-brick pile next to St James's Park Tube station, for a final dinner together before the results came in.

As in 2019, Isaac Levido wanted to thank the people who had worked sixteen-hour days for the past six weeks and thrown everything they could muster into the campaign. The big difference, of course, was that this time, nobody was even contemplating a win.

Among the twenty-five aides gathered in the private dining suite were Sunak's chief of staff, Liam Booth-Smith, and his strategy director, Jamie Njoku-Goodwin; the PM's closest friend and political secretary, James Forsyth; and Rupert Yorke and his partner Nerissa Chesterfield, the Downing Street communications director. From CCHQ, there was media director Alex Wild and head of operations and events Emily Higham, among others.

After the grind of a demoralising campaign, the party had at least laid on a good buffet with plenty of variety – Indian food, salads, salmon, chicken and bottles of red and white wine on the tables. With two hours of voting left, the election race was over. Levido went around the room, praising each person in turn and thanking them individually for their hard work. He had never worked on a tougher election, he said.

'Regardless of whether you win or lose, election campaigns are emotional experiences. People are sacrificing a huge amount and you work so hard,' one person present recalls. 'They're incredibly unhealthy things to do – even if you're eating really healthily. People are just exhausted and particularly in that situation, when the ultimate outcome was not really in question.'[3]

The atmosphere was friendly and supportive. 'It was basically lovely,' one person in the room says. 'We all knew what was coming,' another recalls. But aside from the looming defeat, there was one other shadow that hung over the meal.[4]

Earlier in the evening, Sunak had announced a dissolution honours list, taking much of the political world by surprise, including many in his own team. The honours included a knighthood for Oliver Dowden, Sunak's Cabinet ally and deputy PM, and a damehood for former deputy PM Thérèse Coffey. Former PM Theresa May was made a peer, as was Sunak's chief of staff, Liam Booth-Smith.

Rupert Yorke and a number of others felt the timing was terrible. Just as more than 150 Conservative MPs were about to lose their jobs in a potential extinction-event election for the party, the PM decided to give his top aide a peerage as a reward. The objection was not to Booth-Smith's elevation to the House of Lords, which nobody in the room disagreed with. It was simply regarded as crass timing to announce it on what would be a disastrous day for the party.

The dinner wrapped up and the Tories, with a few glasses of wine inside most of them, wandered back to CCHQ to face their fate.

• • •

Keir Starmer was not at his Kentish Town home on election night. Along with his wife and family, he was at an £18 million penthouse apartment in Covent Garden, owned by Labour peer and donor Waheed Alli.

The media entrepreneur, who was given a peerage by Tony Blair aged just thirty-four, had played a big backroom role as a fixer for

Labour, leading election fundraising activities. Alli's fans in the party say he was critical in filling up Labour's election coffers, as well as in making his own funds and properties available for Starmer and his team.

In the years before the campaign, Alli let Labour officials use his offices in central London for election planning away days. During the short campaign, he provided the Starmer family with a bolthole, a gift estimated to be worth £20,000 in accommodation costs.

That night, Starmer wanted to eat dinner privately with his family and delay the moment their lives would change forever. He took a call around 7 p.m. from McSweeney, who gave him his estimate of the likely result. Based on the party's internal numbers, gathered from teams around the country, McSweeney predicted a majority of close to 200.

Starmer's aides arrived at Alli's apartment late in the evening, at around 9.40 p.m., just twenty minutes before the exit poll was due to be announced. The TV was tuned to the BBC. Under Professor Sir John Curtice's guidance, the exit poll has been astonishingly accurate in recent years. The survey, on behalf of ITV, the BBC and Sky, questions 20,000 people who have just voted at a carefully selected sample of polling stations across the country, calibrated to enable Curtice's team to extrapolate the findings into a national picture.

Starmer, Victoria and their teenage son and daughter huddled together on the sofa to watch. They were about to discover if the past four years of Starmer's efforts to detoxify his party and come up with a convincing offer to voters had paid off.

Among Starmer's most senior and loyal team members in the room were his private secretary Jill Cuthbertson, chief of staff Sue Gray and director of communications Matthew Doyle, who had been on the road with the Labour leader throughout the campaign.

Starmer's sympathetic biographer Tom Baldwin – a former top aide to Ed Miliband – was also there.

At 9.59 p.m., Keir and Victoria wrapped their arms around each other's shoulders, holding hands tightly. Labour staffers had been scarred by past defeats and exit poll shocks that had crushed their hopes before. Nervousness and doubt weighed heavily on them in those final seconds before 10 p.m. The BBC reminded viewers that it was the first July election since 1945 – how would the timing of the vote affect the outcome?

'And as Big Ben strikes ten, the exit poll is predicting a Labour landslide,' presenter Laura Kuenssberg announced. 'Sir Keir Starmer will become Prime Minister with a majority of around 170 seats,' her colleague Clive Myrie added.

Numbers flashed on screen. Starmer's face appeared above the predicted seat tally of 410 for Labour. The Tories were far distant, with just 131.

A cheer filled the room, then silence fell as everyone stared at the TV, stunned. Starmer gave his wife an 'extravagant' kiss and hugged his daughter, before the emotion of the occasion overwhelmed them.[5]

The first to break the silence was Doyle, the communications man: 'Well, we won,' he said.

There was no 'punch the air' moment from the Labour leader. 'It was very emotional but also calm,' one person present recalls.[6] He was happy, clearly, and full of smiles, generously thanking and congratulating everyone. But it was a businesslike display, in the style of a football manager shaking his coaching staff by the hand after a tidy performance in the league.[7] Alcohol was available, but nobody touched it.

• • •

Morgan McSweeney had been growing nervous all day. He had a personal investment in the results, more than most: his wife, Imogen Walker, was standing as a Labour candidate in Scotland. They'd spoken a few times during the day, and McSweeney was using his data feed at his desk in Southwark to keep track of the voting in her seat.

Labour's offices had been largely empty but started to fill up as the evening drew closer to 10 p.m. A big party was under way at Tate Modern, but most staffers wanted to be in the war room for the exit poll. Pizzas arrived in anticipation of a long night, but there was no beer.

As the countdown to 10 p.m. began, McSweeney's team huddled in front of the TV. He almost couldn't watch. What if, despite months of meticulous work, Labour's data was wrong? McSweeney stood and faced the TV with one arm around Hollie Ridley and the other around Teddy Ryan, Ridley's husband, squeezing them tight as the announcement approached. 'It felt like the longest two minutes of my life,' one member of the team at HQ that night says. 'Time just stops for a minute, and then the numbers come up and the room just erupts, it goes mental.' Elated and relieved, McSweeney hugged his colleagues. As jubilant officials wept and celebrated their long-dreamed-of triumph, McSweeney slipped away to talk to his boss.

He stepped out of Labour's Southwark headquarters into the night air and called Starmer from the pavement on Rushworth Street. The exit poll looked 'about right,' he said. Back at Waheed Alli's apartment on the other side of the river, the Wi-Fi had cut out. The man McSweeney's campaigning had first made Labour leader, and now Prime Minister, had to climb to the top floor to try to get a signal.

ELECTION NIGHT

• • •

At the Lib Dem offices in Vincent Square, Dave McCobb's team huddled around the big TV screen, similarly consumed with nerves. Party chief executive Mike Dixon gave a short speech thanking the staffers for their efforts. 'Then we all went quiet for a few minutes,' a party staffer says. 'It was like a penalty shoot-out. I couldn't watch.'[8]

At his semi-detached suburban house in Kingston & Surbiton, Ed Davey sat on the sofa next to his wife Emily as 10 p.m. approached. 'I think we'll have a really good night,' he told her. 'I think we'll get to between forty-five and fifty seats.'[9] That would have been a historic result for the Lib Dems, the party's biggest ever tally of seats gained at a single election by a long way.

When the numbers came up, projecting that Davey's party would win sixty-one seats, an increase of fifty-three, he was 'ecstatic' and 'jumped out of the sofa, hugging Emily'.[10]

McCobb and the HQ team were equally elated. 'Everyone went absolutely nuts,' one party staffer present recalls. 'There was cheering and people jumping in the air and people absolutely overwhelmed by it. A lot of the team were new. But there were also people who'd been through really tough elections and to be there when it actually went well was amazing.'

Another Lib Dem says, 'Some people cried. Some people cheered. I went silent. We had actually done it. We'd worked so hard, for many years.' McCobb, Olly Grender and Rhiannon Leaman went into a small room and called Davey. 'We all just screamed with excitement at each other on Zoom for a bit,' one person present recalls.[11]

• • •

After dinner, Isaac Levido and his senior lieutenants arrived back at CCHQ at around 9.40 p.m. He wanted anyone who worked on the campaign to feel free to join the team in the office on the night, even though all concerned knew it was likely to be a depressing evening. He did not want hard-working staffers to feel abandoned.

But that open invitation meant it was a busy place at Conservative HQ and a ticketed system was operating. People were given security wristbands to wear, as if they were entering a music festival. Downstairs in the basement, a watch party for volunteers was under way, with snacks and drinks. On the main floor, the campaign war room was full. An exclusive reception was under way at the back of the building, for donors and other VIPs. Most people had finished their work, but Dan O'Neill's digital team were sending social media posts right up until the polls closed.

When the exit poll dropped, it showed the huge Labour win with just 131 seats projected for the Tories – a loss of 241. Levido and his senior colleagues were not particularly surprised. 'There was relief in one sense that it was in three figures,' one Tory recalls.[12]

Another says, 'We have literally spent every morning for the last six weeks coming to work and those screens were all having people in the media saying, "Ooh you're predicted to go down to fifty seats." The exit poll was the best poll I'd seen on those screens in six weeks.'[13]

Even so, it spelled out the scale of the disaster. Hundreds of Tory politicians and staff were going to lose their jobs. Levido gave a quick speech to the room: 'Right, people are still working. It's a very disappointing night for the party. Nonetheless, it's going to be a significant moment in the party's history and how we conduct ourselves tonight is going to be very important.'[14]

Liam Booth-Smith and Levido retreated into the privacy of the

ELECTION NIGHT

boardroom, with a couple of the party's pollsters, and called Sunak. They spoke to the Prime Minister for around half an hour, telling him the exit poll looked broadly right, though the Reform prediction of thirteen seats seemed high. They talked him through how the rest of the long night ahead would unfold. It would be painful. It was the end.

Sunak finished the call and went to bed.

• • •

Around the country, politicians on all sides were in the same boat as voters, sitting on their sofas, waiting for the verdict.

In Basildon & Billericay, Tory Chairman Richard Holden had been staying with a local couple who kindly offered him a room for the duration of his campaign. As the exit poll was announced, his first reaction was 'Christ, that's bad' followed by relief that it was not worse. He wondered if so many seats had gone, who had lost. And then he realised the scale of Labour's victory meant his own result must be on a knife edge.

In Wolverhampton, Pat McFadden, Labour's campaign coordinator, was at home watching the exit poll alone at 10 p.m. He felt relief, after fourteen years out of power, that Labour's long exile was coming to an end.[15]

• • •

A two-minute walk from the soft sand and amusements of Clacton beach stands the Royal Hotel. Established in 1872, the grand building on the seafront, with its covered balconies, is a classic example of the style found in Victorian coastal resorts across England.

Reform UK chose it as their base for election night, and by 10 p.m. the festivities were in full swing, with around 150 guests enjoying food and drinks.

Unlike other parties predicted to do well, Reform did not invite the media into its election night event.

The signs had been good for Reform all day. In the afternoon, Lee Anderson, who defected to join Team Farage after he was suspended by the Tories, said he felt confident he had saved his Ashfield seat. He saw the biggest turnout coming in the 'worst estates' in the neighbourhood – they were Reform's people.[16]

In the function room of the Royal Hotel, the exit poll flashed up on a screen, predicting thirteen of Nigel Farage's candidates would win. That would represent a stunning breakthrough into the political mainstream.

'We ignore it,' says Gawain Towler, Farage's longstanding press aide, who was enjoying a dinner of 'steaks' at the time. 'Most people are pissed by then anyway.'

• • •

The first constituency to declare its result always comes from the north-east of England. It is something of a tradition that there is a race between Sunderland constituencies and Newcastle to see who can count the votes the fastest.

In a sports hall in Sunderland, Bridget Phillipson waited for what felt like the longest five minutes of her life for the exit poll. As the incumbent Labour MP, her own result was not in doubt, and at 11.14 p.m., she was declared the winner in the first result of the night. Reform UK's candidate, Sam Woods-Brass, came second with almost 12,000 votes, knocking the Tories into third place.

Wearing a broad smile, Phillipson took the microphone:

Tonight, the British people have spoken. And if the exit poll this evening is again a guide to results across our country, as it so often is, then after fourteen years the British people have chosen change. They have chosen Labour and they have chosen the leadership of Keir Starmer.

She would be named Education Secretary the following day.

• • •

Jacob Rees-Mogg, the former Cabinet minister, arch-Brexiteer and Tory MP for North East Somerset, appeared on the BBC to offer his analysis. The fact that the Tories ousted Boris Johnson was a betrayal of the electorate that gave his party an eighty-seat majority in 2019, he said. 'We do have an increasingly presidential system,' he argued. 'People vote for a Prime Minister, rather than for an individual Member of Parliament.' The Tories, he said, had taken their core voters 'for granted'.

• • •

In the Lib Dem office, McCobb had installed a whiteboard with all eighty-four target seats marked on it. Each row had the name of the candidate, their phone number, the contact details of the lead team member on the ground, and a little box which would be coloured in if the party won it.

At around midnight, he told his colleagues he thought the exit poll had been wrong: 'We are going to do better.'

Morgan McSweeney had been busy tracking the numbers his ground teams fed back to HQ in Southwark. Party spokespeople needed the latest information before appearing on TV to give interviews. But as the man in charge of the election triumph, he was required to show his face elsewhere.

Like other senior colleagues, he had an appointment to meet Labour donors at an election watch party hosted by Waheed Alli. McSweeney jumped in a cab.

• • •

Around 3 a.m., Sunak's chief of staff Liam Booth-Smith rang Sue Gray, his Labour counterpart. He wanted to set up a call with Starmer. The Prime Minister was ready to concede.

Booth-Smith contacted the Downing Street switchboard – which has remarkable powers to find virtually anyone, wherever they are – and asked them to make the arrangements.

• • •

At 3.27 a.m., Nigel Farage won Clacton from the Conservatives. Though it was not a surprise, it cemented the reality of Reform's existential threat to the Tories. In seat after seat, Farage's candidates came in second place behind victorious Labour MPs. In many cases, Reform had taken enough votes from the Conservative candidate to allow Labour to win.

'It's four weeks and three days since I decided to come out of retirement and throw my hat in the ring,' Farage said.

ELECTION NIGHT

I think what Reform UK has achieved in just those few short weeks is truly extraordinary. Given that we had no money, no branch structure, virtually nothing across the country, we are going to come second in hundreds of constituencies ... Something very fundamental is happening. It's not just disappointment with the Conservative Party. There is a massive gap on the centre-right of British politics and my job is to fill it. And that's exactly what I'm going to do.

• • •

Not everything was going Starmer's way.

Standing as an independent candidate in Islington North, Jeremy Corbyn thrashed his Labour rival, winning a seat from the party he once led. In his victory speech, with a white rosette pinned to his jacket, Corbyn thanked his local backers. And he warned that the crisis in Gaza was something the incoming Prime Minister must prioritise.

To applause and cheering, Corbyn declared his constituents were 'looking for a government that on the world stage will search for peace, not war, and not allow the terrible conditions to go on that are happening in Gaza at the present time'.

Starmer, meanwhile, was privately worried. Two of his key frontbench colleagues, Jonathan Ashworth and Thangam Debbonaire, lost their seats.

• • •

At 3.37 a.m., the BBC updated its forecasts by combining the exit poll predictions with the actual results from the first 170 constituencies declared.

The new numbers predicted 405 Labour MPs, down a handful

from the first forecast. The Tories were up to 154, an improvement of twenty-three on the initial exit poll.

In the war room in Conservative headquarters, the mood suddenly lifted. Levido's team were also tracking their own internal data, which suggested a similar positive pattern. In 1997, the Conservatives had won 165 seats and commentators were suggesting it was looking like a similar outcome this time. That would certainly give the next Conservative leader a platform to build from.

Booth-Smith and Levido called Sunak again. The chief of staff said the BBC numbers were 'wild' and urged him not to read too much into them.[17]

• • •

Keir Starmer was in the car on his way to Labour's main victory party, which was under way in the Turbine Hall of the Tate Modern art gallery on the South Bank of the Thames.

The phone rang. It was Downing Street – the Prime Minister was on the line.

'Congratulations,' Rishi Sunak said. 'It's a big job.'

The outgoing Prime Minister offered Starmer any assistance he needed, especially on national security matters. He went beyond that too. 'I'm available if there's anything I can help with or even if you just want someone to talk to,' he said. Sunak disclosed that he had benefited himself from talking to former PMs in the past.

'That's great,' the Labour leader replied.

It was a short conversation, just three or four minutes long. But staffers listening in believed it had been a healthy one. The two leaders spoke to each other with respect and courtesy – the defeated Prime Minister, and the candidate who was about to replace him.[18]

ELECTION NIGHT

• • •

The brief burst of optimism at Conservative headquarters didn't last.

Amid the torrent of Tories being defeated, a stream of ministers were losing their seats, many by thousands of votes. Richard Holden, the party chairman, was facing a recount in Basildon & Billericay, formerly one of the safest Tory seats in the land.

Grant Shapps, the Defence Secretary and former party chairman who helped deliver Cameron's victory in 2015, lost to Labour in Welwyn Hatfield. After wishing the victors well for the sake of the country, he rounded on his colleagues for their failure to remain disciplined.

'What is crystal clear to me tonight is that it's not so much that Labour won this election but rather that the Conservatives have lost it,' Shapps said.

> On door after door, voters have been dismayed by our inability to iron out our differences in private and then be united in public. Instead, we have tried the patience of traditional Conservative voters with a propensity to create an endless political soap opera out of internal rivalries and divisions, which have become increasingly indulgent and entrenched. Today, voters have simply said, 'If you can't agree with each other, we can't agree to vote for you'.

In the main war room, Booth-Smith sat with a beer and read through the draft of the concession speech he had prepared for Sunak to make at his count. The comments seemed right. He and James Forsyth, Sunak's political secretary, had been working on them for the past four weeks.

Many of the Tories' seats fell by small margins. Isaac Levido rued the mistakes the party had made, such as the D-Day debacle or the betting scandal. Without these – or if the wooden TV performer Keir Starmer had agreed to another couple of live debates – the Conservatives could have had a much better night.[19]

• • •

In south-west London, Ed Davey woke and checked the latest numbers. 'We had won a few seats that we hadn't expected and that polls hadn't included, and I thought, we're going to do better than sixty-one,' he recalls.[20]

In Vincent Square, Dave McCobb had been ringing the office bell at key moments as Lib Dem victories were declared. He rang it one more time when the party passed seventy seats.

• • •

At 4.40 a.m., it was time to declare the result in Rishi Sunak's seat of Richmond & Northallerton in North Yorkshire. He stood, grim-faced, on a stage crowded with candidates, including one from the Monster Raving Loony Party and Count Binface, the satirical candidate who likes to take on the PM of the day. Sunak held his seat, with 23,000 votes to his name.

He had an announcement to make to the country. 'Labour has won this general election,' he said. 'And I have called Sir Keir Starmer to congratulate him on his victory.'

Today, power will change hands in a peaceful and orderly manner, with goodwill on all sides. That is something that should give us all confidence in our country's stability and future. The British people have delivered a sobering verdict tonight. There is much to learn and reflect on, and I take responsibility for the loss. To the many good, hard-working Conservative candidates who lost tonight, despite their tireless efforts, their local records of delivery and their dedication to their communities, I am sorry.

• • •

In Clacton, Farage returned to the party at the Royal Hotel to the delight of his lit-up supporters. He thanked everyone and raised a glass, with his customary toast: 'Cheers!' Among those who had come along for the election was the former foreign minister of Finland – Timo Soini, Farage's friend from the European Parliament. 'He'd seen it from Finland; he thought Nigel would win so he wanted to be there,' Towler explains. 'Of course, we were not laughing at all those Tories who thought about joining us and then didn't – red wall Tories who lost their seats, who may well not have lost their seats if they'd had the bollocks to do what they believed.'[21]

• • •

Starmer's car pulled up at the Tate Modern. Morgan McSweeney was there to meet him. Hardly believing what they had achieved, the two men shared a huge hug before heading into the victory party.

'What do you think?' Starmer asked his aide.

'Like, I am happy,' McSweeney replied. 'It's a great result. But it's just a bit irritating it's not as big as '97.'

McSweeney told his boss he expected the size of the landslide to increase from the projected 410 seats but to fall just short of Tony Blair's record haul. 'We don't think it will hit 419. It's so irritating,' he said.

Starmer agreed and the two men continued grumbling about not quite beating Blair in the gallery lift on their way to the event. In the end, Starmer's wife Victoria had to tell them to stop their 'ridiculous' complaints.[22]

Starmer walked out into the crowds of party workers and friends who packed the Turbine Hall, bathed in red lighting for the night. At 5 a.m., Starmer stepped up to the microphone with hundreds of supporters waving flags and Labour posters behind him. The TV tally confirmed Labour had passed the milestone of 326 seats, formally winning a Commons majority.

'Thank you so much for that reception,' the Labour leader said to his cheering supporters, grinning broadly. 'We did it!'

After four years fighting to change the party, Labour can 'restore Britain to the service of working people,' he said. 'Across our country, people will be waking up to the news, relieved that a weight has been lifted, a burden finally removed from the shoulders of this great nation.'

Tony Blair's famous victory line from 1997 – 'A new dawn has broken, has it not?' – was clearly on Starmer's mind. He went on: 'And now we can look forward again, walk into the morning, the sunlight of hope, pale at first but getting stronger through the day, shining once again on a country with the opportunity, after fourteen years, to get its future back.'

It wasn't quite as pithy as a Blair-style soundbite, but Starmer's point was clear all the same.[23]

• • •

At 5.20 a.m., Professor Sir John Curtice, the election expert in charge of the exit poll, declared that the Tories were heading for their 'worst-ever performance', while the Lib Dems were enjoying their best result since 1923. He added that Labour had not won over large swathes of voters, despite its parliamentary landslide:

> But for the rise of the Labour Party in Scotland, which has been truly spectacular, we will be reporting that basically Labour's vote has not changed from what it was in 2019 – in Wales, it is actually down and in England it has barely changed. One has to say this does look like an election that the Conservatives have lost and have lost primarily because of the votes that they have lost to Reform, which has cost the party seat after seat after seat.

In Northern Ireland, high-profile MP Ian Paisley Jr lost North Antrim, the seat his family had held for fifty years, as his Democratic Unionist Party fell back.

In England, Tory casualties kept mounting. Cabinet ministers thrown out included: Justice Secretary Alex Chalk in Cheltenham, Culture Secretary Lucy Frazer in South East Cambridgeshire; Education Secretary Gillian Keegan in Chichester; Penny Mordaunt, the Commons Leader, in Portsmouth North; and Veterans Minister Johnny Mercer, in Plymouth Moor View.

Other former Cabinet ministers also paid the price, including Jacob Rees-Mogg, the staunch Johnson and Truss supporter, and Thérèse Coffey, who had been Truss's Deputy PM.

• • •

When Rees-Mogg lost, the room went wild in Labour HQ.

Party workers fuelled themselves on Domino's pizza and Haribo Tangfastic sweets to stay awake – not that many staffers felt like going to bed. Some washed down their snacks with an occasional celebratory gin and tonic in a can.

On one desk, there was a bell of the kind that a customer in an old-fashioned shop might ring for service. It rang every time Labour won a seat. 'It got to the point where it just kept ringing,' one Labour staffer says.

• • •

'Where is she?'

Isaac Levido was frustrated. In the early hours, reports emerged from the count at a leisure centre in King's Lynn that Liz Truss was on the point of losing her South West Norfolk seat. Television reporters informed viewers that the result was about to be declared. All the other candidates were on stage – and on TV – as was the returning officer. But Truss was nowhere to be seen.

After waiting for several minutes, the crowd in the room started slow hand-clapping. Some Tories wondered if she was ill. A senior Tory recalls colleagues watching the event drag on, thinking, 'Get on the fucking stage and get this over and done with.'[24] The shortest-serving Prime Minister in British history had wrecked the Conservative Party's reputation for economic competence during her brief tenure. Senior colleagues had urged her not to stand for re-election, but she had refused.

At 6.46 a.m., Truss finally took her place at the edge of the stage. The camera zoomed in on her as the returning officer read the result. She lost to Labour by 630 votes. A few isolated cries of 'Yes!' came from the hall. Truss blinked.

In the end, one Tory campaigner remarked, it was probably important for everyone that she did stand, and that she lost – the party and the country could now move on. Another said, 'The public did what the Conservative Party couldn't do, which was to get Liz to step down.'[25]

Truss's ousting was dramatic but not unusual on a dire night for her party. The seats of every one of Sunak's predecessors as Prime Minister since 2010 fell into rival parties' hands: Boris Johnson's former seat of Uxbridge went to Labour; David Cameron's Oxfordshire stronghold of Witney turned Lib Dem; and Maidenhead in Berkshire, which Theresa May had represented for twenty-seven years, fell to the Lib Dems too.

• • •

In Essex, Holden held on. But the Tory chairman had earned an unwanted accolade after two recounts: with a majority of just twenty, Basildon & Billericay was now the most marginal Conservative seat in the country.

After thanking his team, he got in the car to be driven back to the headquarters of the party he had worked for, in various roles, for most of his adult life. The scene inside 4 Matthew Parker Street resembled a defeated army. Loss hung in the air. A few researchers slumped over their desks. Other staffers were tearful. One person had curled up asleep on the floor.

After flying south, Sunak arrived at CCHQ around 8 a.m. and made a speech thanking the team for their gruelling work and acknowledging it wasn't the result anyone there wanted. Holden spoke after the PM. He knew then that he needed to resign.[26]

• • •

It was another rainy morning when Sunak headed into No. 10 for the last time on Friday 5 July.

Jeremy Hunt, who had just clung onto his Surrey seat, was the first to leave Downing Street, posing for photographers on the steps of No. 11 with his wife, three children and their dog.

Inside No. 10, Sunak started to say his goodbyes. He thanked staff individually, spent some time with Cabinet Secretary Simon Case, and his political team, many of whom were in tears. Sunak remained his stoical self, according to those who saw him. He doesn't display much emotion in public, though others were upset around him.

After making a short speech in the Pillared Room where Downing Street officials had gathered, Sunak returned to his private study with Liam Booth-Smith. They had been a partnership – the politician and the aide – forged in the intense pressure of the Treasury during the pandemic. Booth-Smith had later encouraged Sunak to stand for the leadership.

In their final moments together in the No. 10 study, they ran through Sunak's farewell remarks to the nation. Then Sunak's wife, Akshata Murty, opened the study door. It was time.

Sunak walked down No. 10's famous staircase, past the portraits of his predecessors, to applause from the staff. He stopped to shake them all by the hand, with some wanting to hug him as he left. He made unusually slow progress, taking twenty minutes to reach the ground floor.

Before leaving, Sunak had also handwritten personal notes to thank individual officials for their 'hard work and support'. There were forty or fifty of these letters in all. It was in keeping with the way he had handled his officials throughout his time as PM – writing notes of thanks and praise for their work, always 'hugely appreciated' by those who received them.[27]

ELECTION NIGHT

When Sunak reached the bottom of the stairs, he turned to Booth-Smith for a final hug. The aide clapped as his boss walked around the corner towards the door of No. 10. Then Booth-Smith turned and walked the other way, leaving Downing Street by a back door and handing in his pass.

Sunak paused with his wife in the hallway behind the No. 10 door and flicked through his speech one last time. He was ready. The door swung open at 10.40 a.m. and they walked out together, with Murty holding an umbrella this time.

'I will shortly be going to see the King to offer my resignation as Prime Minister,' Sunak said. 'To the country I would like to say, first and foremost, I am sorry.'

Sunak listed some of his proudest achievements – including stabilising the economy, reducing inflation and bringing back growth. Then he turned to Starmer.

> Whilst he has been my political opponent, Sir Keir Starmer will shortly become our Prime Minister. In this job, his successes will be all our successes, and I wish him and his family well. Whatever our disagreements in this campaign, he is a decent, public-spirited man, who I respect. He and his family deserve the very best of our understanding, as they make the huge transition to their new lives behind this door and as he grapples with this most demanding of jobs in an increasingly unstable world.

Sunak expressed his gratitude to his colleagues, his wife and their 'beautiful daughters', saying, 'I can never thank them enough for the sacrifices they have made so that I might serve our country.'

This is a difficult day, at the end of a number of difficult days. But

I leave this job honoured to have been your Prime Minister. This is the best country in the world and that is thanks entirely to you, the British people, the true source of all our achievements, our strengths and our greatness. Thank you.

After twenty months as the Prime Minister's chief of staff, Booth-Smith's final task had been to prepare Rishi Sunak to make his final speech. He didn't need to watch. He had heard it plenty of times in the study that morning already.

His job done, he took a walk by himself around St James's Park. The sun had come out. His feet carried him to The Phoenix, a pub near Buckingham Palace, which was quiet at that time of day. At the bar, he ordered a pint of ale and sat down to drink it alone.[28]

CHAPTER 17

NEW DAWN

For almost two hours on Friday 5 July, the most famous address in British politics was officially unoccupied.

Inside No. 10, the cleaners went to work. A battalion of staff quickly and efficiently moved through the building from room to room, erasing all traces of Rishi Sunak's presence. Photographs of the PM with his team, letters, cards and other mementos were cleared from desks and collected into boxes. As soon as Sunak left for the last time in his government car, his political staff were ushered out via the adjoining Cabinet Office, handing in their security passes, phones and laptops as they went.

Waiting to enter were members of Starmer's new government, sipping coffee in a side room. Morgan McSweeney had put on his smart new suit. On his shirt sleeves he wore the cufflinks he'd had made two years previously, marking the moment in Brighton when Starmer stamped his authority on Labour by changing the party's leadership rules.

It was a reminder, as they moved from the wilderness of opposition into the historic buildings at the heart of government, of just how far they had come.

• • •

Keir Starmer's prime ministerial convoy swept out of the gates of Buckingham Palace and cruised down the Mall. Police outriders held back the traffic to clear the road ahead. The cars turned through Trafalgar Square onto Whitehall as the sun came out.

Crowds of supporters waited for him in Downing Street, lining the pavement outside No. 10. It resembled the scene of flag-waving fans that greeted Tony Blair in 1997. Some felt it was the wrong move, worrying that the atmosphere in Britain in 2024 was more cynical and far less hopeful than when Blair took power. There was a debate among Starmer's top team about whether it would be appropriate to fill the street with ecstatic fans in the same way this time. Starmer insisted that they should do it.

'He saw it as a shared moment with this generation of party staff and activists – they deserved to have their moment, just as the 1997 generation had their moment in the street,' one party source says. 'It was nineteen years since we'd last won a general election.'[1]

The black iron gates of Downing Street swung open and Starmer's government Audi turned in, coming to a stop at 12.38 p.m. He climbed out of the car and into his new life. Elated friends and colleagues greeted the Starmers with cheering and applause, waving union flags and saltires in the air. Sir Keir and Lady Victoria spent the next few minutes greeting their supporters with hugs, handshakes and kisses. Then he stepped up to the lectern to address the nation as its leader for the first time.

'I have just returned from Buckingham Palace, where I accepted an invitation from His Majesty the King to form the next government of this great nation,' Starmer said.

I want to thank the outgoing Prime Minister, Rishi Sunak. His achievement as the first British Asian Prime Minister of our country – the extra effort that will have required – should not be underestimated by anyone. We pay tribute to that today. And we also recognise the dedication and hard work he brought to his leadership. But now our country has voted, decisively, for change, for national renewal and a return of politics to public service.

Starmer promised to begin to rebuild trust in politics:

When the gap between the sacrifices made by people and the service they receive from politicians grows this big, it leads to a weariness in the heart of a nation, a draining away of the hope, the spirit, the belief in a better future that we need to move forward together. Now, this wound, this lack of trust, can only be healed by actions not words. I know that. But we can make a start today, with the simple acknowledgement that public service is a privilege and that your government should treat every single person in this country with respect.

His seven-minute speech over, Starmer returned to greeting his crowd of friends and fans on the pavement before joining Victoria on the doorstep of No. 10. 'Give us a wave,' yelled the press photographers on the opposite side of the street. The couple obliged, taking in the scene before turning to walk through the famous doorway.

On the other side of the threshold, Simon Case, the Cabinet Secretary, welcomed Starmer to No. 10 with a handshake. Applause from civil servants and party aides filled the cramped hallway with a din. Many civil servants were delighted to have one of their own

– a former director of the Crown Prosecution Service – coming in to lead them, after a decade on the receiving end of attacks from Tories who wanted to tear down Whitehall orthodoxy.

As he made his way inside, gripping Victoria's hand, Britain's new Prime Minister paused briefly just once, to acknowledge a backroom party worker whom most viewers watching on television would not have recognised. Morgan McSweeney beamed with pride, clapping hardest of all.

• • •

Simon Case showed Starmer and Victoria into the Cabinet Room. 'Ah,' said the Labour leader. 'I think this is the first time I've ever been in here.' Waiting for them inside were their teenage son and daughter.[*]

Soon Starmer would begin appointing his Cabinet. But first the family spent a few moments together taking stock of where they were and how their world would not be the same now they had made it to Downing Street. The alteration in family life was a preoccupation for Starmer, who worried about the impact his career would have on his children's lives. He wanted them to have a normal life as teenagers, away from the scrutiny of publicity as far as possible. Their names have still not been made public.

In the Cabinet Room, as he caught his breath, Starmer was

---

[*] Starmer relies on Victoria for support and advice, but she has no appetite for the limelight for herself. A Labour source says, 'She's a phenomenal person and politically very, very astute and I'm sure someone he relies on for judgement and advice. I think if he's getting advice from her, he's getting advice from a very good person. They want to protect their families, especially their kids. So, I think she does as much as is needed. She's never wanted to be someone who has taken a more frontline role, like candidates' spouses in the past who have done speeches or have a political project. She doesn't want to do that. She plays the role she's comfortable with and doesn't want to expand on that.'

introduced to the Downing Street 'front-of-house' team. These are the No. 10 officials whose job it is to show guests where to go and to make sure the head of the government has whatever he needs, day and night.

This being Britain, their first duty was to bring the Prime Minister a cup of tea.

CHAPTER 18

LANDSLIDE

BACON ROLLS

Nursing a few hangovers and short of sleep, Labour aides preparing to move into Downing Street on the morning after the election started to question the system of government they were about to inherit. Unlike in the US, where a presidential transition period of around eleven weeks applies between the election and the new administration taking office, there was no time to prepare. They were just thrown into power.

One Labour source explains the scenario confronting them as they turned up at the Cabinet Office building next to No. 10 to start their new jobs on 5 July:

> You wake up, after two or three hours' sleep, stagger your way into 70 Whitehall, get given a bacon roll, a cup of coffee and a pass and get sent into a room with the Prime Minister, who is assembling the government of a G7 nation. There should be a transition of about a week.[1]

The result of the instant transformation from opposition to power is that many at the top of the Labour Party had not come to terms with what they had achieved or reflected on what the election meant. It was a historic and unprecedented result.

Under Morgan McSweeney's remarkable captaincy, Labour won 63 per cent of the seats in the House of Commons with just 34 per cent of the votes cast. The 2024 election was officially the most disproportionate result in history. It was also the most volatile contest on record, according to the British Election Study's initial analysis. That means more voters switched parties this time than at any previous election over the past sixty years.

Starmer's crowning achievement was to make voting Labour seem safe again after the years of radicalism and internal disarray under Jeremy Corbyn. He won by a landslide, a colossal achievement at any time. The fact it was just four-and-a-half years since the party crashed to its worst defeat since 1935 made the scale of victory truly historic.

It was a landslide too for the Conservatives, who discovered that the ground they stood on had given way. They fell to just 24 per cent of the vote, from 44 per cent in 2019 under Boris Johnson. Rishi Sunak's tally of 121 parliamentary seats was the lowest in the party's history, dating back to its foundation in the 1830s. The Tories lost 244 seats in a single five-year term, another unwanted record.

There were dramatic shifts elsewhere too. Smaller parties surged, making fragmentation another key feature of the election. Tactical voting happens at every election but there was more of it this time than in 2019. The unifying motivation for voters to switch between the Lib Dems and Labour was a desire to get rid of the Tories. Both opposition parties benefited as a result.

The Liberal Democrats, who were almost wiped out between 2015 and 2019, finally surged back into the mainstream, winning seventy-two seats in their biggest haul in a century. At just over 12 per cent, their vote share hardly changed, but their highly effective campaign, run by Dave McCobb, was relentlessly focused and efficiently delivered. Ed Davey took a risk and captured voters' affections with his stunts and by opening up about his personal experience as a carer for his son and other members of his family.

Senior Lib Dems also admit that they benefited from the fact that Keir Starmer had made the prospect of a Labour government non-threatening. In 2015 and in 2019 especially, the Conservatives had successfully put off English voters who were tempted to vote Lib Dem with warnings that they risked letting a weak and unpredictable Labour leader (Ed Miliband or Jeremy Corbyn) enter No. 10 under the influence of the Scottish National Party (SNP).

The demise of Nicola Sturgeon and her tarnished tribe played its part in denying the Tories their go-to warning about a Labour–SNP alliance. And the Scottish upheaval paved the way for Labour to win back dozens of seats that it had lost to the SNP in 2015. Its haul north of the border now stands at thirty-seven, up from just one.

Another throwback to 2015 was the return of Nigel Farage as an electoral force in the land. Nine years earlier, he was kept out of Parliament by a Tory operation in South Thanet that was later shown to have broken election law. This time, he got his revenge.

Farage rivalled Clacton-on-Sea's famous pier for landmark status on the promenade as he campaigned to unseat Tory Giles Watling. In the pro-Brexit, down-at-heel Essex resort, he won by his own small landslide. The surge in backing for Farage across the country, however, was anything but minor. Reform took 4.1 million votes, slightly more than UKIP achieved in 2015, making them the third-biggest party in the UK by vote share, receiving 14 per cent. When Farage entered the contest, Labour knew it meant Sunak was sunk. Morgan

McSweeney decided not to fight him. Farage signalled afterwards that he will be targeting Labour next, aiming to overtake the Tories as the official opposition and ultimately win power.

One of the fascinating features about Farage's support was his apparent popularity with young people. TikTok, the short video app adored by younger generations, was full of spontaneously shared clips of a sixty-year-old man in an old-fashioned blazer and tie. This group is traditionally among the most disaffected section of the electorate. In 2024, that sense of disillusionment was more widespread, with around three-quarters of voters aged 18–60 agreeing that 'politicians don't care what people like me think'. The British Election Study, which published the findings, coined the phrase 'the disillusionment election' to sum up 2024's campaign.[2]

The narrative has set in. Professor John Curtice, in his election night commentary on BBC TV, was the first to call it: Labour didn't win this election as much as the Conservatives lost it. But that does not tell the full story of the landslide of 2024. There were three key factors that shaped the result: the legacies the parties inherited, the leadership at the top of the campaigns and luck.

THE LEGACIES

The first and most important factor that shaped the 2024 election was the way the two main party leaders handled the legacies they inherited.

Keir Starmer initially made a show of trying to accommodate the hard left in his party who had led Labour to two successive defeats. But when that did not placate them, and as his own failures mounted up, he moved decisively into a purge. Starmer's lieutenants neutralised and cut out candidates who were not from their centrist stable and ripped up the party's leadership rules to lock out the Corbynites for the long term. Corbyn himself was ejected from the party altogether.

Then, with Deborah Mattinson's voice ringing in their ears, McSweeney and Starmer set about winning back the 'hero voters' her research had identified. These 'red wall' residents who abandoned Corbyn to lend their vote to Boris Johnson in 2019 were the voters who would put Starmer in power.

After stumbling in his first year, the former chief prosecutor remained totally focused on professionalising his party and doing whatever it took to win. He kept telling the country that he had 'changed' Labour and deserved the chance to change Britain too. Certainly, the steady tone of his sometimes-pedestrian oratory (which was often derided as boring) embodied the kind of solid stability that both Corbyn's Labour and successive chaotic Tory governments had failed to provide. Starmer apparently recognised that being forgettable can be attractive in a political leader, promising in his first speech as PM to 'end the era of noisy performance' and 'tread more lightly on your lives'.

For Rishi Sunak, the story unfolded in reverse. Unlike Starmer, he went from ruthless to hopeless. After spearheading a wave of resignations that ultimately toppled Johnson in July 2022, he found himself unable to make headway with voters when he finally got the top job himself three months later.

Another critical difference with Starmer was that Sunak could not – or would not – shake off the legacies of his two toxic predecessors. Johnson's hypocrisy in defending Dominic Cummings's trip to Barnard Castle and engaging in lockdown-breaking parties during the pandemic dragged the Tories below Labour in the polls, and they never recovered.

But it was Liz Truss's catastrophic 49-day rule that vaporised any hope of a Tory fightback and gave Labour's Rachel Reeves her big chance on the economy. Truss's terrifying gamble on unfunded tax cuts (after a little-noticed but vastly more expensive energy bill relief package) sent bond markets into a tailspin. Having lost control of the economy she had promised to grow, she fired her Chancellor and then quit herself, humiliated by a more resilient lettuce. The Truss crisis meant that, rightly or wrongly, the Tories were blamed for high interest rates that would hit millions of homeowners when their fixed-rate mortgage deals ended.

Panicking Tory MPs sent for Sunak. Much to the relief of Whitehall, the Bank of England and the markets, they didn't force him into a drawn-out contest for the votes of the Conservative members, crowning him leader within days.

It was at this point when many former aides and Cabinet ministers say Sunak could and perhaps should have done more to signal a clean break with the past. Looking back, rueful Tories wonder whether he should have thrown Truss and Kwarteng (and maybe Johnson) out of the party, in the same way Starmer treated Corbynites and Johnson dispensed with Brexit rebels.

But Sunak was not in a position of strength, lacking even a mandate from his own members. With Conservative MPs deeply jittery and amid constant talk of leadership challenges, Sunak's officials worried he might not make it to Christmas. On top of that, the need to reassure the markets meant dealing out drastic punishments to other Tories and stoking civil war in the party would have been highly risky. A calm presence was needed and that fitted with Sunak's temperament.

When the election came, voters treated it as 'a referendum on the Conservative Party's time in office,' according to one senior Tory.[3]

The mood of the electorate, clearly, was for a new start. As Isaac Levido says, 'The British public were dissatisfied with the status quo. So whichever party ultimately presented itself to the public at the election as the status quo was going to lose.'[4]

In defeat, Rishi Sunak was generous. Many on both sides describe him as a thoroughly decent person who worked harder than anyone. In office, he liked to make deals, seek compromises and find answers. One of his proudest achievements was the Windsor Framework, which followed complex negotiations with the EU and delivered a reworked post-Brexit plan for goods trade with Northern Ireland. Another was his intervention in the Silicon Valley Bank collapse to protect British tech firms. And then there was the giant furlough scheme and other pandemic policies he designed while at the Treasury. Neither Sunak nor his team were from the divisive, fire-starting Dominic Cummings school of party management.

Keir Starmer wasn't either, but he was able to be tough when he had to be. He won the Labour leadership with an inclusive offer to the bruised and battered Corbynite left. When that didn't work, he moved to kill off their influence for good.

LEADERSHIP

During his four years in charge of Labour, Starmer cemented his authority and consolidated his centrist faction's power. As the polls moved his way and his team prepared their campaign machine, he grew even stronger.

Rishi Sunak had limited room for manoeuvre at the start and got weaker as the election approached. His first few months were his best chance to impose himself on his party and the public. But it was never clear to anyone, even in his top team, what he really wanted to do. They still aren't able to say what his vision was.

Sunak was famously hard-working. He was a demanding boss too. Ministers and officials knew that if they were not on top of the detail, it would be an uncomfortable meeting. He was at home among the fine print of policy and did not naturally like to delegate. When it came to deciding the date of the election, he overruled even Isaac Levido, the talented strategist he had hired to run the campaign. He remained intimately involved in preparing key policies in the Tory manifesto in a way that some predecessors did not.

Keir Starmer was more comfortable outsourcing big tasks, including the design of Labour's election campaign. He gave Morgan McSweeney, Levido's counterpart, all the freedom he wanted.

As far as his team was concerned, Starmer was the perfect candidate. He didn't interfere with the detail of campaign decisions and did as he was told. Exactly the same was said of David Cameron's relationship with Lynton Crosby in 2015. Both men deserve credit for recognising their limits and trusting highly talented campaign directors to do their jobs.

By contrast, Rishi Sunak overruled his chief election strategist on the biggest decision of all – when to call the election. Of course, this is the politician's decision in the end. But the fact that so many in the Cabinet and beyond believed it was a terrible mistake showed the logic of an early vote was not as clear as Sunak and his closest allies believed. Where McSweeney learned the lessons of Labour's defeat under Ed Miliband in 2015, Sunak had forgotten key lessons from Theresa May's disastrous snap election gamble in 2017. Labour was ready for the fight. The Tories, again, were not.

As a leader, Sunak often struggled to let go. He was prone to getting stuck in the weeds, unable to delegate or to break free of

Chancellor mode. As one aide put it, the parts of the Conservative policy offer he cared most about were fiscal and economic credibility.[5] In private, he was genuinely deeply frustrated that Labour were not being honest about their plans to put up taxes. But he never set out a lasting vision explaining why his promise to cut taxes was a good thing. It was just supposed to be self-evident. Clearly, that was a bad misreading of the public mood.

The leadership of the campaign directors was also key. Whenever they are asked what they admired most about the Labour operation, senior Tory strategists, aides and ministers all say the same thing: the discipline.

Isaac Levido read the riot act to Sunak's Cabinet at the start of 2023, telling them to stop briefing the media and start showing the discipline required to win. It made little difference. What discipline the Tories possessed after 2019 disappeared along with Boris Johnson's ability to stick to his own Covid rules. It never returned.

As a professional, Levido carried on and did his best. There is evidence that switching tactics to focus voters' minds on avoiding a Labour supermajority helped save Tory seats. The £2,000 tax attack on Labour and the Diane Abbott selection row were the only parts of the campaign that had McSweeney's team seriously worried.

But the D-Day debacle and the gambling scandal probably cost as many, if not more, seats than Levido's nimble shifting of gears before polling day was able to save. Trying to keep Tories on message and everyone aligned when opinion polls showed disaster was inevitable was like pushing water uphill. For that, Labour must thank Britain's failing pollsters.

By contrast, McSweeney and Pat McFadden ran a highly disciplined operation from their Pret sandwich-fuelled 'cell' in Southwark. McSweeney's rule was absolute. Many Labour insiders attribute their success to his relentless focus and natural flair for running a campaign. Almost nobody spoke out of turn, ever. The 'small target' or 'Ming vase' strategy was defensive, designed to make sure Labour avoided messing up. It meant saying as little as possible. The buttoned-up McFadden was a regular on broadcast interviews, precisely because he could be relied upon never to make news.

McSweeney knew all about the need to stick to the message, having worked with Peter Mandelson and studied the methods of Lynton Crosby, the sage of Tory election strategists, who wrecked Ed Miliband's campaign by winning a majority for David Cameron in 2015. Levido, Crosby's former colleague, knew it too, but his demoralised and ill-disciplined candidates just would not comply.

LUCK

There was something else driving Labour's obsession with not speaking out of turn. It wasn't just about seeing and accepting the logic of message discipline. It was a psychic scar that ran the length of the party from top to bottom. It throbbed in the solitary moments, when anxious aides were trying to get to sleep after a seventeen-hour day, and twinged again in those heavy seconds before the exit poll dropped. It was fear. However hard they had worked, and whatever else might be true, the fear was always there that Labour is a party that just doesn't win. And that fear spawned anxiety and even superstition.

David Evans, Labour's general secretary during the election campaign, described breaking out in a 'cold sweat', haunted by Neil Kinnock's failure to beat John Major in 1992. McSweeney designed a sensible sleep routine to ensure he got enough rest during the brutal six-week campaign. It fell apart on day one. His mind whirred with a thousand thoughts and anxieties, and he couldn't switch off. McFadden, the campaign coordinator, was another who felt it might be bad luck to look too far ahead. Labour must not appear to be 'measuring the curtains' in anticipation of victory. The public (and the gods) could grow angry.[6]

Starmer himself would not countenance any talk of life in Downing Street before the election. That was partly to guard against complacency. But the vehemence of his attitude, even in private, was surprising to close aides. When one colleague tried to discuss future staffing plans for government, he replied, 'None of us know what we're going to be doing after the election. It's silly to even have this conversation. I don't know what I'm going to be doing.'[7]

The perils of taking victory as read will have been deeply embedded in Starmer's psychology as a sports fan. In football, if a team relaxes before the final whistle blows, disaster in the form of conceding a late goal often follows.*

• • •

The Conservatives have been described as the most ruthless election-winning machine in Western political history. They are by far Britain's most successful party, winning the most seats in eighteen out of the twenty-nine elections since 1918. Their lust for power is legendary and has made them expert at decapitating failing leaderships and going on to win. Labour has the reputation of being unable to dispose of its worst leaders (Corbyn survived for more than four years) and suffering at the ballot box as a result.

---

* Football fans are particularly prone to superstition. Nick Hornby, the writer, describes the lengths to which fans can go in his 1992 memoir *Fever Pitch*. In one scene, he describes how a ritual of biting the head off a sugar mouse was believed to bring his team luck on the pitch.

What was clear this time was that Keir Starmer, a fiercely competitive lawyer, was utterly determined to win power. His whole team wanted victory more than they wanted anything else. The Tories were weary after a decade of turmoil and had had enough. 'I don't think anyone would think it was a good campaign and we were just unlucky,' says Grant Shapps.[8]

Discipline in the Conservative Party had fallen apart. MPs were voting with their feet and staying away from Parliament. Some seventy-five Tories decided to stand down rather than face the angry voters. Some in Sunak's Cabinet believe he was also weary and just wanted out, though he could not have worked harder to try to make the campaign a success. In the end, however, a huge number of Tories simply did not want to be there. The country, as it happened, agreed.

Conservative candidates and even Cabinet ministers complained to the media every day about their own ailing campaign. The party was hopelessly divided after years of internal strife, first over Brexit, then Covid and then over whether Boris Johnson should stay or go..

For the Tories, the money ran short too. A decision was taken not to throw all the cash the party had at the final weeks of the campaign, in order to make sure it wasn't bankrupt after a bruising defeat. That probably had the effect of making the defeat heavier, by denying Levido the chance to buy more advertising and send out more direct mail to voters as polling day approached. Thanks to flattering polls, and a highly effective fundraising operation by Waheed Alli, Labour had a war chest that was the envy of the Tories.

Donors queued up to make new friends with the left. Labour took more in donations than all the other parties combined during the election campaign, receiving £9.5 million between 30 May and 4 July, compared with £1.9 million for the Tories, £1.7 million for the

Lib Dems and £1.6 million for Reform.[9] The impact was predictably clear. In the words of one jealous Conservative, Labour had 'fuck-you money' to burn.[10]

• • •

In politics and in life, you need a slice of luck to succeed. It is also true that to some degree, you make your own good fortune by being open to opportunities when they come and moving on from failures in the past. Starmer got lucky by finding a great campaign chief in Morgan McSweeney, who understood the truth of this. McSweeney studied Labour's failed election campaign of 2015 intently. Among the crucial lessons he learned was that resilience was key: successful parties do not try to 'control the past' when things go wrong, as they always will. Instead, they regroup and focus on 'winning the next hour'.[11] That takes self-discipline and strength. McSweeney's campaign had them both. Despite the hard work of staff and volunteers, the Tories had neither.

Starmer was also more than fortunate to find himself leading Britain's main opposition party at a time when the ruling Conservatives were irreparably unpopular after fourteen years in office. Voters were beyond tired of the government's psychodrama and with politics in general, after a decade that included four general elections and referendums on Scottish independence and, explosively, Brexit.

But Labour's campaign leaders made their own luck too. They saw their chance had come and were determined not to let it go this time. They possessed a desire to win that was missing from too many Conservatives, especially those in Parliament.

Sunak could not catch a break. He called the election in part because he believed there was no point waiting for things like the economy or the national mood or the Rwanda programme to get better – because they would probably just keep getting worse. The public had stopped listening to the government, anyway.

The bad luck continued. When Sunak's tax attack on Labour was taking off, the D-Day debacle knocked it out of the headlines. He could have fought back, but he apologised instead, arguably reinforcing the idea that he'd betrayed veterans.

Once the D-Day story had faded, Tories close to the top of the campaign were caught up in allegations they had placed insider bets on the date of the election. The furore wiped out another week for frustrated CCHQ staffers.

Over the weekend that followed the election, Rishi Sunak didn't do what many would have wanted to and hide from view. Instead, he sat patiently and set about calling every one of the 175 Tory MPs who had lost their seats. He asked them how they were and apologised profusely for his failed campaign.

In truth, Sunak's team had given up hope long before a single vote was cast. In the words of one bruised Tory Cabinet minister, 'they became scared of the future'. Voters consigned them to the past.[12]

EPILOGUE

GOVERNMENT

The question for Starmer is whether he'd even thought about the future at all.

Several senior figures in the Labour administration agree with the aide quoted at the beginning of the previous chapter that the famously 'brutal' UK handover of power should be softened with a formal period of transition. But incoming governments are not supposed to be completely unprepared, as Labour seems to have been.

It was the job of Sue Gray, Starmer's chief of staff and a Whitehall veteran, to get Labour ready for power. She brought in her friend Waheed Alli, in charge of the party's election campaign fundraising, to help. He worked with her on designing both the grid for Labour's first 100 days and the organisation of special adviser roles inside No. 10. That now looks ironic. Those first 100 days were in fact dogged by negative headlines about Gray's allegedly micromanaging and obstructive operating mode, and her salary, and about Alli's boundless generosity in providing thousands of pounds to Starmer and his wife for new clothes, among other 'freebies'.

In the weeks leading up to the election, Alli accompanied Gray in what were known as 'access talks' in Whitehall. These meetings between the opposition and senior civil servants are intended to allow shadow ministers to give Whitehall officials notice of their priorities for government. Ideally, the more detailed they are, the better to help a new government hit the ground running. In previous years, these talks have begun as many as eighteen months before polling day. Rishi Sunak, as is conventional, granted permission to allow Labour to begin talks with the civil service in January 2024.

But Labour was reluctant to get involved. Officials in some departments were surprised not to be in more demand. The talks were often minimal and took place in extreme secrecy. Shadow ministers (as they then were) were not even allowed to discuss the matter with each other.

When the election was called, Starmer's team was 'caught out by the timing' and scrambled to intensify the talks with civil servants – usually the permanent secretaries in relevant government departments. 'We did accelerate the pace,' one of those involved recalls. 'We had to rapidly move through things.' It meant ministers needed to break away from the campaign to present their plans for power to Whitehall officials. Then towards the end of the short campaign, the shadow ministerial team had to stop access talks again and throw themselves into the final phase of the ground war.[1]

It's understandable that Labour wanted to focus first and foremost on making sure they won. But why did they not prepare Whitehall more thoroughly for what they wanted to do in the first weeks and months after taking office?

It was a worry for some that Gray was among the senior figures who were reluctant to engage in access talks, and the hold-up was frustrating. 'We were told not to speak to other teams about what we were doing,' one source says. 'We were at one level saying, "We've got to be ready for the election at the same time as the local elections in May," but then we were also saying, "There's no need to have access talks." Those two things were totally contradictory.'[2]

The excuse that the party bosses gave to frustrated underlings was that they did not want to look like they were taking victory for granted or be seen to be 'measuring up the curtains'.

Staffers got the impression that Gray did not trust the civil service to keep Labour policies confidential. A Labour Cabinet minister says:

> There was a concern that, whereas in the past, shadow ministers could have been confident that it would stay entirely confidential, that might not be true this time round. I think there was a nervousness around that, from Sue's point of view. That's not without merit ... but it was more important actually that if we did win the election, we were ready to go. We just had to take the hit on 'You look like you're measuring up the carpets'. The answer was straightforward: 'This is just what happens as part of the democratic process.'[3]

Some suspected Gray worried about 'dysfunction' she'd witnessed within the civil service, due to the way the Conservatives under Boris Johnson and Liz Truss had treated officials in government, savaging the Whitehall 'blob' for obstructing their priorities. Gray's concerns were apparently shared by other senior figures, including Pat McFadden and Jonathan Ashworth, from the shadow Cabinet Office team. One minister privately described access talks consisting of just one half-hour meeting with a permanent secretary.

Keir Starmer valued Sue Gray precisely because he could trust her to take care of preparations for government and ensure his new administration, if Labour's luck held, delivered what it promised.

She had what he lacked: experience of Whitehall. Nobody was better placed to know which levers to pull from No. 10 to get a result in some remote civil service office that would make sure policies were delivered.

Gray had other problems. Persistent reports of tensions with Morgan McSweeney and others boiled over into a flurry of stories in the newspapers after the party won power. The denials from Labour insiders were consistent but never wholly convincing.

After taking office, Gray found herself in the firing line for complaints. Eventually, it became too much and in early October, she resigned. There were reports that Starmer had been ready to fire her if necessary. He replaced her as his chief of staff with McSweeney, who had the job before. Starmer moved him then, some say, because it wasn't working – though others insist it was because the election campaign was more important. Whatever the reason, McSweeney proved a brilliant campaign director. Running a government is a very different task. He will be a prime target for criticism if Labour does not rediscover the discipline and focus that he brought to the party's bid for power.

'You always get these figures who get built up within the administration to be larger-than-life personalities,' one senior Labour official says. 'It's inevitable that there's always someone who becomes the lightning-rod figure for decisions that are ultimately made by the leader. People find it easier to blame the member of staff than they do to blame the leader themselves when they get a decision they don't like.'[4]

• • •

There doesn't need to be a conflict between campaigning and governing. It is possible – and preferable – to campaign in accordance with the values you will bring to government. Equally, parties that forget why and how they got elected tend to lose their way. As Downing Street chief of staff, McSweeney has the chance to bring the hunger and drive his team displayed in their hunt for a majority to deliver on Labour's promises now they are in office. That will require a searching honesty and looking hard at the vulnerabilities that are masked by Labour's success.

Having won a landslide, many of Starmer's senior officials took the opposite approach. In place of their pre-election nerves was an apparently unshakeable conviction that their victory spoke for itself. The landslide majority was the answer to any doubt, dissent or criticism. The fact Labour won so many seats with such a low share of the vote was just life under the first past the post electoral system. It was irrelevant even to ask what it might mean for trust in politics, the legitimacy of the mandate or even the strength of the party's electoral position in the longer term, they said.[5] But others inside Starmer's government do see the dangers.

'In the first week or so, there was a lot of hope and optimism – and I think that was wonderful – but the risk is you end up looking a bit self-congratulatory if you're not careful,' says Bridget Phillipson, the Education Secretary.[6]

It would clearly be unfair to judge a fledgling Labour government on the strength of its first few months in office. But the rapid downgrade of Starmer's personal ratings and the internal feuds that played out in public have worried Labour's newly elected MPs – many of whom will be defending small majorities at the next election. Seasoned Whitehall officials said they could not remember such disunity so soon after such a thumping victory.

Disquiet spread rapidly on policy too. Rachel Reeves sparked a revolt over the removal of the winter fuel allowance for pensioners, among other things. More cuts and tax rises are expected in her first Budget. Tories will gleefully claim that this confirms their warnings about Starmer's secret tax-hike agenda during the campaign. In truth, neither side was open enough with voters and there was a 'conspiracy of silence' about tax and spending, according to the Institute for Fiscal Studies. It will be harder to rebuild trust in politics as a result.

Phillipson argues that Labour has to explain to voters how long it will take to fix the difficulties the country faces. Labour has 'an amazing opportunity' to win a second term and truly transform the country 'if we do things right in the next four years,' she says. But a persistent risk is likely to be voter cynicism. 'I think the challenge in part in the election was that the public [was] thinking, "Well, none of you can sort this out."'

• • •

In the days following Labour's victory, Sue Gray remarked to a friend that she thought Starmer was 'born to do this job'. Gray herself didn't last long and increasingly, questions are being asked about Starmer's own abilities. He was flat-footed at key moments in the election campaign when he came under pressure. It took too long (his own team says) to resolve the Diane Abbott selection dispute, and he failed to rebut Rishi Sunak's claims about Labour's tax plans quickly enough in the first TV debate.

Starmer's tendency to be slow to address problems has continued in office. He likes to wait and to delegate, which some allies fear shows too passive an attitude to leadership. In opposition, especially with the Tories imploding, it didn't matter too much. But Labour strategists still worry that the party was always 'reactive' and that

Starmer was reluctant to get on the front foot with a message or a plan. Even as he walked into No. 10, some allies feared his new government would be vulnerable to losing focus and could find itself shunted off-course by events.[7]

It's never good when a Prime Minister is asked if they are really in charge. For a new one to have to insist 'I'm completely in control' just two months after winning a historic landslide is deeply unfortunate. And to lose his chief of staff after a relentless torrent of briefing and criticism a few weeks later is a sign of a leadership struggling to get to grips with the job.

So far, the question of whether Starmer will fight the next election as Labour's leader has not arisen. If things don't improve, it will. Starmer says his defining goal is to restore trust in politics. He can't afford to delay. The 2024 election shows voters are more volatile and disillusioned and less patient than they used to be. With Farage, the Lib Dems and the Greens now on the scene – and the Conservatives turning hard right too – there are more interesting options to choose from than in the past.

As Boris Johnson found out, there is a new truth in British politics: a big win can be quickly forgotten.

APPENDIX 1

THE RESULTS

Party	Seats	Net +/-	Votes	Vote share %
Labour	411*	+209	9,708,716	33.7
Conservative	121	-244	6,828,925	23.7
Lib Dem	72	+61	3,519,143	12.2
SNP	9	-39	724,758	2.5
Sinn Féin	7	–	210,891	0.7
Independent	6	+6	564,042	2
DUP	5	-3	172,058	0.6
Reform UK	5	+5	4,117,610	14.3
Green	4	+3	1,843,124	6.4
Plaid Cymru	4	–	194,811	0.7

Other parties: SDLP won 2; TUV 1; Alliance 1; UUP 1

Source: Richard Cracknell, Carl Baker, Louie Pollock, 'General election 2024 results', House of Commons Library, Research Briefing No. 10009, 24 September 2024, https://commonslibrary.parliament.uk/research-briefings/cbp-10009/

---

* Not including the Speaker.

APPENDIX 2

KEY DATES FOR THE 2024 ELECTION

12 December 2019 – Boris Johnson's Conservatives win an eighty-seat majority, consigning Jeremy Corbyn's Labour Party to its worst result since 1935. Corbyn resigns.

23 March 2020 – Johnson orders first national pandemic lockdown, with Chancellor Rishi Sunak announcing the furlough scheme three days earlier.

4 April 2020 – Keir Starmer is elected Labour leader.

6 May 2021 – The Conservatives win the Hartlepool by-election, taking the seat from Labour.

1 July 2021 – Labour narrowly holds Batley & Spen in a crucial by-election for Starmer.

17 June 2021 – The Lib Dems win the Chesham & Amersham by-election. The seat had been held by the Tories since it was created in 1974.

26 September 2021 – Starmer wins key vote on leadership rule changes in a defining showdown with Labour's hard left.

3 November 2021 – After Tory MP Owen Paterson breached lobbying rules, MPs vote to postpone his thirty-day suspension from Parliament, sparking uproar and claims Johnson is eroding standards in public life.

30 November 2021 – First reports emerge of lockdown-breaking parties in Downing Street.

24 February 2022 – Russia invades Ukraine.

25 May 2022 – Sue Gray publishes her report into parties at Downing Street during lockdown, criticising leadership and a culture of impunity at No. 10.

6 June 2022 – Boris Johnson survives a confidence vote by Tory MPs but more than 40 per cent vote against him.

5 July 2022 – Sajid Javid resigns as Health Secretary. Rishi Sunak resigns as Chancellor, saying the public expect the government to be run 'competently and seriously'. A record number of ministers resign over the next two days.

7 July 2022 – Boris Johnson resigns, triggering a Conservative leadership contest.

5 September 2022 – Liz Truss is elected Conservative leader, becoming PM the next day.

APPENDIX 2: KEY DATES FOR THE 2024 ELECTION

8 September 2022 – Buckingham Palace announces the death of Queen Elizabeth II, aged ninety-six.

23 September 2022 – Chancellor Kwasi Kwarteng delivers the 'mini-Budget'. Measures amount to the biggest tax cuts since 1972. Market turmoil follows.

14 October 2022 – Truss sacks Kwarteng, appoints Jeremy Hunt as Chancellor, and reverses some measures in the mini-Budget.

20 October 2022 – Liz Truss resigns just forty-five days after winning the Tory leadership. She ends her term as PM on 25 October after forty-nine days in Downing Street, becoming the shortest-serving Prime Minister in British history.

25 October 2022 – Rishi Sunak becomes the first British Asian Prime Minister after rival candidates withdraw in a fast-tracked Tory leadership contest.

27 February 2023 – Sunak and European Commission President Ursula von der Leyen agree on new post-Brexit trade rules for Northern Ireland, known as the Windsor Framework.

4 October 2023 – Sunak makes a speech to the Tory conference in which he casts himself as the 'change' candidate.

7 October 2023 – Hamas attacks Israel, killing more than 1,100 people.

9 October 2023 – Rachel Reeves tells the Labour Party conference that as Chancellor she would cut waste and promises an 'era of economic security'.

13 November 2023 – Sunak fires Home Secretary Suella Braverman in a reshuffle that sees ex-PM David Cameron appointed Foreign Secretary.

15 November 2023 – The Supreme Court rules Sunak's Rwanda asylum policy is unlawful.

2 May 2024 – The Tories lose 474 councillors in a dire set of local elections.

22 May 2024 – Sunak announces the general election will be held on 4 July.

26 May 2024 – The Conservatives announce plans to bring back national service. Jeremy Corbyn is blocked from standing as a Labour candidate and announces he will run as an independent in Islington North.

26 May 2024 – Rachel Reeves rules out raising income tax or National Insurance in an interview with the BBC. She does not rule out spending cuts.

2 June 2024 – Diane Abbott says she wants to stand for Labour as a candidate in the election, after a row over media reports that she would not be selected.

3 June 2024 – Nigel Farage announces he will take over as Reform UK leader and contest Clacton-on-Sea.

APPENDIX 2: KEY DATES FOR THE 2024 ELECTION

4 June 2024 – Sunak claims Starmer will put people's taxes up by £2,000 during ITV leaders' debate in Salford.

6 June 2024 – D-Day anniversary commemorations in Normandy. Sunak misses the international event. David Cameron is photographed with Joe Biden, Emmanuel Macron and Olaf Scholz in Normandy.

7 June 2024 – Rishi Sunak apologises for partially missing D-Day amid a backlash.

11 June 2024 – The Tories launch the party's manifesto at Silverstone.

12 June 2024 – *The Guardian* reports that Craig Williams, parliamentary private secretary to Rishi Sunak, put a £100 bet on a July election three days before the announcement.

13 June 2024 – Labour launches its manifesto at the headquarters of the Co-op in Manchester.

17 June 2024 – Defence Secretary Grant Shapps admits that a Tory win is not the most likely outcome and warns against handing Labour a 'supermajority'. Reform UK launches its manifesto, or 'contract', in Wales.

19 June 2024 – Two big pollsters, Savanta and YouGov, predict Tory wipeout.

26 June 2024 – Sunak and Starmer go head-to-head in their second TV debate, broadcast by the BBC, in Nottingham.

28 June 2024 – Nigel Farage hits out at Channel 4 after the broadcaster reported on racism among party activists. One was filmed calling Sunak a 'P***'.

2 July 2024 – Boris Johnson gives a speech in London, in a last-ditch attempt to boost the Conservative campaign.

4 July 2024 – Polling day.

5 July 2024 – Keir Starmer becomes Prime Minister at the head of a Labour government.

NOTES

INTRODUCTION
1. Interview, Labour source
2. Private information
3. Georgina Sturge, '2024 general election: Turnout', House of Commons Library, 5 September 2024, https://commonslibrary.parliament.uk/general-election-2024-turnout/

CHAPTER 1: KING BORIS
1. Tim Ross, 'Sajid Javid holds Boris Johnson's fate, and the torch of Thatcherism, in his hands', *New Statesman*, 15 September 2021, https://www.newstatesman.com/politics/conservatives/2021/09/sajid-javid-holds-boris-johnsons-fate-and-the-torch-of-thatcherism-in-his-hands
2. *Laura Kuenssberg: State of Chaos*, 'Johnson', series 1, episode 2, BBC Two, 18 September 2023
3. Interview, government source
4. Interview, senior official
5. Interview, Steve Baker
6. Interview, senior official
7. Interview, Tory aide
8. Interview, Tory source
9. Interview, senior Labour strategist
10. Interview, senior Tory
11. 'Findings of second permanent secretary's investigation into alleged gatherings on government premises during Covid restrictions', Cabinet Office, 25 May 2022, https://assets.publishing.service.gov.uk/government/uploads/system/uploads/attachment_data/file/1078404/2022-05-25_FINAL_FINDINGS_OF_SECOND_PERMANENT_SECRETARY_INTO_ALLEGED_GATHERINGS.pdf
12. *Laura Kuenssberg: State of Chaos*, 'Johnson', series 1, episode 2, BBC Two, 18 September 2023
13. Ibid.
14. Ibid.

CHAPTER 2: TRUSSONOMICS
1. Harry Cole and James Heale, *Out of the Blue: The inside story of the unexpected rise and rapid fall of Liz Truss* (HarperCollins, 2022)
2. Interview, Tory source

3 Interview, Tory source
4 Cole and Heale
5 Ibid., p.270
6 Interview, Truss adviser
7 Cole and Heale, p.286
8 Interview, government source
9 Interview, Treasury official
10 Interview, Tory aide
11 Interview, Tory adviser
12 Interview, senior official
13 Marcus Ashworth, 'The $4 Trillion UK Bond Salesman Has Left the Building, Bloomberg, 12 July 2024
14 Interviews, government sources
15 Interview, senior government official
16 Interviews, senior officials
17 Interview, government aide
18 Interview, government source
19 Private interviews
20 *Laura Kuenssberg: State of Chaos*, 'Johnson/Truss', series 1, episode 3, BBC Two, 25 September 2023
21 Interview, Truss adviser
22 On the Friday afternoon, Truss had given a dismal press conference announcing the U-turn on corporation tax, which she later described as 'like officiating at my own funeral'. Liz Truss, *Ten Years to Save the West* (Biteback, 2024), p.275
23 Truss, p.275
24 Interview, government source
25 Truss, p.276
26 Interviews, Conservative sources
27 Interviews, Conservative sources
28 Interview, Tory source
29 Cole and Heale, p.309
30 Private information
31 *Laura Kuenssberg: State of Chaos*, 'Johnson/Truss', series 1, episode 3, BBC Two, 25 September 2023
32 Interview, ex-Cabinet minister
33 Interview, Tory aide
34 Interview, government official
35 Interview, senior official

CHAPTER 3: THE LAWYER

1 Shabana Mahmood, interview with Rachel Wearmouth. 'Shabana Mahmood: "All I do these days is talk to Tory voters"', *New Statesman*, 26 July 2023, https://www.newstatesman.com/politics/preparing-for-power/2023/07/shabana-mahmood-interview-labour-tory-voters
2 Interview, Labour aide
3 'Sir Keir Starmer, Leader of the Opposition', *Desert Island Discs*, BBC Radio 4, 15 November 2020
4 *Newscast*, 'Leader Profiles: Sir Keir Starmer', BBC News, 14 June 2024
5 Quoted in Tom Baldwin, *Keir Starmer: The Biography* (William Collins, 2024), p.96
6 Interview, Labour source
7 Interview, Labour source
8 Interview, Deborah Mattinson
9 Interview, Labour source

NOTES

10 Interview, Deborah Mattinson
11 Ibid.
12 Interviews, Labour sources
13 Interview, Labour official
14 Interview, Labour official
15 Interview, Labour staffer

CHAPTER 4: THE BANKER
1 Michael Ashcroft, *All to Play For: The Advance of Rishi Sunak* (Biteback, 2023)
2 Ibid.
3 Interviews, Tory sources; Kate Ferguson, 'Bridge of Spies', *The Sun*, 16 March 2024, https://www.thesun.co.uk/news/26738575/boris-johnson-rishi-sunak-secret-summit/
4 Interview, Tory MP
5 Interview, Steve Baker
6 Prime Minister's Office, 'Rishi Sunak's first speech as Prime Minister: 25 October 2022', gov.uk, 25 October 2022, https://www.gov.uk/government/speeches/prime-minister-rishi-sunaks-statement-25-october-2022
7 Interview, government official
8 Ashcroft, *All to Play For*, p.36
9 Emily Schultheis, 'Rishi Sunak's California escape hatch', POLITICO, 19 June 2024, https://www.politico.com/news/2024/06/19/rishi-sunak-california-00164050
10 Interview, Tory minister
11 Interview, Tory source
12 Interviews, Tory sources
13 Interview, senior adviser
14 Interview, senior official
15 Interview, Cabinet minister
16 Interview, senior Conservative
17 Interview, Tory aide
18 Interviews, Cabinet ministers
19 Interview, Steve Baker
20 Interviews, Tory sources
21 Interview, Tory strategist
22 Interviews, government sources
23 Interview, government source
24 Interview, Tory source
25 Interviews, government sources
26 Interview, senior Tory
27 Interview, Tory source
28 Interviews, Tory sources
29 Interview, Tory aide

CHAPTER 5: TEARS AND RAIN
1 Interviews, multiple sources
2 Interviews, Tory sources
3 Interviews, Cabinet ministers
4 Interview, Cabinet source
5 Interview, Tory source
6 Interview, Labour official
7 Interview, Labour source
8 Interview, Labour adviser

CHAPTER 6: ON THE GROUND
1. Interviews, Tory sources
2. Interviews, Tory campaign sources
3. Interviews, Tory sources
4. Interview, Tory campaign source
5. Interview, Labour official
6. Interviews, Labour sources
7. 'Dominic Raab dismisses allegations against diary secretary', BBC News, 2 May 2018, https://www.bbc.co.uk/news/uk-politics-43979681
8. Interviews, Tory campaign sources
9. Oscar Bentley and Lauren Tavriger, 'Tories fighting defensive campaign, analysis shows', BBC News, 26 June 2024, https://www.bbc.co.uk/news/articles/crggg3ongnyo
10. Interviews, Tory sources
11. Interview, Labour official
12. Interviews, Labour campaign sources
13. Interviews, Labour staffers
14. Interview, senior Labour official
15. Interview, senior Labour figure
16. Interview, Tory adviser
17. Interview, Steve Baker
18. Interview, senior Tory
19. Interview, Tory source
20. Interviews, Labour sources
21. Interviews, Tory sources
22. Interview, CCHQ source
23. Interview, Tory volunteer
24. Interview, Naz Shah
25. Interview, Thangam Debbonaire
26. Interview, Labour source

CHAPTER 7: DIGITAL
1. Interview, Labour staffer
2. Tim Ross, *Why the Tories Won: The inside story of the 2015 election* (Biteback, 2015), pp.107–21
3. Interview, Labour insider
4. Interview, Labour campaign official
5. Interview, Labour source
6. Interviews, Tory sources
7. Interview, Tory official
8. Who Targets Me has some fascinating detail analysing the spending of parties on digital, which also gave a strong indication in real time about which seats the parties were targeting. These figures are from analysis published on 1 July 2024. See 'UK campaign analysis: 19th–25th June', Who Targets Me, 1 July 2024, https://whotargets.me/en/uk-campaign-analysis-19th-25th-june/
9. Interview, Tory official
10. Interview, Tory staffer
11. Graeme Demianyk, 'Tory Anger As Party Uses BBC Presenter's "Middle Finger" Gaffe To Attack Labour', Huffington Post, 7 December 2023, https://www.huffingtonpost.co.uk/entry/conservative-party-bbc-meme-middle-finger_uk_65721714e4b001ec86a747a4
12. Interviews, Tory sources
13. Interview, Gawain Towler
14. Interview, Tory sources
15. Conservative analysis
16. Interview, Labour official

NOTES

CHAPTER 8: CHANGE
1. Interview, Tory source
2. Interview, Tory adviser
3. Interview, Isaac Levido
4. Interview, Cabinet minister
5. Interview, Labour source
6. Interview, Tory aide
7. Interview, Labour source
8. Interview, Labour source
9. Interviews, Tory campaign sources
10. For Lammy's thoughts on compulsory civic service, see David Lammy, 'English identity, civic nationalism and a compulsory civic service', Labour List, 23 April 2020, https://labourlist.org/2020/04/english-identity-civic-nationalism-and-a-compulsory-civic-service/. For Blunkett's, see David Blunkett, 'I've seen national service work – Labour should champion it', The i, 31 May 2024, https://inews.co.uk/opinion/david-blunkett-national-service-work-labour-should-champion-3082120
11. Interview, Steve Baker
12. Labour Party, 'Change: Labour Party Manifesto 2024', https://labour.org.uk/change/
13. Interview, Labour source
14. Interview, senior Labour figure
15. Interviews, Tory officials
16. Ibid.
17. Interview, Tory aide

CHAPTER 9: TRUST
1. Interview, Deborah Mattinson
2. Interview, Pat McFadden
3. Interview, Labour official
4. Interviews, Labour sources
5. Interview, Labour source
6. Interviews, Tory sources
7. Interview, Labour official
8. Interviews, Labour sources
9. Interviews, Labour sources
10. Interview, Labour source
11. Interview, government official
12. Interview, government official
13. Interview, Grant Shapps
14. Interview, Deborah Mattinson
15. Interview, Labour source
16. Interview, Labour source
17. Interviews, Labour sources
18. Interview, Labour official
19. Interview, Labour source

CHAPTER 10: D-DAY
1. Interview, Tory aide
2. Interview, Tory source
3. Interview, government official
4. Ibid.
5. Dan Bloom, 'No fighting on the beaches, please', London Playbook from POLITICO, POLITICO, 6 June 2024, https://www.politico.eu/newsletter/london-playbook/no-fighting-on-the-beaches-please/

6   Interview, Labour source
7   Interview, senior Tory
8   Sam Francis, 'Cameron side-steps questions on Sunak's D-Day exit', BBC News, 13 June 2024, https://www.bbc.co.uk/news/articles/crgg1n519410
9   Interview, Tory source
10 Interview, Sunak ally
11 Interview, Sunak aide
12 Interviews, Tory sources
13 Interview, senior Tory adviser
14 Alix Cuthbertson, 'Rishi Sunak issues apology for returning from D-Day ceremony early', Sky News, 7 June 2024, https://news.sky.com/story/rishi-sunak-apologises-for-returning-from-d-day-ceremony-early-13149195
15 Harry Cole and Thomas Godfrey, 'There's no defence for Rishi leaving D-Day early, blasts veterans' minister as even HE slams PM's "significant mistake"', *The Sun*, 7 June 2024, https://www.thesun.co.uk/news/28357710/rishi-leaving-d-day-mistake-johnny-mercer/
16 Interview, senior Tory minister
17 Interview, Labour staffer
18 Ibid.
19 Interviews, senior Tories
20 Interview, Labour sources
21 Interview, Deborah Mattinson

CHAPTER 11: BAD BETS
1   Interview, Tory source
2   https://www.bbc.co.uk/news/articles/c844je9nq890
3   Interview, Tory source
4   Interview, Tory source
5   Anna Lamche, 'Election betting scandal: Met Police ends investigation', BBC News, 23 August 2023, https://www.bbc.co.uk/news/articles/c4gd7qxwvjz0
6   Interviews, Tory sources
7   Interviews, Tory sources
8   Interview, senior Tory
9   Interview, senior Tory

CHAPTER 12: ENTER FARAGE
1   Interviews, Labour staffers
2   Interview, Gawain Towler, Reform UK media adviser
3   Interview, Tory campaign official
4   Interview, Gawain Towler
5   Interview, Gawain Towler
6   ITV News, 'Nigel Farage reacts to "scary" milkshake incident', YouTube, 4 June 2024, https://www.youtube.com/watch?v=O1Mfy2NyknY
7   Interview, Gawain Towler
8   Interview, Gawain Towler
9   'UK election: Sunak's rage at Reform racism – latest updates', POLITICO, 28 June 2024, https://www.politico.eu/article/uk-election-latest-updates-2024-live-rishi-sunak-keir-starmer-nigel-farage/
10 Interview, Isaac Levido
11 Interview, Gawain Towler
12 Interview, senior Tory
13 Interview, senior Tory
14 Interview, Labour source

NOTES

15 Interviews, Labour officials
16 Interview, Labour strategist
17 Ollie Corfe, 'Revealed: The real extent of Reform's damage to the Tories', *Daily Telegraph*, 6 July 2024, https://www.telegraph.co.uk/politics/2024/07/06/the-true-cost-of-reform-conservative-election-result/
18 Adam Hawksbee, Shivani H. Menon, 'Levelling Up in Practice: Clacton Interim Report', Onward, 7 February 2023, https://www.ukonward.com/reports/clacton-interim-report/
19 Written exchanges with Labour source
20 Interviews, Tory sources

CHAPTER 13: FALL GUY

1 Interview, Ed Davey. Babarinde was elected as a Lib Dem MP on 4 July
2 Noah Keate, 'Lib Dems win big – and we rank Ed Davey's 19 top campaign stunts', POLITICO, 4 July 2024, https://www.politico.eu/article/19-crazy-ed-davey-campaign-stunts-and-1-serious-moment/
3 Interview, Ed Davey
4 Interview, Lib Dem source
5 Interviews, Lib Dem sources
6 Interviews, Lib Dem sources
7 Interview, Dave McCobb, Lib Dem campaign director
8 Ibid.
9 Interview, Lib Dem official
10 Interview, Ed Davey
11 'Sir Ed Davey takes a hammer to "Tory blue wall" after by-election win', Sky News, 18 June 2021, https://news.sky.com/video/wacaday-sir-ed-davey-takes-down-a-blue-wall-literally-after-by-election-win-12335630
12 Interview, McCobb
13 Interview, Lib Dem official
14 Interview, Lib Dem source
15 Interview, Lib Dem official
16 Interview, Ed Davey
17 Liberal Democrats, 'Ed's story', YouTube, 5 June 2024, https://www.youtube.com/watch?v=d6LJEUKdjNI

CHAPTER 14: SCOTLAND

1 Interview, Labour source
2 Interview, Labour campaign source
3 Interview, Labour source
4 Interview, Starmer aide
5 Interview, Gordon McKee
6 Andrew McDonald, 'Humiliated, Scotland's independence warriors lick their wounds', POLITICO, 31 July 2024, https://www.politico.eu/article/scottish-national-party-lick-wounds-united-kingdom-general-election/
7 Interview, Kirstie McNeill
8 Interview, McKee
9 Interview, Labour source
10 Interview, Labour source

CHAPTER 15: POLL AXED

1 Interview, Conservative source
2 Interview, Tory official
3 Isaac Levido et al., 'GE2024 - Mid-Campaign Strategic Imperatives', 10 June 2024

4   Ibid.
5   Ibid.
6   Ibid.
7   Interviews, Tory sources
8   Isaac Levido et al., 'GE2024 – Mid-Campaign Strategic Imperatives', 10 June 2024
9   Grant Shapps interview, Times Radio, 12 June 2024
10 Interview, Tory source
11 Interview, Tory aide
12 Interviews, Tory sources
13 Interviews, Tory sources
14 'Second YouGov 2024 election MRP shows Conservatives on lowest seat total in history', YouGov, 19 June 2024, https://yougov.co.uk/politics/articles/49809-second-yougov-2024-election-mrp-shows-conservatives-on-lowest-seat-total-in-history. In their press release cited here, YouGov incorrectly stated 425 seats would be an increase of 125 on Labour's 2019 total. It would be an increase of 223, given Labour won 202 seats in 2019.
15 Savanta UK, X, 19 June 2024, https://x.com/Savanta_UK/status/1803458931462906002
16 Interviews, Tory sources
17 Interview, senior Tory
18 Politics UK, X, 18 June 2024, https://x.com/PolitlcsUK/status/1803065343780241464
19 '2024 General Election: Best for Britain's Impact', Best for Britain, August 2024, https://assets.nationbuilder.com/b4b/pages/6303/attachments/original/1725885189/2024_GE_Impact_Report.pdf?1725885189
20 Ibid.
21 Interview, Dave McCobb
22 Interview, Labour strategist
23 Interview, Deborah Mattinson
24 Interviews, campaign sources
25 Interview, Martin Boon
26 For YouGov's full explanation for the changes, see 'Using MRP for our voting intention polling', YouGov, 4 June 2024, https://yougov.co.uk/politics/articles/49614-using-mrp-for-our-voting-intention-polling
27 Interview, Lord Hayward
28 Interview, Isaac Levido
29 Interview, Labour source
30 Interview, Isaac Levido
31 Interview, Martin Boon
32 'Our 2024 Election Polling: Lessons Learned', More in Common, 31 August 2024, https://www.moreincommon.org.uk/latest-insights/our-2024-election-polling-lessons-learned/
33 'The 2024 General Election', British Polling Council, 11 September 2024, https://www.britishpollingcouncil.org/the-2024-general-election/
34 Interview, Tory source
35 Interviews, Tory sources
36 Final internal tracker poll summary, Tory campaign

CHAPTER 16: ELECTION NIGHT

1   Interviews, Labour sources. Starmer only talked through the draft speeches for a victory. His team didn't bother him with notes for other outcomes on the day.
2   Interview, Dave McCobb
3   Interview, senior Tory
4   Interviews, Tory sources
5   Tom Baldwin, 'Stunned silence, hugs and a very big kiss: at home with the Starmers on

NOTES

election night', *The Observer*, 7 July 2024, https://www.theguardian.com/politics/article/2024/jul/07/election-starmers-pm-biographer-4-july-starmer-family
6 Interview, Labour aide
7 Interview, Labour source
8 Interviews, Lib Dem sources
9 Interview, Ed Davey
10 Ibid.
11 Interviews, Lib Dem sources
12 Interview, senior Tory
13 Interview, Conservative campaign source
14 Interviews, Tory sources
15 Interviews, Tory and Labour sources
16 Interview, Gawain Towler
17 Interviews, Tory sources
18 Interviews, Labour and Tory sources
19 Interviews, Conservative sources
20 Interview, Ed Davey
21 Interview, Gawain Towler
22 Interviews, Labour sources
23 Interviews, Labour sources
24 Interview, senior Tory
25 Interview, Tory campaign official
26 Interviews, Tory sources
27 Interviews, senior Tories and officials
28 Interviews, Conservative sources

CHAPTER 17: NEW DAWN
1 Interview, Labour official

CHAPTER 18: LANDSLIDE
1 Interview, Labour source
2 Jane Green and Marie-Lou Sohnius, 'We're all Disillusioned: Age and Political Disaffection in the 2024 UK General Election', British Election Study, 18 September 2024, https://www.britishelectionstudy.com/bes-impact/were-all-disillusioned-age-and-political-disaffection-in-the-2024-uk-general-election/
3 Interview, senior Tory
4 Interview, Isaac Levido
5 Interview, Tory aide
6 Various interviews with Labour sources and other private information
7 Interview, Labour source
8 Interview, Grant Shapps
9 Daniel Wainwright, 'Labour got more donations than other parties combined', BBC News, 15 July 2024, https://www.bbc.co.uk/news/articles/cg3j131327yo
10 Financial accounts published by the Electoral Commission show the Conservatives reported income of £59.4 million and expenditure of £41.5 million for the year ending December 2023. Labour reported a similar income of £58.6 million but higher expenditure than the Tories of £59.5 million. See 'UK political parties' financial accounts published', The Electoral Commission, 22 August 2024, https://www.electoralcommission.org.uk/media-centre/uk-political-parties-financial-accounts-published
11 Interview, Labour source
12 Interview, Tory minister

EPILOGUE: GOVERNMENT
1 Interviews, Labour government sources
2 Interview, Labour source
3 Interview, Labour Cabinet minister
4 Interview, senior Labour official
5 Interviews, Labour officials
6 Interview, Bridget Phillipson
7 Interview, senior Labour source

ACKNOWLEDGEMENTS

The authors would like to thank the wonderful team at Biteback Publishing for taking a risk on this book coming together and staying with it to make it possible within just four months of the election. In particular, we would like to thank Catriona Allon for her patience and excellent line editing – Cat's care and attention saved us from numerous errors and we both owe her a great debt. Any mistakes that remain are ours. Massive thanks to James Stephens and Olivia Beattie, who backed the original idea wholeheartedly and, as always, provided great support along the way. Thanks also to Suzanne Sangster for her advice on publicity.

Tim Ross would like to thank: my editors and colleagues at POLITICO for their encouragement and interest in this book, for generously allowing me the time to work on it and helping to promote it so well, especially Jamil Anderlini, Christian Oliver, Laura Greenhalgh, Kate Day, John Harris, Jack Blanchard, Matt Honeycombe-Foster, Karl Mathiesen, Stefan Boscia, Dan Bloom, Emilio Casalicchio, Ian Wishart, Barbara Moens, Sonya Diehn, Ali Walker, Emma Krstic, Stephan Faris and Joanna Roberts. Frank Prenesti gave a thoughtful and thorough editor's attention to chapter drafts. Tom McTague and Brendan Carlin provided generous advice and help at key moments.

My family and friends are owed the greatest thanks for putting up with my absences (and my presences), especially Billy, Joey, Daisy, Bumble, assorted Stockwells, Rosses and the friends I haven't seen enough. Cincinnati CC had to survive another season without slowly accrued, single-figure scores from their chairman. My amazing Mum and Dad gave me invaluable feedback and endless encouragement, as they always have done. Most of all, this book is for my wife Amy, who read, reread and improved every chapter (still no byline) and encouraged me to write it in the first place. Thank you for keeping me going when nobody else could and for keeping everyone else going when I couldn't.

Rachel Wearmouth would like to thank her family, in particular her sisters Lorna and Janet and mother Jennifer, as well as friends Jessie, Anne, Tom and Mark. She is also grateful to editors at *The i* for taking some news lines from the book. Her whippet Mavi has been endlessly patient in waiting for his walks, even when the final edits were being done from a campervan in the Lake District. To anyone she can't mention, hopefully you know who you are and how much your support has meant over the past year.

This book would have been impossible without the contributions we received from numerous people involved in the story of the 2024 election. Thanks to all the ministers, MPs, candidates, advisers, party staffers, officials and others who gave us their time and honest accounts because they believed the story was worth telling properly. We can't thank them by name, but they know who they are and we won't forget them. Among those who agreed to give us interviews on the record, we would like to thank the following: Steve Baker, Martin Boon, Ed Davey, Thangam Debbonaire, Robert Hayward, Isaac Levido, Dave McCobb, Pat McFadden, Gordon McKee, Kirsty McNeill, Deborah Mattinson, Bridget Phillipson, Grant Shapps and Gawain Towler.